Wakefield Press

VICE-REGAL

For Graham & Karen,
Love & Best Wishes,

Philip

By the same author

Pictorial History of Australia's Little Cornwall
The Story of HMS Fisgard
The Cornish Miner in Australia: Cousin Jack Down Under
Cornish Carols from Australia
The Cornish Farmer in Australia
Tregantle and Scraesdon: Their Forts and Railway
Cyril Noall's Cornish Mine Disasters (ed.)
The Making of Modern Cornwall: Historical Experience and the Persistence of 'Difference'
Cyril Noall's The St Ives Mining District: Volume Two (ed. with Leonard Truran)
Cornwall Since the War: The Contemporary History of a European Region (ed.)
Cornish Studies (ed.) (a series of twenty-one annual volumes, 1993–2013)
The Conservation Value of Metalliferous Mine Sites in Cornwall (ed. with Nicholas Johnson and Adrian Spalding)
Cornwall
The Cornish Overseas
New Directions in Celtic Studies (ed. with Amy Hale)
Cornwall For Ever! The Millennium Book for Cornwall (ed.)
A Vision of Cornwall
Cornwall's History: An Introduction
Cornwall: A History
A.L. Rowse and Cornwall: A Paradoxical Patriot
The Cornish Overseas: A History of Cornwall's Great Emigration
Making Moonta: The Invention of 'Australia's Little Cornwall'
D.H. Lawrence and Cornwall
John Betjeman and Cornwall: 'The Celebrated Cornish Nationalist'
Regional Australia and the Great War: 'The Boys from Old Kio'
The Maritime History of Cornwall (ed. with Alston Kennerley and Helen Doe)
Australia in the Great War
One and All: Labor and the Radical Tradition in South Australia
Emigrants and Historians: Essays in Honour of Eric Richards (ed.)
Cornwall: A History (revised edition)
A History of Sussex
'Repat': A Concise History of Repatriation in Australia
Australia, Migration and Empire: Immigrants in a Globalised World (ed. with Andrekos Varnava)
More Than The Last Shilling: Repatriation in Australia 1994–2018
The Cornish Overseas: A History of Cornwall's Great Emigration (revised edition)
Cover Plus The Care: A Centenary History of the Defence Service Homes Insurance and Loan Schemes
Cornwall's History
Pictorial History of Australia's Little Cornwall (revised edition)
Cornwall in the Age of Rebellion 1490–1690 (ed.)

VICE-REGAL

A HISTORY OF THE GOVERNORS
OF SOUTH AUSTRALIA

PHILIP PAYTON

Wakefield
Press

Wakefield Press
16 Rose Street
Mile End
South Australia 5031
www.wakefieldpress.com.au

First published 2021

Edited by Julia Beaven, Wakefield Press
Designed by Liz Nicholson, Wakefield Press
Typeset by Jesse Pollard, Wakefield Press
Printed by Finsbury Green, Adelaide SA

ISBN 978 1 74305 853 4

A catalogue record for this
book is available from the
National Library of Australia

Wakefield Press thanks
Coriole Vineyards for
continued support

Supported by
Government of
South Australia

CONTENTS

Foreword by
STEVEN MARSHALL PREMIER OF SOUTH AUSTRALIA

The retirement of the Honourable Hieu Van Le AC is a timely opportunity to look back over the history of South Australia's Governors. From the earliest days of European settlement to now, Governors have played a central role in the State's life.

As a Government we are proud and respectful of the history and role that the Westminster system plays in our governance. As well as performing constitutional functions, such as the opening of Parliament or giving Assent to Bills passed in both Houses, Governors have provided a sense of cohesion, stability and continuity in the State, especially in times of crisis such as two World Wars, the Depression years, and more recently the COVID-19 pandemic. They have travelled widely across the State, meeting people from all walks of life.

South Australia proudly leads the nation, appointing the first Aboriginal Governor and the first female Governor, both significant demonstrations of the State's commitment to honouring its history and recognising diversity. Government House, the second-oldest building in Adelaide and an architectural gem, is a visible symbol of grace and stability as well as a physical expression of the importance of the vice-regal office. It is also the venue for numerous functions hosted by the Governor and attended by people from across the South Australian community.

This highly readable account, where Philip Payton chronicles the evolution of the vice-regal role from 1836 to the present day, tells the story of the State's Governors against the background of South Australia's rich history. This is a remarkable book, widely researched and vivid in the telling of the account of the State's Governors. I commend it warmly to all South Australians.

Steven Marshall,
Premier of South Australia

Chapter 1

PORTRAIT OF AN OFFICE AND A HOUSE

As P.A. Howell remarked in a lecture delivered to the Historical Society of South Australia in August 1977, in 'addition to their importance to the political, constitutional and social historian, the Crown's representatives in South Australia have been a fascinating set of individuals'.[1] Intriguing and often forceful characters, occasionally with a dose of eccentricity, these Governors have played a surprisingly varied life in the role of the State. Behind the simple chronology of one Governor replacing another, lies a rich history. It reflects the subtly (and sometimes not so subtly) changing nature of the appointment over time, from the Imperial administrators who ran the colony before responsible government in 1856, through Federation, the impact of two world wars, the Depression years, and much else, to today when Governors are quintessentially and indisputably South Australian in their identification and allegiance, yet still maintaining their primary function as representative in this State of the Queen of Australia, Her Majesty Queen Elizabeth II.

All this makes for entertaining as well as illuminating history, especially when the stories of individual Governors (and sometimes their wives and families too) are set against the wider background of political, constitutional and social developments in South Australia from foundation in 1836 until today, including the Governors' relationships with the peoples and places of the State. Some Governors were deemed highly successful by public opinion, or at least by politicians and the press, while others seemed less well attuned to the norms and aspirations of the State. Earlier Governors often saw their appointment as just one episode in an Imperial career that would take them to several other destinations within the British Empire. Later Governors would typically see their appointments as the culmination of their life's work in service of Australia, particularly South Australia. It is a story laced with telling and sometimes amusing (even shocking) anecdotes, revealing the human dimension of the governorship, but it remains a chronicle of a distinguished office central to the institutional being of South Australia.

Role and powers of the Governor

Today, the role and powers of the Governor are derived specifically from the *Australia Act 1986*, legislation which, among other things, was designed to address various anomalies left over from the Federation of Australia in 1901.[2] Before Federation, South Australia had been a British colony in its own right, as had the other five Australian colonies, each with its own Governor representing the Crown. Federation created another tier of government, with the colonies becoming States, and with the office of Governor-General instituted to represent the Crown in the newly unified Commonwealth of Australia. However, as constitutional historian Peter John Boyce has observed, the role of State Governors 'was largely unaffected by the federation of the six colonies in 1901, creating a constitutional anomaly which was not removed until 1986'.[3] As late as 1981, for example, as Boyce notes, a memorandum from the UK Foreign and Commonwealth Office to the House of Commons at Westminster could still describe the Australian States as 'self-governing dependencies of the British Crown', a constitutional status that had been unaltered by Federation.[4]

Moreover, Federation had not undone the Governor's existing role as 'watchdog of the United Kingdom government and the Crown', and after 1901 the Imperial government continued to rely on intelligence from the State Governor relating to trade and business opportunities, defence infrastructure (including ports, railways and aviation), and reports on social and political developments of interest. As Howell observed, all 'Governors remained agents of Downing Street and Whitehall'.[5] In 1926, Australia was formally recognised in the British Government's Balfour Declaration as a self-governing 'Dominion' within the Empire-Commonwealth. The Declaration also acknowledged that the Governor-General directly represented the Crown and could in no sense be considered an agent or representative of the British Government itself. Yet no such clarity was afforded the role of State Governor.[6] The 1926 Declaration was a result of the Imperial conference in London that year, at which the Commonwealth of Australia – but not the Australian States – had been represented. The argument advanced at the time, therefore, was that the Declaration 'could only be applicable to the party attending', namely the Commonwealth, and, as legal experts Castles and Harris have concluded, as 'a result the constituent parts of the Australian Federation continued to be regarded in a constitutional sense very much as if they were still nineteenth century colonies'.[7]

One consequence of this was that, until 1986, the appointment of each Governor did not necessarily rely solely on the advice of the State Premier but could be subject to possible intervention by the British government.[8] A telling insight into the anomalies that this ambiguity could throw up was provided by the experience of Don Dunstan, State Premier in the late 1960s and 1970s. According to Boyce, 'state premiers were not meant to correspond with British authorities except through the governor, and, as young Premier of South Australia, Don Dunstan was scolded by the then Governor, Sir Edric Bastyan [1961–1968], for having dared to telephone a Whitehall official to inquire about progress with the selection of a new governor'.[9] Dunstan himself recalled the incident slightly differently, writing in his memoirs in 1981 that, anxious to know what was happening regarding the appointment of a new Governor, he decided to contact the relevant British Secretary of State 'as a fellow member of the Labour movement and rang him privately on an old-boy basis and said could he put the rush on it'. However, the Minister in question decided not to respond informally, but instead contacted the Governor directly (as protocol demanded) to inform him that the Queen was away and that it would be some time before matters could be completed. As Dunstan went on to explain, the 'Governor rang me – or rather got his aide to ring me and then came on the phone himself. He was in a fury . . . How dared I communicate with the Secretary of State except through him'.[10]

Dunstan's experience was one of a number of developments that helped pave the way for the *Australia Act*, or rather Acts, of 1986, passed jointly by the parliaments of the United Kingdom, the Commonwealth of Australia, and the Australian States. It was also no coincidence that Sir Edric Bastyan proved to be the last non-Australian appointed as State Governor of South Australia. As Boyce noted, Dunstan 'was the first to indigenise [*sic*] the vice-regal office and tap into a pool of eligible local talent.'[11] The innovation had been a long time coming. As early as 1926, five of Australia's six State Governments had requested that henceforth all gubernatorial appointments be confined to Australians, echoing Prime Minister W.M. 'Billy' Hughes' insistence during the First World War that all officers appointed to commands in the Australian Corps be Australian.[12] However, while the British had bent to Hughes' demand in the exigencies of war, they refused to sanction such a significant change in vice-regal arrangements, which remained largely 'Imperial' until the Dunstan era.[13]

There had been those who had wondered after Federation whether the role of State Governor was still relevant or would be allowed to lapse. Hallam Tennyson (1899–1902), for example, had been offered the governorship of South Australia in January 1899 but hesitated initially as he feared that after Federation the post might be subordinated to that of Governor-General or even abolished.[14] In October 1919, the Governor-General himself, Sir Ronald Munro Ferguson, complained to the Secretary of State for the Colonies in Britain that the 'position of State Governors has been undermined by the constant belittling of their office by a powerful section of the Press who [*sic*] never cease to refer to them as "rubber stamps", and to taunt them with having no employment save that of opening Flower Shows'.[15] In June of the following year, Sir William Archibald Weigall (1920–1922) arrived in Adelaide as State Governor, and in less than twelve months had decided that his office had become an anachronism.[16] He served for only one year and 356 days.[17]

Paradoxically, perhaps, it fell to Don Dunstan half a century later to articulate the continuing constitutional significance of the vice-regal role in South Australia. As Howell put it, with a slight hint of irony: 'No one has more highly lauded the value of having a State Governor than a former

Premier of South Australia, the Hon. Don Dunstan AC QC. He claims that the office "is a practical necessity", integral to our form of government'.[18] As Dunstan himself had argued in 1977, in an early contribution to the republic debate, in 'the Westminster System it is quite essential as a protection to the populace that there be a Head of State independent of Legislature, Judiciary and Executive. Without such an office one of the essential checks in the Constitution would be missing'.[19] If this sounded rather high-minded and dauntingly theoretical, then Dunstan offered from his own experience as Premier several examples to show the importance of having a 'head of state' who was in the position to ask difficult and searching questions, not least during Executive Council meetings. Indeed, a Governor was entitled to require Ministers to provide detailed information on all matters submitted for his or her approval, and if ministerial papers arrived too late for the Governor to read them before a meeting of the Executive Council, then he or she could defer discussion until another time. Moreover, past Governors had on occasion detected flaws in Bills presented for Royal Assent – a sentence that did not quite make sense, perhaps, or a provision that appeared to conflict with existing legislation – requiring the Bill in question to be returned to parliament for rectification. In this way, the Governor of South Australia was far more than a mere 'rubber stamp'.

Since 1986, His or Her Excellency the Governor has always been appointed by the Crown upon the recommendation of the Premier, which is made directly (and not via Canberra). Likewise, the Governor exercises the Crown's powers and functions in State matters, except when Her Majesty happens to be in South Australia. Even then, the constitution directs that she may perform such duties as opening parliament or giving Royal Assent, only if requested to do so by the Premier. Section 7 of the *Australia Act* confers upon the Governor the so-called 'prerogative powers' of the Crown, emphasising that 'all powers of her majesty in respect of a State are exercisable only by the Governor of the State'.[20] These include: to summon, prorogue and dissolve parliament; to recommend measures to parliament; to make grants or leases of Crown land; to appoint Ministers and dismiss them; to assent to Bills passed by both Houses of Parliament; to appoint judges, royal commissioners and the higher public servants; and to exercise the prerogative of mercy by issuing pardons to prisoners or remitting fines and sentences imposed by courts.[21]

In practice, these 'prerogative powers' are exercised on the advice of Ministers and the Premier, and meetings of the Executive Council, at which the Governor presides, are held to confirm the decisions of the Cabinet and the advice of Ministers about appointments, resignations, and the publication of official notices.[22] Before 1986, certain 'reserve powers' were held personally by the Governor, so that should he or she see sufficient cause to dissent from Ministerial advice given through the Executive Council, then *in extremis* these powers could be exercised in opposition to the opinion of the Council.[23] However, the Royal Instructions that had invested these powers in the Governor were withdrawn in 1986, when, alongside the provisions of the *Australia Act*, Her Majesty issued new Letters Patent reconstituting the office of State Governor. Yet the Governor was still required to safeguard peace, order and good government in the State, which implied the continuance of certain 'reserve powers', even if not explicitly defined. Hypothetically, these might be exercised on rare occasions when a Governor found it necessary to act as 'umpire' in a crisis which parliament had been unable to resolve. For example, in a 'hung parliament' the Governor might appoint the Premier, using his or her own discretion to decide the matter. Likewise, he or she might reasonably dismiss a Premier who had lost the confidence of parliament, or was acting unlawfully. The Governor might even refuse to dissolve the House of Assembly, despite a request from the Premier, if there was sufficient cause to resist the Premier's advice.

Just how much of this residual 'reserve power' remains in practice today is extremely unclear, especially as the *Australia Act* offers no guidance. As might be expected, this ambiguity has been a subject of 'endless debate' (as Howell has described it) between constitutional experts, but it is generally agreed that such 'reserve powers' (should they exist) would only be used in 'extreme circumstances'.[24] Oddly, despite this intense interest in their potential 'reserve powers', the continuing role of State Governors (or successor appointments in a republican system) received only cursory attention during the debate leading up to the 1999 referendum, suggesting a constitutional conundrum that commentators found just too difficult to tackle.[25] More recently, constitutional expert Anne Twomey has begun to address the conundrum, postulating that if Australia ever voted to become a republic, there could be two possible outcomes as far as the States are concerned. If it was determined that there was only 'one Queen' in Australia, she argues, then the Crown would lapse in each State as well as in the Commonwealth. However, if it was considered that the Crown existed separately in each State, then each of these States would 'retain its own Crown and break up relationships later'. But, as Twomey has wisely observed in round-table discussion on the topic, such possibilities have thus far attracted little serious attention, and 'I think that's something that needs a lot more thought and a bit of consensus-building'.[26]

Added to the weight of his or her constitutional obligations, the Governor today is required to undertake a number of ceremonial duties, including the opening of parliament, administering oaths of office, and holding investitures. Additionally, there are numerous public and private engagements, some at Government House in Adelaide, but many elsewhere in the city and in all parts of the State, making the office of Governor accessible in even the remotest areas. The Governor is also patron of a great many community, charitable and voluntary organisations, and is often invited to attend their various events, from annual general meetings to balls and conferences. The Governor is asked to launch new books, and to present awards and prizes. Government House hosts numerous social functions, the Governor entertaining prominent members of the community and distinguished visitors to the State, as well as thousands of ordinary citizens from all walks of life. Garden parties and receptions are opportunities for the Governor to meet representatives of organisations such as the Red Cross and the Salvation Army.[27] Taken together, the Governor's duties are wide-ranging and complex, and to assist him or her in case of temporary absence or illness is the Lieutenant-Governor, nominated by the Premier.

In a broader sense, the Governor is a symbol of stability, unity and continuity, and offers what has been described as 'moral leadership', giving encouragement to those working for the benefit of the State and its heritage and well-being.[28] The dignity of the office is reflected in the title 'His/Her Excellency', and in June 2014 the Queen, following a recommendation from the Premier, accorded all current, future and living former Governors with the title 'The Honourable' for life.[29] The Governor also has his or her own Standard, which is the Flag of South Australia with the State Badge (a piping shrike in a golden disk) surmounted by the St Edward's crown. When the Standard is flown at Government House, or on a vehicle or at an event, it indicates that the Governor is present.

Government House(s)

Government House is itself a reflection of both the dignity and functions of the office of Governor. Situated at the corner North Terrace and King William Road, and set in the midst of immaculate gardens, it is the oldest Government House in Australia and the second oldest building in Adelaide. Its handsome proportions and elegant interior have long attracted admiring comment. During Hallam Tennyson's incumbency, for example, the Duke of York and Duchess of Cornwall (later George V and Queen Mary) visited Adelaide as part of their tour of Australian capitals following the opening of the new Commonwealth Parliament in Melbourne. The Duchess declared, or so it was said, that 'they were more comfortable at Government House, Adelaide, than in any other viceregal residence in Australia'. It was an accolade remembered fondly almost a quarter of a century later by the *Register* newspaper, which added that 'If an unbiased travelled person were asked for his opinion on the subject of Government House, its site, and its surrounding walls, his answer would certainly be, "A most excellently situated and snug little viceregal residence, with just a touch of the homeland in its boundary walls"'.[30]

There were, the *Register* admitted, politicians who periodically coveted the attractive site, hoping to use it for alternative purposes, with proposals for the Governor to be housed elsewhere, suggested venues being Rostrevor, Morialta and Torrens Park. But such interventions merely confirmed the utility of the site and House and its sheer appropriateness as vice-regal residence. As the *Advertiser* put it in 1934, reviewing Government House's 95-year history, it is 'the most historic building in Adelaide' and 'has been the setting for many brilliant pageants ... It contains the most complete collection of full-length paintings of Royal personages in Australia, and probably the finest set of portraits of Queen Adelaide, after whom Adelaide was named, in the world'. For good measure, the newspaper also echoed the widely held belief that, 'Although by no means the largest it is admittedly the most comfortable Vice-Regal residence in Australia'.[31]

Later, in 1995, P.A. Howell was aghast at resurfacing suggestions that Government House should be put to new uses. 'Since the 1920s', he wrote with scarcely concealed annoyance, ' there have been suggestions from time to time that the Governor could be moved to a house in the suburbs . . . and Government House thrown open to the people as a museum or art gallery or so on, or else replaced with a modern building more suitable for such new purposes'. But demolition was 'totally out of the question', he insisted, as Government House 'is not only the oldest [sic] and most historically significant building in the State, but also one of the most interesting architecturally. Its surrounding gardens are integral to its attractions'. Similarly, Howell dismissed any notion that new uses would save money. 'Toilet blocks and other new facilities would have to be built', he explained, while cleaning and maintenance costs would rise, and the single policeman on the gate would have to be replaced by an army of security guards. As Howell concluded, 'most people now consider that it [Government House] must be preserved at all costs', adding emphatically: 'It is arguable that there is no other purpose to which Government House could be put that would be of greater value to South Australians . . . This will remain true regardless of whether we become a republic or not'.[32]

Howell had stressed the continuing relevance of Government House to the life of South Australia as the new millennium approached. Historian K.T. Borrow added a further, yet more historical perspective, when he observed that 'Government House, over the years, has become, like the Old Gum Tree [at Glenelg, where Governor John Hindmarsh (1836–1838) read his founding Proclamation], symbolic of South Australia's early days', another reminder, if any were needed, of historic continuity in the vice-regal role.[33] As Borrow noted, the South Australian Commissioners in London, responsible for planning what was then the new colony, had sent out a prefabricated wooden structure to be erected as the Governor's first residence. But the structure was deemed unsuitable on arrival, and was never put up. Instead, an impromptu building had to be made from first principles on a site thought to be somewhere between the present railway station and the River Torrens.

Construction work was undertaken by Marines ('semi-jacks' in Naval parlance of the day) from HMS *Buffalo*, Hindmarsh's command that had brought him to South Australia. John Hill, the warship's boatswain, was apparently the only member of the ship's company who knew how to thatch, and, so it is said, he received his discharge from the Navy on the strength of this skill, attaching himself to the Governor's retinue as gardener.[34] Delays occurred due to a shortage of nails, and there was some controversy when, allegedly without permission, sailors cut down native pines in the Park Lands for use as rafters in what was now dubbed pejoratively (as well as accurately) as 'Government Hut'.[35] When completed, the building measured 27 feet by 50 feet, and consisted of three rooms. The walls were made of timber slabs and wattle-and-daub. The ceiling was calico, and the roof thatched with reeds.

The story goes that the Marines, being maritime men, had neglected to include a chimney in their design. James Young, an early colonist, recalled years later that the 'first Government house [*sic*] was built by the Marines brought out by Captain Hindmarsh, but they had forgotten to put in a chimney, and afterwards had to build one outside; a more unsightly building would be hard to imagine'.[36] Nathaniel Hailes, another early settler, was even more scathing:

> Government House was an extraordinarily uncouth and repulsive structure . . . It resembled a moderately large barn which seemed as if it had been brought by main force into contact with the tall ugly external chimney. This interesting architectural peculiarity His Excellency explained to me had been created by the party of marines who accompanied the first Governor, Captain Hindmarsh. The 'semi-jacks' forgot that chimneys are indulged in on shore, and war-steamers had not then come into use, so a chimney had subsequently to be erected outside the wall and an aperture made in the masonry to communicate therein.[37]

Despite its aesthetic shortcomings, this first Government House served its purpose well enough, although when Governor George Gawler (1838–1841) – Hindmarsh's replacement – arrived in October 1838 he complained the accommodation was unsuitable for his family. Thought was given briefly to erecting the prefabricated wooden structure previously abandoned but it was soon apparent that many of the components were now missing, and that to build a new timber building would actually be more expensive to erect than a stone structure.[38] Accordingly, in November 1838 it was announced that a new Government House would be built, using a plan prepared in London by the architect Edward O'Brien and modified in the colony by George Strickland Kingston, assistant to the Surveyor-General, William Light. Gawler convened a committee of taste, drawn from prominent settlers, to evaluate the plans, not least the costs, but on the day only one invitee, Henry Jones, turned up. He was strongly of the opinion that work should commence at once, and so, as Borrow has put it, Jones 'thus became an unwitting actor in the long chain of events which was to lead to Gawler's recall'.[39] Initial tenders for the work suggested the cost would be in the region of £7000, a not insignificant sum.[40]

In February 1839 the contract for the construction of new Government House was let to the builders Messrs East and Breeze, and less than a month later the foundations had been completed. By now Gawler had decided to proceed with only about two-thirds of the building, reducing the estimated cost to £5700. New Government House was soon rapidly taking shape, and what is today the east wing of the present building was completed and occupied in May 1840. Government House is thus probably the second oldest continuously occupied house in South Australia, after the Quakers' 'meeting house' in Pennington Terrace, North Adelaide, first used by the Society of Friends in mid-1839. When completed, the new Government House comprised the present main drawing room, morning room and Hindmarsh dining room, while upstairs there were three bedrooms, a dressing room and two small servants' rooms. Kitchens were situated in a detached building.[41]

At the same time as work had continued apace on the new building, there was an attempt to refurbish the original 'Government Hut'. The thatching was repaired, some zinc roofing supplied, the chimney repointed, and interior plastered. When this was complete, it was decided to move various papers and records from the new Government House to the old – a fatal decision, as shortly after midnight on 12 January 1841, 'Government Hut' was in flames. Nathaniel Hailes claimed to have observed the conflagration, reporting acidly that 'I watched the destruction of this primitive palace by fire. The building was no loss, but unfortunately official documents in adjoining offices were consumed'.[42]

The *Register*, reporting the conflagration, noted with regret that the 'thatched building occupied by Governor Hindmarsh, as his residence, and more recently used as the Private Secretary's Office, was destroyed by fire on Tuesday evening last'. The newspaper also mourned the loss of 'many papers of great private value to the Governor', and published a letter to the editor from one self-styled 'Eye Witness' who expressed his 'Strong suspicion that the fire was wilful'. To the accusation of arson was added criticism of the firemen who attended the blaze, 'Eye Witness' opining they were 'totally ineffectual', their efforts 'indifferent and almost ridiculous'.[43] Even in the moment of its destruction, it seemed, the old 'Government Hut' continued to attract controversy and opprobrium.

Governor Gawler also thought the fire was deliberate. More unsettling still was news in February 1841 that Gawler's bills had been dishonoured (see p. 35), adding to the charges of profligacy, extravagance and financial incompetence that had dogged him since his decision to build new Government House. Not surprisingly, when his successors as Governor, George Grey (1841–1845) and then Frederick Holt Robe (1845–1848), arrived in South Australia they deemed it necessary to spend as little as possible on the building. Nonetheless, Government House and its domain presented an increasingly attractive prospect, especially as the newly planted gardens began to mature. In 1846 *The Royal South Australian Almanack* gave cautious approval:

> Government House, a commodious but unfinished pile of building, on the
> Park Land, opposite North Terrace, is constructed principally of the stone
> of the country, and is pleasantly situated in the centre of a considerable

enclosed space, at a slight elevation above the river [Torrens], and a short distance from its banks. The grounds appertaining to it are beginning to assume the appearance of a garden, and will probably present a pleasing and refreshing promenade in the course of twenty years or so, if the same progress is continued to be made as hitherto.[44]

In the same year, as the colony's finances began to improve, consequent upon the recent discovery of copper at Kapunda and Burra Burra, the first section of stables was erected, fronting King William Road (to be demolished in 1926), said to be on the site of old 'Government Hut'. In September 1849, work began on the stone wall around the domain of Government House, stepped on the eastern side, the whole with red-brick capping. As South Australia prospered, after initial dislocation, as the 'Granary of Australia' during the Victorian goldrush, so new funds became available for major additions to Government House. Governor Sir Henry Fox Young (1848–1854) argued briefly for the construction of a new Government House, closer to the Torrens, but it made practical as well as financial sense to extend the existing building. The new work extended the earlier accommodation westwards, and included the small drawing room, the main south-facing entrance hall, the adjoining Adelaide room, the ballroom and the large dining room. Upstairs, three additional bedrooms facing south and a bathroom were added. It is also possible that the Governor's study and two large bedrooms over the large dining room were added at this time.[45]

Further improvements were made in the years 1863–1869, principally to the servants' quarters, including the demolition and replacement of earlier rooms, together with the addition of a new kitchen and scullery. In 1872, a conservatory (today the library) was built next to the ballroom, and in 1878 the billiard room, the Private Secretary's office, the porter's hall (now called the Western Entrance) and strong room were added. In 1874 the old guard room was replaced by a substantial guardhouse, while a new west wall was built to allow for widening of King William Road.[46]

In 1899, shortly after the arrival of Hallam Tennyson as Governor, Audrey Lady Tennyson, his wife, wrote to her mother Zacyintha Boyle in England to describe Government House. 'The garden is extremely pretty & plenty of trees with 3 or 4 gardeners', she exclaimed. 'It is quite a comfortable house . . . having been repainted and papered – great big square bright rooms & we are all very comfortably housed much more roomily than at home and we have 3 spare rooms & a maid's room for *relations* only or officials!!!'[47] She continued, in intricate detail:

> There are two entrances, the one in the pictures with a portico is the public one & people come in there and write their names in that hall in a huge red leather book . . . In this hall there is nothing but the table, two carved chairs with silk on one side, & two large ditto on the other & big mahogany & gilt doors on each side and at the end; the right hand door leads into one of three drawingrooms – the end ones facing the entrance to the state diningroom, & the left hand side into a very nice room called the Admiral's room . . . Facing these doors from the hall are more folding doors into the ballroom & across the ballroom . . . are other folding doors into H's library & business room, & then the billiard room & staff rooms are beyond with their bedrooms over.[48]

'The ballroom has been newly decorated', she added, 'it's a long room & a large picture of the Queen & gilt brackets and mirrors & red settees all round'. Upstairs, there were 'large wide carpeted passages . . . My sittingroom has a balcony over the portico – it opens into my bedroom'.[49] Overall, Lady Tennyson concluded, summing up first impressions of Government House: 'We are very agreeably surprised with it – the rooms are very large, lofty and airy'.[50]

It was in this condition that Government House entered the twentieth century. It was not until during and immediately after the Second World War that major renovations were again undertaken. In 1941–1957 the bathrooms in the main part of the building were refurbished, and in the 1970s a new kitchen block was built between the dining rooms and staff area. Part of this modernisation was prompted by the anticipated Royal visit in 1973, when some of the rooms on the first floor of the original East Wing were rearranged and updated to form a separate suite for the Queen and Duke of Edinburgh.[51]

The story of Government House had been one of continuous improvement, the building increasingly well appointed and ever better suited to the Governor's requirements. Yet for successive Governors and their families, only recently arrived from Britain and unfamiliar with the fierce, dry heat of the South Australian summer, Government House could sometimes take on an oppressive atmosphere. In November 1900, for example, Lady Tennyson wrote from Government House to her mother to complain about the weather:

> This is our 4th day of heat & the upper rooms are getting unbearable . . .
> The heat of the air this morning driving to church and walking back was so
> tremendous it prevented keeping one's eyes open properly & the pavements
> literally scorched one's feet. My hat-pins were burning when I took them
> out tho' hidden among folds of chiffon & lace. But everyone goes on the
> same, Lord Richard to his polo, Capt. Maurice to his drilling on a scorching
> ground in full sun, & the boys & Hallam & one of the others, lawn tennis.[52]

Despite the stiff upper lips and goings out in the midday sun, it had been resolved early on that Governors and their entourages should have the opportunity to escape the baking heat of the Adelaide Plains and seek instead the relative cool of the neighbouring Mount Lofty Ranges. In an echo, perhaps, of the niceties of British rule in India, it was decided in the late 1850s that the Governor of South Australia should have an official summer residence in balmier climes. The site chosen was on government land acquired (somewhat dubiously) in 1840 by Governor Gawler in what is now Belair National Park. The vice-regal retreat, known rather confusingly today as 'Old Government House', was designed by the architect Edward Hamilton and his associates and built by Charles Farr from local sandstone, with red-brick quoins coming from the nearby Blackwood brickworks. Completed in 1860, the summer residence comprised two main rooms (a dining room and a bedroom), a small office, bathroom, dressing room and cellar. An especially attractive feature was the large five-sided bay window in the dining room, with French doors opening to a spacious terrace. There was also an indoor plunge pool, reputedly the first in South Australia.[53]

'Old Government House' remained in use as the official summer residence until 1880, when it was superseded by the far grander Marble Hill, also located in the Mount Lofty Ranges, between Ashton and Cherryville. Transferred initially to the Department of Woods and Forests Nursery, and in 1961 to the National Parks and Wildlife Reserves, Old Government House is today looked after by the Friends of Old Government House and open to the public on occasions. Although the building had served its purpose well, providing a haven away from the city heat, the three Governors who used it – Richard Graves MacDonnell (1855–1862), Dominick Daly (1862–1868), and William Jervois (1877–1883) – found its modest proportions rather limiting.[54] Indeed, in 1878–1879 Governor Jervois had occupied the more substantial two-storeyed bluestone Heathfield House at Port Eliot as his temporary official summer residence, benefitting from its larger size as well as the sea breezes of Encounter Bay.

It was Jervois who, soon after his arrival in the colony in 1877, began planning the new summer residence at Marble Hill. He secured government funding for the project, and was intimately involved in its execution, personally selecting the site and overseeing the building's design. An officer in the Royal Engineers, Governor Jervois had previously constructed formidable fortifications across the British Empire, and was in his element directing the building of a Victorian Gothic pile in the style of a Scottish baronial castle. His architect was William McMinn. The original design was for a palatial forty rooms but only twenty-six were completed. Despite the building's grandeur, the rooms themselves were quite modest in size, including a drawing room, morning room, and dining room. Especially noteworthy was an impressive staircase of kauri pine and blackwood.[55]

All fifteen Governors who held office from 1880 to 1955 spent at least part of their summers at Marble Hill. Not surprisingly, Lady Tennyson was particularly fond of the location. When she and her husband Lord Tennyson, by now appointed Governor-General of Australia, revisited Marble Hill in 1902, they expressed an interest in purchasing the property, should it ever become available.[56] George Le Hunte (1903–1909) began the delightful tradition of entertaining local children at Marble Hill, and Lady Bosanquet, wife of Le Hunte's successor, Day Bosanquet ((1909–1914), hosted annual picnics for pupils from nearby primary schools.[57] During the First World War, Henry Galway (1914–1920) offered Marble Hill for use as a military hospital, but it was considered too remote. In the Second World War, Malcolm Barclay-Harvey (1939–1944), a noted railway historian and train enthusiast, installed a miniature railway in the gardens. Not to be outdone, his wife, Lady Muriel, named one of her racehorses Marble Hill.[58] Her son, David Liddell-Grainger (stepson of Malcolm Barclay-Harvey), was enchanted by the location, recalling an early visit when the beds of dahlias and cannas – not to mention the garden paths – had become completely overgrown. 'When we came here these had been neglected and were overgrown at least 6 foot high with broom, pea and eucalypt', he remembered. 'It was a case of arming oneself with a machete, finding the start of a path and just continuing on until you got somewhere.'[59]

By the early 1950s major renovations were underway at Government House in Adelaide, and in 1954 the original acetylene gas lighting at Marble Hill was replaced by electricity in anticipation of the current Governor, Robert George (1953–1960), together with his wife, family and servants, moving into the summer residence full-time until the refurbishment of Government House was complete. All his and Lady George's possessions were moved to Marble Hill in anticipation of a longer than usual stay, as well as clearing the decks for unimpeded work at Government House. On 2 January 1955 ('Black Sunday') disaster struck. The temperature rose steadily through the day, reaching 107°F (42°C) by 1 pm, with winds of up to forty-five miles per hour fanning a bushfire that had started at nearby Anstey's Hill. Marble Hill was soon ablaze, and although the Governor and his sons fought valiantly to save the building it was to no avail. Motor cars standing by for a retreat of last resort were also engulfed by flame, and, at the Governor's direction, the fifteen family and staff at Marble Hill sheltered under the protection of a retaining wall, covering themselves with wet blankets. The fire swept over them, causing only minor injuries, but Marble Hill was all but destroyed, as were the personal belongings of Sir Robert and Lady George.[60]

Despite its idyllic location, Marble Hill had been prone to bushfires from the beginning. As early as February 1882, just two years after it had been completed, the building was threatened by encroaching flames. In the hot summer of 1900, Lady Tennyson was mesmerised by the approaching fires, writing to her mother on 25 January to explain that 'we had a terrible bushfire & were really only saved by the wind mercifully shifting right round as it was rushing up the hill close to the tennis court'. But she found the spectacle a 'magnificent sight as it was at night. The hills opposite were covered with *hundreds* of trees alight . . . looking like a huge town beautifully illuminated – I shall never forget it'.[61] In the following year, the fires again menaced Marble Hill, Lady Tennyson recording that they 'simply had bushfires raging all round us, really a most wonderful sight, all the hills bursting with great volumes of smoke & great clouds of smoke rolling along the gullies'.[62] Twice during his residency, Governor Bosanquet had to organise the defence of Marble Hill against the flames, on one occasion the *Register* noting that 'big trees were as matches before the advancing fire'.[63] During the 1930s there were more such dangerous moments, not least during the devastating 'Black Friday' fires of 1939.

Although Marble Hill had been earmarked for comprehensive refurbishment, the government of the day baulked at the cost of rebuilding from scratch after the disaster of January 1955. Thereafter the site lay fallow, until the National Trust for South Australia acquired the ruins in 1973, restoring the stables and other buildings for public access as well as rebuilding the tower in the main house. In 1992, however, the National Trust relinquished the site, which reverted to the State Government. In 2007, the government called for expressions of interest, and in 2009 the property was sold to private owners under a heritage agreement requiring, among other things, that Marble Hill be rebuilt, this time with adequate bushfire protection. Today, restoration work continues apace.

P.A. Howell considered that, as a vice-regal residence, Marble Hill was a 'costly white elephant' which had done little to enhance the dignity of the vice-regal office or assist the Governor in his duties.[64] Yet Howell recognised that the roles of Governor and Government House itself were intimately entwined, the latter the real focus of gubernatorial activity and the centre of the institutional and civic life of the State. To understand this intimacy was to appreciate much of consequence that had happened in South Australia since foundation. In his lecture to the Historical Society of South Australia in August 1977, as he mused on the 'varieties of vice-regal life', Howell asked his audience: 'Despite the current vogue for "history from below", a school of writing which is proving so very fruitful, may one venture to suggest that what has recently been lampooned as "the Government House verandah view" of history is worth a closer look?'[65] The answer was, surely, yes.

Chapter 2

FOUNDATION

For naval deeds in middy's clothes,
The sapient Whigs poor Hindmarsh chose,
But being rather pugnacious,
Recalled him in a way ungracious.
They Gawler chose, whose merit tested,
On acts of early valour rested.
Then Russell looked for one more keen.
One who colonial life had seen –
And then the province came in sooth
Grey-headed in the dawn of Youth.[1]

This ditty, an abridged version of a much longer doggerel poem, was reputedly written by A.H. Davis, a prominent journalist in Adelaide in the colony's early days.[2] It was an attempt to capture the defining characteristics of South Australia's first three foundational Governors – Hindmarsh, Gawler, Grey – and to summarise their experiences in office. (Lord John Russell, also mentioned, was Secretary of State for War and the Colonies in the British Government from 1839–1841, responsible for gubernatorial appointments across the Empire). The verse does indeed reflect the relative fortunes of these foundational Governors, or at least how their careers were perceived by observers – then and, to some extent, now. How each of them came to be Governors of the new colony is integral to the story of South Australia's foundation.

To begin with, South Australia was formally a Province, a distinctive title that reflected the peculiar origins of the colony. Established uniquely by Act of Parliament in the United Kingdom in 1834, South Australia was the brainchild of Edward Gibbon Wakefield and his associates in the South Australian Association, which adopted the planners' prescription that land sales in the new colony be used to fund assisted emigration in a system which came to be known as 'systematic colonisation'.[3] By applying this 'systematic' method, the Association argued, a balance would be achieved in the supply of land, labour and capital in the new colony. Wakefield has received a bad press from historians, not only for the flaws that appeared in his scheme in practice, but because in hindsight he seemed an unscrupulous character – a fraud, deceitful propagandist, and manipulator.[4] Yet the most recent assessments have offered a revised opinion. Eric Richards considers that 'Wakefield was a prophet of his times', and his success should be measured not by his shortcomings but by the fact that he did indeed attract 'extraordinarily good-quality emigrants' to South Australia, at a time when the Australian colonies generally were shunned as brutalised, corrupt and impossibly distant. Moreover, in achieving this, 'a perfect balance of the sexes' and of age, family structure, and occupational spread had been struck in the colony's early years.[5]

Wakefield should also be seen as a child of his time, as should the South Australian Association and indeed the new Province itself. These were the 'Reforming Thirties', which had resulted in the *Great Reform Act 1832*, when the franchise was extended in the United Kingdom and some of the worst electoral malpractices addressed. But there were still many who clamoured for enhanced social and economic mobility and greater civic and religious liberty.[6] Such individuals were attracted to the new colony, not least those Nonconformist Protestants who advocated the separation of Church and State and resented the payment of tithes to the Anglican Church, along with the other disabilities they suffered. These Dissenters, as they were known, were prominent among those who planned and advocated the foundation of South Australia, and were notable too among its early colonists, giving the Province its reputation as a 'Paradise of Dissent', as historian Douglas Pike called it.[7]

The *South Australia Act 1834* made provision for a Governor, who would hold executive power and make laws in the name of the Crown, but there would also be a set of Commissioners back in Britain who would be responsible for the survey and sale of lands and for emigration. A Resident Commissioner, based in the colony, would be answerable to the Commissioners for these land surveys and sales as well as emigration, a role that in any 'normal' British territory would have been invested in the Governor. A lawyer, James Hurtle Fisher, was appointed to this powerful position.[8]

Initially, Colonel Charles Napier, who had fought at Waterloo, was proposed as South Australia's first Governor. But, wisely no doubt, he recognised the potential for conflict between Governor and Resident Commissioner, and did not wish his powers to be limited by the Commissioners' activities, either at home or in the colony. Accordingly, he declined the post. As he put it, to have accepted it 'would be to work with a halter round my neck . . . I have no ambition to be at the head of a milk and water colonial government and while fancying myself a Governor discover that I was only a football'.[9] There were also moral objections. The *South Australia Act 1834*, Napier protested, was nothing less than an attempt 'to seize by force' a territory whose annexation would deprive 'an inoffensive race of people of their property, without giving them the slightest remuneration'.[10]

The *South Australia Act 1834* had assumed the planned colony to be unoccupied, and even the newly formed 'Society for Providing Religious Instruction among the Dissenters in the Proposed New Colony of South Australia' imagined the whole continent was only 'peopled by a few wandering savages'.[11] Yet integral to the spirit of the 'Reforming Thirties' was a growing concern in Britain for the plight of Indigenous peoples at the hands of European expansion and empire building. Evangelical Dissenters, notwithstanding the sentiments of the Society for Providing Religious Instruction, were especially troubled. In 1835, for example, Sir Thomas Fowell Buxton, the well-known evangelical Whig Member of Parliament, who had played a prominent part in the abolition of slavery (and whose grandson of the same name would later become Governor of South Australia [1895–1899]), was appointed chair of a Select Committee into the condition of 'Aboriginal' peoples in British possessions.[12] When the Committee reported two years later, it lamented that Indigenous 'territory has been usurped, their [Indigenous] numbers diminished; their character debased ... European vices and diseases have been introduced among them'.[13]

Such concerns almost stalled the South Australian project. Lord Glenelg, the Secretary of State for War and the Colonies, demanded assurances about the treatment, rights and welfare of the Aborigines in the proposed colony, and the Commissioners rushed to promise that Aboriginal lands would be safeguarded and that a Protector would be appointed to look after the specific interests of Indigenous people. Lord Glenelg was inclined to insist that the Act be amended to explicitly include such measures, which would have caused considerable (possibly catastrophic) delay, but finally he relented, bowing to pressure from the impatient Commissioners to proceed.[14]

John Hindmarsh
(18 December 1836 – 16 July 1838)

Meanwhile, a Governor had been appointed. This was John Hindmarsh, a Captain in the Royal Navy (hence the 'middy' – Midshipman – reference in Davis' ditty), who had lately returned from Egypt where he had been attempting to persuade the Pasha to place his fleet under British command. Hearing from Napier that he had refused the post of Governor, Hindmarsh hastened to express his own interest in the appointment. The Colonial Office was impressed. Hindmarsh, it reported, was 'zealous, good-tempered, anxious to do the right thing, brave and well used to hardship'.[15] Accordingly, he received his commission as Governor and Commander-in-Chief of the Province of South Australia on 14 July 1836, and shortly after set sail for the colony in his ship HMS *Buffalo*, along with his family, the Resident Commissioner James Hurtle Fisher and *his* family, and some 160 emigrants.

John Hindmarsh was a Royal Navy man through and through, and this is a clue to his leadership style, not least as South Australia's first Governor. He was born in Chatham, the Naval dockyard town in Kent, the son of John and Mary Hindmarsh, and was baptized there in St Mary's church on 22 May 1785.[16] His father, John Hindmarsh senior, was a gunnery officer in HMS *Bellerophon*, the ship young John joined in March 1793 as his father's servant. It was the beginning of an illustrious career in the Royal Navy. Hindmarsh served in the West Indies, saw action in the battle of the Glorious First of June in 1794, and was likewise in the thick of it off Cadiz in 1797. In August of the following year, he was at the battle of the Nile when the *Bellerophon* was menaced by the approaching French warship *L'Orient*, which had been engulfed by fire. All the other officers on deck had been killed or wounded, so Midshipman Hindmarsh, still only a teenager, took charge, ordering the cutting of the anchor cables and raising a spritsail to break free of the blazing hulk. The incident gave Hindmarsh a reputation for gallantry, and Horatio Nelson referred to it when Hindmarsh received his promotion to Lieutenant in April 1803 in HMS *Victory*. Hindmarsh had suffered a contusion during the action at the Nile, which resulted in him later losing an eye, rather like Nelson himself.

Hindmarsh's career as Naval hero continued apace. In May 1801 he had been transferred to HMS *Spencer*, taking part in the battle of Algeciras Bay, and in August 1803, newly promoted Lieutenant, he was appointed to HMS *Phoebe*, which was tasked with patrolling the French coast and participated in the storming of the forts at Toulon and the destruction of French ships in the Aix Roads. The *Phoebe*, with Hindmarsh embarked, was also at Nelson's famous victory over the combined French and Spanish fleets at Trafalgar on 21 October 1805. Next, Hindmarsh became First Lieutenant (second-in-command) of the sloop HMS *Beagle*, part of the Channel Squadron which saw action at Walcheren on the Scheldt estuary, as well as participating in the battle of the Basque Roads. In late 1809 he joined HMS *Acasta*, which patrolled on the Cape Station (southern Africa), and in the following year was sent in HMS *Nisus* to the East Indies Station, where he assisted in the conquest of Mauritius, and at the capture of Java commanded the boats sent to silence the shore batteries. Promoted Commander in 1814, he joined the senior ranks of the service, but with the end of the Napoleonic Wars, was placed 'on the beach' on half-pay, an opportunity to spend time at last with his wife Susannah Wilson Edmeades, whom he had married in 1809, and their children.

By March 1830, Hindmarsh was back at sea, in command of the frigate HMS *Scylla* on the Mediterranean Station. Promoted Captain in

1. The 'Old Gum Tree' at Glenelg, Holdfast Bay, with Governor Captain John Hindmarsh Royal Navy reading his Proclamation, 28 December 1836 (courtesy State Library of South Australia (SLSA) B19466).

2. 'Government Hut', the first Government House in Adelaide, sketched from the River Torrens by Mary Hindmarsh (the Governor's daughter) in 1837 (courtesy SLSA B4941).

3. An early anonymous sketch of 'Government Hut', c.1836 (courtesy SLSA PRG 280/1/38/84).

4. Government House, Adelaide, 1845, watercolour by S.T. Gill (courtesy Art Gallery of South Australia).

5. Government House, Adelaide, east view, from a sketch by F.R. Nixon, 1846 (courtesy SLSA B9483/10).

6. Government House, c.1867 (courtesy SLSA B2791).

7. Marble Hill, the Governor's summer retreat in the Adelaide Hill, c.1879 (courtesy SLSA B3094).

8. The ruins of Marble Hill, following its destruction by bushfire in 1955 (courtesy SLSA B63439).

9. 'Old Government House', Belair, c.1887 (courtesy SLSA B63015/41).

10. Government House in 1901, showing the oldest part of the building on its eastern side (courtesy SLSA B 9091).

11. Her Majesty Queen Elizabeth the Queen Mother planting a tree at Government House during her visit to South Australia in March 1966 (courtesy SLSA PRG 1662/5/4).

12. Above: Captain John Hindmarsh Royal Navy, first Governor of South Australia (courtesy SLSA B11165).

13. Left: Susannah Hindmarsh, wife of the first Governor, from an ivory miniature painted by George Milner Stephen (courtesy SLSA B7010).

14. Above: Lieutenant Colonel George Gawler, second Governor of South Australia (courtesy SLSA B14428).

15. Right: Maria Gawler, wife of the second Governor, c.1855 (courtesy SLSA B45262).

16. Left: Captain George Grey, the third Governor (courtesy SLSA B5969).

17. Below: Eliza Lucy Grey, wife of the third Governor, from a portrait by William Gush, c.1840 (courtesy SLSA B6436).

18. Left: Governor Lieutenant Colonel Frederick Holt Robe (courtesy SLSA B3753).

19. Right: Governor Sir Henry Edward Fox Young, c.1850 (courtesy SLSA B3754).

20. Governor Sir Richard Graves MacDonnell, c.1871 (courtesy SLSA B3755).

21. Above: Governor Sir Dominick Daly (courtesy SLSA B990).

22. Right: Caroline Maria, Lady Daly, wife of Governor Daly, c.1861 (courtesy SLSA B10204).

23. Above: Governor Sir James Fergusson, (courtesy SLSA B3758).

24. Left: Edith, Lady Fergusson, wife of Governor Fergusson, c.1865 (courtesy SLSA B493).

25. Above: Governor Sir Anthony Musgrave (courtesy SLSA B27293).

26. Right: Jeanie Lucinda, Lady Musgrave, wife of Governor Musgrave (courtesy SLSA B8769).

27. Joyce Harriet Musgrave, and her younger brother Dudley, sometime before her death by scalding in Government House in October 1874 (courtesy SLSA B22388).

28. Governor Lieutenant General Sir William Francis Drummond Jervois, c.1881 (courtesy SLSA B6984).

September 1831, he was again on half-pay by December of that year but was soon engaged to prepare the paddle-steamer *Nile* at Blackwall Yard on the Thames in east London for delivery to the Egyptian Navy. Hindmarsh travelled as a passenger in the *Nile* on its journey to Alexandria, the ship being commanded by Colonel William Light, who had served in the Royal Navy but gained his reputation in the British Army during the Peninsular Wars (he was a favourite of Wellington). Light was soon to be appointed Surveyor-General of South Australia, on Hindmarsh's recommendation, so the voyage together in the *Nile* must have been an agreeable and fruitful experience. Once in Egypt, however, Hindmarsh failed in his endeavour to place the Pasha's Navy under British command, and he returned home anxious to find a new project – which he did.

'Bluff Jack Hindmarsh', as he was sometimes known, commanded HMS *Buffalo* on its expedition to South Australia in the manner he would any warship, exercising Naval discipline and expecting unquestioning obedience, which some of the embarked passengers found irksome. Many of the emigrants under his stewardship had never been on the ocean before, and some of them found Governor Hindmarsh's jocular but ill-judged references to 'landlubbers' patronising and offensive. Some began to question his competence. Even his secretary, George Stevenson, became increasingly irritated by Hindmarsh's behaviour. 'The poor man does not know his own mind for two hours altogether', Stevenson confided in his journal, as Hindmarsh continually and seemingly haphazardly altered course. The sails were trimmed at night, Stevenson observed, so the ship made slow progress, and Hindmarsh allowed his dogs to run wild and nip passengers at will. He habitually resorted to 'violence and ruffianism' and 'profane and abominable oaths', Stevenson alleged.[17]

Yet early in the voyage, Hindmarsh had been distracted by his wife's illness. Even before the ship had left Spithead, off Portsmouth, Susannah had been incapacitated by severe seasickness, so much so that later the ship's surgeon almost despaired of her life. But despite his burdens and responsibilities – the loneliness of command, made worse by Susannah's affliction – Governor Hindmarsh could on occasion also display good humour and kindly sentiment. Shortly after the *Buffalo* set sail from Spithead, the whole ship's company and passengers assembled on the upper deck to witness the celebration of three weddings. The formalities completed, the newly married couples and bridesmaids were entertained by Hindmarsh in his cabin, while there was wine served on the quarter-deck and singing and dancing.[18]

Several emigrant ships had arrived in South Australia ahead of Governor Hindmarsh and HMS *Buffalo*, the original intention being to base the new colony on Kangaroo Island. But the locality proved unsatisfactory, not least a result of poor water supplies, and William Light, who had arrived with the advance parties, proceeded to the mainland to explore possible alternatives. He was much impressed with the country around Holdfast Bay but carried on to investigate Port Lincoln, which Hindmarsh had already earmarked as a potential capital. However, Light discovered this site too was unsatisfactory, and hastened back to Holdfast Bay, examining the extensive harbour at what would become Port Adelaide, and selecting a site inland for the proposed capital, Adelaide, which he later surveyed. When Hindmarsh eventually visited the locality, he found it acceptable, although grumbling that it was in his opinion too far from the Port.[19]

On 28 December 1836, HMS *Buffalo* anchored in Holdfast Bay and Governor Hindmarsh came ashore to read his famous Proclamation, which established his Government in the Province. Significantly, a major part of Hindmarsh's Proclamation was his insistence that his duty to protect the colonists extended equally to the Aboriginal population, which was to be afforded the privileges of British subjects. This, of course, reflected the grave concerns that Lord Glenelg had already expressed, and it was no coincidence that Hindmarsh named his landing place at Holdfast Bay after the Secretary of State. As Hindmarsh put it:

> In announcing to the Colonists of His Majesty's Province of South Australia the establishment of the Government, I hereby call upon them to conduct themselves at all times with order and quietness, duly to respect the laws, and by a course of industry and sobriety, by the practice of sound morality, and a strict observance of the ordinances of religion, to prove themselves to be worthy to be Founders of a great and free Colony. It is also, at this time especially, my duty to apprise the Colonists of my resolution to take every

lawful means for extending the same protection to the native population as to the rest of His Majesty's subjects, and my firm determination to punish with exemplary severity all acts of violence and injustice which may in any manner be practised or attempted against the natives, who are to be considered to be as much under the safeguard of the law as the Colonists themselves, and equally entitled to the privileges of British subjects. I trust therefore, with confidence to the exercise of moderation and forbearance by all classes in their intercourse with the native inhabitants, and they will omit no opportunity of assisting me to fulfil His Majesty's gracious and benevolent intentions towards them by promoting their advancement in civilisation, and ultimately the blessing of Divine Providence, their conversion to the Christian Faith.[20]

Hindmarsh's Proclamation won the appreciation of Lord Glenelg – 'Lord Glenelg congratulates Capt. Hindmarsh on the foundation of the projected Colony, and approves the Proclamation issued for the protection of the Aborigines'[21] – and the expectation of conversion to Christianity mirrored the aspirations of the Society for Providing Religious Instruction among the Dissenters of the Proposed New Colony of South Australia. Although the Society believed the Province was only sparsely settled by Indigenous peoples, it argued that the establishment of the colony offered not just 'the prospect of covering its surface with a moral and religious people' but provided 'the only means by which the present natives may become acquainted with the doctrines, and subject to the influence, of Christianity'.[22]

Hindmarsh's anxiety that the protection of the law be extended to the Aborigines as British subjects appeared to match the Society's evangelical fervour in adjudging Indigenous peoples ripe for conversion. However, such sincere intentions were fraught with their own contradictions. It was naïve to expect that British law would correspond to Aboriginal conceptions of legitimate behaviour, and when Aboriginal people were deemed to have contravened British law, they would suffer the consequences. Aboriginal notions of land ownership and land management were beyond the understanding of British law (and the colonists themselves), while the desire to 'civilise' and promote Christianity undermined and ultimately threatened to destroy an ancient culture and unique way of life with its own beliefs, creation stories, territorial and kinship allegiances, social relationships, languages, ceremonies, art forms, economy, and much else. If the first years of the colony's existence seemed to be marked by the apparently good relations between settlers and the Indigenous people, it was not so much a result of Governor Hindmarsh's exhortations but rather that the Kaurna of the Adelaide Plains were overawed by the presence of so many immigrants.[23]

Hindmarsh's Proclamation at Glenelg had dwelt extensively on the rights of Aboriginal people before the law. But within a few months the inherent difficulty in applying British law to Indigenous people became all too apparent. In mid-1837, the corpse of one Driscoll, a whaler, was found close to Encounter Bay. He had last been spotted by settlers accompanying an Aborigine named Reppindjeri (or 'Black Alick' as the colonists called him), together with Reppindjeris's two wives. The Aborigines had apparently agreed to act as Driscoll's guide but the relationship turned sour when they were confined against their will on a whaling vessel (Reppindjeri was even imprisoned in a barrel for a time). It was also alleged that Driscoll had attempted to sexually assault one of the wives, and had then been killed by an enraged Reppindjeri. The whalers and settlers of Encounter Bay demanded justice, and Reppindjeri was duly arrested. He languished in custody for four months while Hindmarsh pondered how best to handle the case. The Advocate-general, Charles Mann, the Governor's legal adviser, considered it was absolutely necessary to try and then hang Reppindjeri. But he wondered whether this could be done legally, because the only witnesses to the alleged murder were Aborigines whose testimony, he opined, was probably not admissible in a British court. Fortuitously, as it turned out, Reppindjeri escaped never to be seen again, thus saving Governor Hindmarsh from the unpalatable dilemma of matching due legal process as defined by his Advocate-general to the spirit of his own recent Proclamation.[24]

Unlike Charles Napier, Hindmarsh had underestimated or not understood the division of powers created in the new colony, with governance split between his own role as Governor and the position of the Resident Commissioner, James Hurtle Fisher. Despite his earlier good relations with William Light, Hindmarsh resented Light's authority as Surveyor-General. Hindmarsh also disliked John Brown, the Emigration Agent (who was likewise answerable to the Resident Commissioner), reporting that Brown sneered at his 'authority and person with disrespect and contempt'.[25] He was equally scathing about George Strickland Kingston, Light's assistant, and Colonial Secretary Robert Gouger, and complained about what he saw as Fisher's high-handed behaviour.[26] Not surprisingly, factions began to form, one around Hindmarsh and his Secretary Stevenson, the other around Fisher, the latter including Light, Kingston, Brown and Gouger. Hindmarsh may have bridled at his lack of power, but Fisher, a shrewd legal practitioner, knew exactly the extent of his own authority. As Paul Sendziuk and Robert Foster have concluded: 'While Hindmarsh was South Australia's first Governor, Fisher – in control of funds – effectively led the colony's first government.'[27]

Inevitably, the Fisher faction saw itself as beleaguered democrats defending the principles that underpinned the Province's foundation, while Hindmarsh was characterised as a pugnacious autocrat. By December 1837, the European population of the colony had swollen to about 3000, putting increased pressure on the surveying process, with demands that land be made available as soon as possible for agricultural purposes. Kingston was sent to Britain to secure further assistance with the surveys, and with him he took a letter from the colony's leading luminaries requesting that Hindmarsh be relieved of his governorship. Not surprisingly, the Commissioners agreed, and pressed their case in the Colonial Office. Lord Glenelg, who recognised the impossible position in which Hindmarsh had been placed by the *South Australia Act 1834*, acquiesced and arranged the Governor's recall, issuing the fateful order in February 1838. Hindmarsh accepted his dismissal without rancour and, with the exception of the small clique that had undermined him, the colonists felt little bitterness towards him when he set sail for Britain in July 1838.[28]

Despite his several difficulties, Hindmarsh's pioneering role as first Governor was not easily forgotten. Indeed, his Proclamation was swiftly adopted as one of South Australia's foundational myths, a source of pride (not least for its apparent recognition of Aboriginal rights), the 'Old Gum Tree' at Glenelg becoming a traditional place of pilgrimage and remembrance. The anniversary of 28 December became Proclamation

Day – or Commemoration Day, as it was also known – and was celebrated as a public holiday, with ceremonies at the Old Gum Tree to recall the original event and Hindmarsh's fine words. Before Federation, South Australia increasingly regarded itself as an embryonic 'nation', part of the Empire but distinctive when compared to other Australian colonies, and Proclamation Day was its 'national day'.[29] In this way, the collective memory of Governor Hindmarsh and his noble Proclamation underpinned the fashioning of an imagined South Australia, Hindmarsh's lasting contribution to the colony and State assuming a significance that went far beyond his relatively short tenure as Governor.

Hindmarsh's departure from South Australia was not the end of his career. In 1840 he was appointed Governor of Heligoland, the somewhat unlikely British possession set in the North Sea. In a mirror of his South Australian experience, he found the colony's tiny population riven by factions, and as before he was accused of despotic behaviour, not least by those who controlled the archipelago's fishing fleet. To pass the time he developed an interest in ornithology, and at length his governorship mellowed into a benign paternalism which provided sound administration in troubled times. He was knighted in 1851 and promoted Rear Admiral on relinquishing his position in 1856. He retired to the genteel seaside town of Hove in Sussex, but after his wife Susannah passed away in 1859, Hindmarsh moved to London where he died on 29 July 1860.

George Gawler
(17 October 1838 – 15 May 1841)

Meanwhile, back in 1838, the Colonial Office had amended the *South Australia Act 1834* so that in future the positions of Governor and Resident Commissioner would be merged, the combined authority now vested in the Governor himself. After Hindmarsh's departure, George Milner Stephen, the colony's new Advocate-general, had been appointed temporary Acting Governor. He was replaced as South Australia's second substantive Governor by Lieutenant-Colonel George Gawler, who arrived in the Province on 12 October 1838 with his wife Maria and five children in the emigrant ship *Pestonjee Bomanjee*.

Like Hindmarsh before him, Gawler had distinguished himself in the wars against France and Napoleon. Born at Chudleigh in Devon, he had attended the Royal Military College before being commissioned as an Ensign in the 52nd Regiment in October 1810. Gawler soon found himself in the midst of the Peninsular War, arriving in Lisbon in 1812 and leading a storming party during the capture of Badajoz in south-western Spain. He was wounded in the knee during this bloody encounter and was mentioned in dispatches by Wellington; shortly after he was promoted Lieutenant. In August 1812 Gawler participated in the subsequent march on Madrid, and was again wounded. He saw further action at Vittoria in 1813 and Toulouse in 1814; at the battle of Waterloo in 1815 Gawler led his company in repeated attacks on the French Imperial Guard. Thereafter, he served in the army of occupation in France for three years but was granted extended leave when his eyesight began to suffer.[30]

Gawler returned to duty in 1819, his health restored, but he was now a changed man. During his enforced absence, Gawler had studied the religious philosophy of Revd William Pacey, an evangelical Protestant prominent in the movement to abolish slavery and the author of a number of theological works, notably his *View on the Evidences of Christianity*, published in 1794. Gawler was much persuaded by Pacey's *Evidences*, and decided to commit his life to active evangelism. In 1820 he married the like-minded Maria Cox, noted for her piety and religiosity, and she went with Gawler when his regiment was posted first to Ireland and then to New Brunswick, in Canada. Here they threw themselves into local society, organising a Sunday school, Bible-reading class, lending library, and other 'improving' activities. Back in Britain, Gawler was promoted Captain in 1825 and became a Major in 1831. In August 1834 he purchased the rank of Lieutenant-Colonel, but in the same year resigned from his regiment. In 1833 he had published a pamphlet *The Close and Crisis of Waterloo*, about the culmination of that great battle, and in 1837 issued a second treatise, *The Essentials of Good Skirmishing*, evidence that his conversion to evangelical Christianity had by no means dimmed his enthusiasm for things military, or the military way of doing business.

George Gawler's mix of distinguished military service (Davis' 'acts of early valour') and commitment to evangelical Protestantism, commended him to the Whig Government of the day, as did his support for the *Great Reform Act 1832*, which he had expressed while stationed briefly in Bristol to maintain law and order during the Act's turbulent passage. More than John Hindmarsh, George Gawler was a product of the 'Reforming Thirties', and he was invited to apply for the position of Governor of South Australia. He accepted with alacrity but even before he left home shores, Gawler began to realise the enormity of the task that lay before him. He discovered that his authorised expenditure in the colony was at present limited to just £8000 per annum, with the right to draw an additional £2000 (later increased to £4000) to prevent destitution. A further £5000 could be drawn in a major crisis, such as bushfires or insurrections and attacks by pirates. When Gawler arrived in the Province, he found to his dismay that the total authorised expenditure for 1838 had already been exceeded. Salaries of Government officials remained unpaid for the third quarter, with at least one official drawing emergency rations to ward off starvation.

To this financial crisis was added the continuing delays in surveying. The colonists were living off their own capital, with little or no land under the plough and little pasturing of sheep or cattle. Gawler recognised the need for decisive action. To overcome the crippling shortage of finance, he decided (without prior authorisation) that moneys could be drawn against the land fund accumulated from sales, which in turn allowed an increase in his surveying staff. Light, protesting ill health, resigned as Surveyor-General, and was replaced by the energetic Lieutenant Edward Charles Frome. Progress was dramatic, so that by the end of 1840, some 2700 acres were under cultivation with 6000 settlers on the land.

At the same time, Gawler initiated expenditure on a public works program. A devotee of the political economist Adam Smith, he believed that government spending would stimulate economic development. He sanctioned the construction of police barracks, customs house, wharf, hospital and gaol, as well as houses for public officials and outstations for police and surveyors. A good road was built to link Adelaide with the Port. To many colonists this activity looked like sound investment in much needed infrastructure, although eyebrows were raised when this expenditure was extended to construction of the new Government House, the first signs of what would soon be seen as profligacy and extravagance. But, for now, Gawler remained popular among the almost 15,000 settlers by the end of 1840 (including a sprinkling of German immigrants), although some found him a rather dour fellow, with his disapproval of card games, dancing, and horseracing. He considered strong spirits the gateway to crime, although he was content that gentlemen should drink wine, except on Sundays. But he closed public houses at 10 pm, causing annoyance for many, and made gambling, cockfighting and home distillation illegal.[31]

Like Hindmarsh before him, Gawler had arrived in the Province with the welfare of the Aborigines uppermost in his mind. When he addressed the colonists on the subject, he mused: 'What a state of ignorance these poor creatures are in!' He urged the settlers to be 'cautious and forbearing' in their relationships with the Aborigines, asking them to 'remember the many fatal occurrences in other colonies' and to 'refrain from improper intercourse with their women, and with all your power keep them from that detestable and ruinous vice, drunkenness, that scourge of the civilized world'.[32] Shortly after landing in the colony, he organised a gathering for the Kaurna people, attended by 200 Aboriginal men, women and children. William Wyatt, the interim Protector of Aborigines, acted as translator, as Gawler explained the virtues he wished the Indigenous people to adopt. They should love God and embrace Christianity, learn English, wear clothes, build huts, do useful work, and respect white men and women and people from other tribes. But if they were injured by a white person, then the Protector would see that justice was done. Plates of beef and mugs of teas were handed out, along with gifts of rugs, blankets, frocks, caps, dishes and cups.[33]

In spirit, Gawler's gathering was akin to Hindmarsh's Proclamation, with a determination to protect the Aborigines matched by an insistence that they be introduced to Christianity and 'civilized' European ways. The question of Indigenous land rights, which had exercised Lord Glenelg in the aftermath of the *South Australia Act 1834*, also claimed Gawler's early attention. By July 1840, a new set of surveys had been completed and were offered for selection. Gawler gave instructions for some sections to be reserved for Aboriginal people, a decision that provoked an outcry among those settlers who felt they already had to wait too long to be allocated land. Gawler explained patiently that the Aborigines were the original owners of the land, and that it was his duty to protect their rights, but he effectively backtracked by deciding the Indigenous people were not yet sufficiently advanced to undertake farming, and that land would be held in trust until they were. From now on, it was apparent, the expansion of the frontier would be about appropriation rather than sharing.

Relations between settlers and Aborigines were further strained by the *Maria* incident in June 1840.[34] On 7 June the brig *Maria* had left Adelaide bound for Hobart, with twenty-six crew and passengers. Three weeks later the ship had the misfortune to be wrecked off the south-east coast of South Australia. All hands safely made it ashore, and began to make their way up the Coorong in the direction of Encounter Bay. They were assisted by members of the Milmenrura clan, a group of the Ngarrindjeri people, but somehow the relationship collapsed, and all twenty-six survivors were killed. As in the earlier case of Reppindjeri, there were no European witnesses to the massacre, and again it was thought that Indigenous evidence was inadmissible in court (as they could not understand an oath). Although Gawler had accepted that Indigenous people were British subjects, he resolved his dilemma by declaring that the Milmenrura were a 'hostile tribe, that is ... *a nation at enmity with Her Majesty's Subjects*'.[35] Accordingly, he despatched the Police Commissioner, Major Thomas O'Halloran, to investigate and conduct a summary trial, which he did. Two Aborigines were selected from those apprehended by O'Halloran, and were hanged on the beach where the murders had been committed. For these actions, Gawler was roundly criticised by the *Register*. He replied by emphasising that the case was 'beyond the limits of ordinary British justice' and could only be dealt with 'on the principles of martial law'.[36]

Confrontations with the Aboriginal populations became yet more overt as sheep and cattle were driven overland from New South Wales to stock the newly surveyed properties. Those overlanders travelling the route along the River Murray routinely reported violent contacts with groups of Aborigines, and in April 1841 a large Indigenous force attacked a party near Lake Bonney, dispersing some 5000 sheep and 800 cattle. Gawler reacted by sending in Thomas O'Halloran but the Police Commissioner was ordered back to Adelaide when the surprise news came through that Gawler had been recalled to London.

Word of Gawler's spending had by now found its way to London – in 1840, with a total income of £30,000, his expenditure had run to £174,000 – and the Commissioners were astonished when they learned that the entire land fund of £300,000 had gone. They were no longer prepared to honour Gawler's bills, and it was decided he should be recalled. The new Governor, George Grey, arrived unexpectedly in Adelaide in May 1841, carrying with him the letter from Lord Glenelg's successor, Lord John Russell, announcing Gawler's formal recall. In the immediate aftermath, it did indeed appear that Gawler had been recklessly profligate, a verdict encouraged by Governor Grey himself as he struggled with the crisis he had inherited. Some settlers had already quit the colony, fearful of its imminent collapse. When James Penn Boucaut, one-time Premier and Supreme Court judge, returned on a visit to his native Cornwall in 1892 he met an old man in Saltash who had emigrated to the Province in its early days but had returned home shortly after 'because of what he took to be the smash-up of South Australia when Governor Gawler's bills were dishonoured'.[37]

But Gawler's investment was already beginning to bear fruit, the bumper harvest of 1841 a result of the agricultural expansion consequent on the increase in surveys. There was also a mineral boom, the first inklings of which had been apparent during Gawler's time but did not reach its full potential until after his departure. In May 1841, a silver-lead mine had been opened at Glen Osmond, in the foothills. It was christened 'Wheal Gawler' after the Governor ('wheal' being a Cornish prefix meaning 'working'), in anticipation of its supposed economic importance to the infant colony.[38] Other mines sprang up in the locality, the first metalliferous workings in Australia, their discovery and development catching the attention of investors on the world stage. As Seymour Tremenheere explained to the Royal Geological Society of Cornwall, these new South Australian mines could compete directly with those of Cornwall and elsewhere. As he put it: 'The wool-ships [sailing to Europe] on account of the lightness of the cargo are obliged to take in a large quantity of ballast, and therefore glad to take the lead and copper ore at a merely nominal rate of freight.' This, he added, 'was considered as bringing their mines, as it were, actually into Europe, or at all events as placing them upon equal footing with European mines'.[39] These Glen Osmond mines never quite lived up to their promise – this was left to the fabulously rich Kapunda and Burra Burra copper mines, discovered during Governor Grey's term of office.

George Gawler had been recalled before these positive outcomes had become apparent. Although a sympathetic Select Committee in Britain had already acknowledged that it was difficult to imagine any way in which his expenditure might have been significantly reduced, he was nonetheless subject to withering public criticism. 'Bewildered, angry, in the end pathetic', according to his biographer, Gawler 'tried to get from the government some public acknowledgement of the value of his work'.[40] He was refused a knighthood and requests for further public appointments were turned down. He shifted his attentions, therefore, to charitable works and writing. He championed the cause of the resettlement of the Jews in Palestine, and among his publications was *The Emancipation of the Jews*, which appeared in 1847. He was promoted full Colonel in the same year, to his great satisfaction, and in 1849 toured the Holy Land. He resigned from the Army in 1850, and retired to Southsea in Hampshire where he died of pneumonia on 7 May 1869.

George Grey
(15 May 1841 – 25 October 1845)

In one of those curious coincidences of history, Gawler's successor, George Grey, was born during the Peninsular War at Lisbon in Portugal on 14 April 1812. This was barely a week after his father, Lieutenant-Colonel George Grey, had been killed in the battle of Badajoz, the same action in which George Gawler had been wounded and for which he was decorated.[41] Grey's mother, Elizabeth Anne Vignoles, remarried in 1817, and young George was soon sent away to boarding school, which he hated, eventually joining the Royal Military College, Sandhurst, in 1826. As an Ensign in the 83rd Regiment, Grey was posted to Ireland in 1830, and was promoted Lieutenant in 1833. He did not much enjoy soldiering in Ireland but was moved by the plight of the Irish peasantry, and wondered whether the solution to their distress was emigration, especially the 'systematic colonisation' theory, which had recently caught his attention. More generally, he was enthused by stories of exploration in Australia, especially the exploits of Charles Sturt.

In 1836, George Grey approached the Colonial Office with a proposal that he should lead an expedition to determine a site for possible British settlement in north-western Australia. He won the support of the Royal Geographical Society, and with a small team set out in HMS *Beagle* in July 1837, journeying via the Cape where he was joined by HMS *Lynher*. The party arrived at Hanover Bay in what became the Kimberley region, the country of the Worrorra people, at the end of the year, and began to move inland in January 1838. Their progress was impeded by floodwater and resistance from large numbers of Aborigines. On 10 February, Grey was speared by an Indigenous Australian, and was for a time quite ill, although recovered sufficiently two weeks later to resume his exploration. He named the Glenelg River and other local features before returning to Hanover Bay in April 1838, to be picked up by the *Beagle* and *Lynher*, which took the explorers to Mauritius to recuperate.

By the September, Grey was in Perth, the capital of Swan River Colony (later Western Australia), intending to resume his exploration. In February 1839 he sailed for Shark Bay, again in the north-west, and was deposited on Bernier Island with three whale boats, with which he planned to navigate the coast. To Grey's dismay, the party found the island entirely devoid of water, and to escape their predicament they attempted a hazardous landing on the mainland, losing a boat and a large quantity of supplies. All hopes of further exploration were abandoned, and the party turned southwards along the coast in the remaining two boats, with the aim of reaching Perth. However, both boats were wrecked in the heavy surf at Gantheaume Bay, and Grey and his men were forced to complete on foot the 300-mile trek that lay ahead, surviving only through the help given by the Whadjuk Noongar people as the party traversed their country. Grey arrived in Perth on 21 April 1839, with all but one of the others turning up shortly after. The missing fellow was never found.

Grey's exploits in Western Australia were deemed sufficiently worthy for him to be promoted Captain and appointed resident magistrate at King

George Sound, where he met Eliza Lucy Spencer, daughter of the previous magistrate. The couple were married at Albany on 2 November 1839. Having been badly wounded by Aborigines, yet also saved from thirst and starvation by kindly Indigenous people, Grey developed an ambivalent view of Aboriginal society. During his spell at King George Sound he published his *Vocabulary of the Dialects spoken by the Aboriginal Races of South-Western Australia*, demonstrating his facility with local Indigenous languages and a regard for Aboriginal culture. Yet he also believed that the only way to save these people from extinction was for them to abandon their traditional lifestyle and embrace instead Christian ways, finding employment alongside European settlers, and sending their children to boarding schools to be educated properly.

In 1840, George Grey was ordered back to Britain. He and Eliza journeyed via Adelaide, where for three weeks they were entertained in Government House by Governor Gawler and his wife. Grey made the most of his sojourn in South Australia, seeking out every influential person in the colony, making sure his name was known. Gawler had boasted proudly of his achievements in growing the Province's infrastructure but, on his return to Britain, Grey promoted instead a narrative of extravagance and waste.[42] Back in England, Grey was now ensconced in Brighton, the popular resort on the Sussex coast, where he busied himself writing his two-volume *Journal of Two Expeditions of Discovery in North-West and Western Australia in the Years 1837, 38 and 39*, which was published in London in 1841. Then, learning that the Commissioners' funds had been exhausted, and that parliament was being asked to pick up South Australia's debts, he wrote earnestly to Secretary of State, Lord Russell. Grey criticised the existing regime in the colony (but refrained from mentioning Gawler by name), and effectively put himself forward as prospective Governor, stressing the need for prudent economy and his desire to work closely with the Colonial Office. Having already made a reputation for himself in Australia ('One who colonial life had seen', as Davis' doggerel put it), and with his knowledge, albeit fleeting, of Adelaide, Grey seemed the ideal man for the job.

George Grey arrived in Adelaide on 10 May 1841, and assumed the governorship of South Australia five days later. He was only twenty-nine years old, ambitious, single-minded and headstrong. Among the immediate difficulties that confronted him was the death of his and Eliza's only child, aged five months, just a month after their landing in the colony. The long voyage with a new babe in arms could not have been easy for Eliza, and she may have resented the infelicitous timing of the journey, as well as mourning her infant's early demise so shortly after arrival in South Australia. At any rate, her relationship with Grey deteriorated, and the marriage was not a happy one. They separated in 1860 en route to the Cape (Grey accused Eliza of flirting with an Admiral, the final straw), and were only reconciled (grudgingly) later in life.

Grey found the condition of the colony less parlous than he had expected (Gawler's policies were at last having an effect, although Grey was loathe to acknowledge it). But there was still a sense of crisis (immigration had been suspended, for example), which needed to be addressed. Grey looked for ways to cut costs, now the government works and backlog of surveys had been completed, and pared down departments, amalgamating some and abolishing others. He made government more efficient but his cutbacks were not popular with those who found themselves unemployed, such as those labourers thrown out of work when construction was halted on the road linking Adelaide and Mount Barker. Nor was Governor Grey popular when he introduced charges – 'taxation without representation', as his critics complained – and he enraged local merchants when he refused to pay bills that Gawler had incurred. Some colonists decided to abandon South Australia, moving to the eastern colonies or New Zealand. Eventually, under considerable pressure, Grey drew drafts to pay outstanding debts, in doing so incurring the displeasure of the Colonial Office.[43]

Governor Grey became no less popular as time went on. The *Southern Star*, with Shakespearean flourish, declared: 'Think upon Grey and let thy soul despair.'[44] Others called for Grey's resignation, or for him to be recalled, and there was much hostility to his *Police Act*, which prohibited a wide range of public disturbances. The beating of carpets in streets became an offence, as did excessive ringing of doorbells, keeping unmuzzled dogs, selling or exhibiting obscene publications, and singing bawdy songs. For being drunk in public on a weekday, the punishment was a night in gaol plus a five-shilling fine, increased to ten shillings for a Sunday.[45]

Alongside his difficulties with the settlers, Governor Grey had also to deal with fierce Aboriginal resistance. The overlanders again requested protection. Grey despatched Major O'Halloran and the new Protector of Aborigines, Matthew Moorhouse, to assist a beleaguered overland party, only for them to arrive at the scene too late, four of the overlanders having been killed. Grey mustered a further expedition, led by Moorhouse and Sub-Inspector of Police, Bernard Shaw. Just over the New South Wales border, on the Rufus River, they encountered a force, several hundred strong, of the Maraura people. Although Grey had emphasised that the Aborigines be treated as British subjects, and despite Moorhouse's instruction that firearms should only be used as a last resort, there was an unauthorised and seemingly spontaneous outbreak of gunfire, resulting in at least thirty Aboriginal deaths. Grey ordered an inquiry into the incident; a Bench of Magistrates decided the actions were 'justifiable'.[46] Port Lincoln, only recently settled, was also the scene of frontier clashes. The Battara people attacked remote stations, killing several settlers, and Grey was obliged to send in a unit of the 96th Regiment to support local police and provide reassurance for the colonists.[47]

Despite his several difficulties, Governor Grey could point to the success of his policies, as he understood them. He noted the increase in cultivated land, which had grown from 2503 acres in 1840 to 19,790 acres in 1842 and 28,690 acres in 1843. Much of this agricultural land was given over to wheat, producing enough for domestic consumption with a surplus for export. Revenue now equalled expenditure, or nearly so, and Grey was gratified by the reduction in both crime and the number of public houses – in his estimation, the two were linked. To these results of economic planning and financial stringency was added a strong dose of good fortune– the discovery of copper at Kapunda in 1842 and at Burra Burra in 1844.[48] As Francis Dutton explained in his *South Australia and its Mines*, published in 1846:

South Australia was already rapidly advancing towards a prosperous state;
it had recovered from the shock it sustained during the years of depression,
which had retarded, though not crushed, its rising importance; the settlers,
generally, were fast getting out of debt, though none of them were rich,

when new impetus was given to their industry, by the discovery, in 1843 [sic], of rich mineral deposits in different parts of the Province, made doubly important by the fact, that, in South Australia, no reserves are made by the Government with regard to minerals; by which means the owner of the soil was at liberty to extract those metallic ores from the ground, unfettered by Government interference.[49]

In fact, although the Kapunda mine lay within an existing pastoral property that had already been surveyed, the Burra Burra discovery was in wild outback country, a hundred miles north of Adelaide. This did indeed require Government intervention. Governor Grey insisted upon a special survey of 20,000 acres at £1 per acre, payable in cash, before any mining could commence, and two rival groups in Adelaide – known colloquially as the 'Nobs' and the 'Snobs' – scrambled to raise this vast amount of money. Eventually, they joined forces to meet Grey's requirements, and, the special survey completed, the Nobs (including Francis Dutton) drew the southern section, and the Snobs the northern.[50]

The Princess Royal mine, situated in the southern section, was initially very successful but at depth the copper deposits proved disappointing. By 1851 the mine's financial resources were all but expended, and the land was sold as a sheep run. The northern section, by contrast, proved fabulously rich, and this became the far-famed Burra Burra mine, where work started on 24 September 1845. The Cornish miners called their initial working 'Great Wheal Grey', after the Governor, and by October they were raising sixty tons of copper ore per week – mostly malachite and azurite – which assayed at an incredible 71.25% copper. This success placed South Australia at the centre of the rapidly expanding international mining frontier, and led, among other things, to an upsurge in immigration, mainly of Cornish miners and their families, together with a wave of prosperity and optimism that lasted until the Victorian goldrush in 1851.[51]

The Burra Burra bonanza, together with the strong performance of Kapunda and a string of other mines across the colony, ensured that George Grey's period as Governor ended on a high note, at least in the estimation of those, such as Francis Dutton, who were doing well out of the copper boom. Early on, as Dutton recalled, 'Tumultuous meetings were held, seditious language was used, and on one occasion several hundred men in an organized body marched up to Government House, threatening personal violence'.[52] But later, according to Dutton, at 'the very time' of his impending departure from South Australia, the results of Grey's 'admirable and enlightened' administration were coming to fruition, reflected in 'the cordial and unanimous confirmation of the good opinion already so generally felt for him in the colony'.[53]

As Dutton explained, 'the Home Government had determined upon conferring upon him [Grey] the honourable, though arduous task of the administration of the colony of New Zealand'.[54] New Zealand was in a parlous state, according to Dutton, and once again Captain Grey was the man for the job. Grey relinquished the governorship of South Australia on 10 October 1845, and arrived in New Zealand to take up his new post in the November. He found the north of the colony in uproar, where an indignant Maori population complained that the British were honouring neither the letter nor the spirit of the Treaty of Waitangi. Hone Heke, who had led the Maori signatories of the Treaty in 1840, felt undermined and betrayed as he saw his authority slip away and his lands eroded. 'God made this country for us,' he protested to Governor Grey shortly after his arrival, explaining that he had agreed to be 'all as one' with the Governor, sharing power, but that this just accommodation had been ignored in practice. Grey failed to placate Heke, and war gripped the colony from 1845 until 1847 when at last the Governor was able to secure peace of a sort, as power tilted away little by little from the Maoris to the colonial Government and settlers.[55]

Grey was knighted for his efforts in 1848 but he proved no more popular with the settlers of New Zealand than he been with those of South Australia in the early days. Among other things, they expected progress towards representative and eventually responsible government. Intriguingly, Grey was opposed to self-government on the grounds that it would inevitably exclude the Maoris. But, paradoxically, he also wished to curtail the power of the Maori chieftains, making himself directly responsible for Maori affairs, and he tried to engage Maori participation in a range of governmental and civic activities, such as the provision of schools and hospitals. Eventually, in

1853, New Zealand did gain representative government, a result of Imperial intervention, with a Legislative Council nominated by the Governor and an elected House of Representatives.[56] In the same year, Grey was recalled to Britain.

In the following year, however, Sir George Grey was appointed Governor of Cape Colony. With his experience of Indigenous affairs in both South Australia and New Zealand, he aimed to create a harmonious society based on the expansion of white settlement and the counter-balancing accommodation of the black population. His vision likewise extended to the creation of a unified, self-governing federation of South Africa, something that was not achieved until more than half a century later, his outlook now determinedly Imperialist. He was recalled to Britain in 1859 but was promptly sent back to the Cape in the following year, only to be appointed to New Zealand for a second time in 1862, the Colonial Office hoping his experience would enable him to resolve the conflict that had broken out once more between Maori and settler. In July 1863, Grey launched a ruthless assault on the Waikato region, south of Auckland, which finally broke the back of Maori power in that locality, in the process opening up more land for colonial settlement.[57]

Grey was eventually recalled to Britain in 1868. But he was not finished yet. He aspired to a parliamentary political career, and in 1870 proposed to stand as an Independent Liberal in a by-election consequent upon the death of the sitting Liberal MP. He was persuaded to withdraw, when it was pointed out that he was likely to split the Liberal vote. From there it was back to New Zealand, ostensibly to retire, but he was soon elected to the House of Representatives, where he served for twenty years, including a term as Premier (1877–1879). Subsequently, he toyed with the prospect of Imperial federation (which might even include the United States, he thought), and he supported the federation of the Australian colonies, but was against New Zealand joining. In 1891 he attended the Australian Federal Convention, where, according to his biographer, 'with senile garrulity' he championed the notion of one-man-one-vote, then embarking on a tour of the eastern colonies to advocate democracy and social equality.[58]

In 1894, Sir George Grey returned to Britain for the last time. He died on 18 September 1898, and was buried in St Paul's Cathedral in London. His had been an astonishing career. A man of contradictions, he professed liberal ideals, including an affection for Indigenous peoples (he learned Maori as well as several Aboriginal languages), but as Governor – in South Australia, in Cape Colony, and in New Zealand – he was often autocratic and confrontational, and not afraid to shed blood. Personal as well as political relationships suffered. Yet during his time as the third of South Australia's foundational governors, he had turned the colony's fortunes around, partly by sound administration but also by good luck, although usually to the advantage of the settlers and rarely to that of the Aboriginal population.

Chapter 3

RESPONSIBLE GOVERNMENT

From South Australia's conception, early self-government had been a principal aim, the assumption, enshrined in the *South Australia Act 1834*, being that by the time the settler population had reached 50,000 steps would be taken to establish an elected assembly.[1] The numbers increased steadily through the mid- and late-1840s – 25,893 in 1846, 31,153 in 1847, 38,666 in 1848 – exceeding the threshold in 1849 when the population rose to 52,904 people.[2]

This increase was matched by a growing clamour for self-government. The early governors had ruled with the assistance of an appointed Council, which until 1842 had consisted of three Crown nominees. In that year, the British Parliament passed an *Act to Provide for the Better Government of South Australia*, which, as well as redefining the Province as an ordinary Crown colony, created a Legislative Council made up of the Governor and three official and four non-official members also nominated by the Crown, the former being public servants and the latter selected from prominent colonists. Although this marginally increased the influence of leading colonists in how South Australia was run, the Governor remained responsible to the British Government rather than to his Legislative Council.

Despite the expanding population, Governor Grey during his term of office had been opposed to any extension of the Legislative Council that might allow popular representation, and he firmly discounted any possibility of a bicameral system in which an elected lower house might complement the upper.[3] This was despite a strongly worded petition presented to him in April 1844, in which it was insisted that 'the Wakefield principle could not be worked without representation'. The petition, drawn up by leading colonists, demanded the 'unfettered influence of powerful, faithful, and enlightened men who would act as between the Government and the people', arguing that 'the colony was now self-existing and self-supporting and ought to be permitted to be self-legislating'. This would require, it was asserted, 'popular representation'.[4]

South Australia's first essay in local government, the Adelaide Municipal Corporation, also foundered on the shoal of Grey's indifference. In 1840 towns with a population of 2000 or more were allowed to elect their own councils, and Adelaide duly availed itself of this opportunity. The new Corporation was able to levy its own rates but its independence was restricted by the requirement to submit all by-laws for gubernatorial approval. Grey made it clear that he would tolerate no alternative source of authority in the colony, and offered no help when the Corporation, with its chronic lack of funding and no real public achievement, quietly expired. In mid-1843, the Corporation suffered the ignominy of its furniture being seized for non-payment of debts, and it disappeared from public view thereafter.[5]

Frederick Holt Robe
(22 October 1845 – 2 August 1848)

Frederick Holt Robe, who was sworn in on 25 October 1845, replaced George Grey as Governor. A naturally conservative figure, with a military background like his predecessors, Robe was not inclined to encourage either colonial self-government or the development of local government, and on these matters found himself at loggerheads with the colonists, just as Grey had been. He behaved, according to one newspaper, 'like some man-of-war captain of the old school addressing a mutinous crew'.[6] More recent assessments of Robe as Governor are not dissimilar. P.A. Howell thought Robe 'strong minded', and E.J.R. Morgan in the *Australian Dictionary of Biography* decided that Robe's 'attributes made him ill-fitted to control aspiring colonists who demanded independence and an increasing share of their own government'.[7] He was, according to Morgan, 'not wholly a success as governor, he failed through duty too rigidly applied to a society in ferment'. Less charitable was the summing-up of Alex C. Castles and Michael C. Harris, who concluded that Robe was 'a stuffy second-rater as far as his administration was concerned, a pro-consular type ... with little love or real understanding of colonial affairs'. Indeed, he 'found self-aggrandisement in the pomposity of office, and alienated an important section of the community'.[8]

What had Robe done to deserve the condemnation of posterity? He was born in 1802, the fourth son of Colonel Sir William Robe and his wife Sarah, and joined the Army at the age of fifteen. He became an Ensign in 1817, was promoted Lieutenant in 1825, and Captain in the 87th regiment in 1833. In 1840–1841 he was part of the Anglo-Turkish force that saw action in Gaza, and for his services was promoted Brevet-Major in the field. Robe was Assistant Military Secretary in Gibraltar in 1845, and was surprised when he was appointed Governor (formally Lieutenant-Governor) of South Australia. He accepted the post reluctantly, as he had limited administrative experience and knew little of colonial affairs. Robe was comforted by the promise of a long handover from Governor Grey but when he arrived in the colony in the emigrant ship *Elphinstone*, he found to his dismay that Grey was departing in the same vessel for New Zealand. Robe was on his own, except for his Legislative Council where he could count on the support of the official Crown nominees but was regularly in conflict with the non-official appointees.

Robe's conservative predisposition made him resistant to the colony's democratic aspirations but his enduring unpopularity stemmed from his role in two important issues of the day. The first was the question of royalties payable on minerals extracted from previously sold Crown land. Francis Dutton had spoken too soon (see p. 41) when he declared that the Government had no direct financial interest in mineral exploitation. Robe considered that a royalty of one-fifteenth on the value of ores raised would generate funds that could then be used to support immigration. Predictably, leading colonists protested that this was contrary to the principles on which South Australia had been founded, and just two months after he had arrived, Robe was presented on 29 October 1845 with a petition to Queen Victoria of 700 signatures, calling for the plan to be abandoned. He agreed to pass it on. A thousand demonstrators gathered outside Government House to voice their opposition to mineral royalties, speaker after speaker condemning the proposal. The Colonial Office in Britain added fuel to the fire, instructing Robe in May 1846 to withhold the sale of potentially mineralised land for a year.[9]

In September 1846, the Royalty Bill was introduced before the Legislative Council. It was carried on its second reading on 2 October 1846, Robe deploying his casting vote, but immediately thereafter the non-official members walked out, amid cheers from the public gallery, leaving the Council meeting without a quorum. The Legislative Council met a week later, with the 'non-official' members attending at Robe's insistence, and the Governor again forced through the legislation, using his casting vote. Then, extraordinarily, he withdrew the Bill and it was allowed to lapse. Having asserted his authority, Robe was wise enough to bow to the strength of feeling in the colony, recognising this was a divisive issue and for many a matter of principle which would not go away.

Equally divisive was the question of state aid to religion. Frederick Robe was a High Church Anglican, who, needless to say, instinctively and unquestioningly approved of the Church of England as the Established Church within England itself. From the moment he had first heard of his appointment to South Australia, he had been troubled by the reportedly indifferent state of religious practice in the colony. The British House of Commons had warned of the apparent 'religious destitution' of the colony and Robe felt that should state aid be made available to encourage religious instruction, then it ought properly be limited to the Church of England.[10] However, he soon became sufficiently aware of the religious plurality of South Australia to recognise that this would not do. Accordingly, Robe devised a plan in which state aid would be given to denominations proportionate to their membership numbers.

As in the mineral royalty controversy, there were those who saw the scheme as an affront to the principles underpinning the colony's foundation. The Dissenters took the lead in voicing their opposition but they were joined by many Anglicans and some Catholics. A South Australian League for the Maintenance of Religious Freedom was formed, and numerous petitions were presented to the Legislative Council, together with one to the Queen herself. The Colonial Office took note of the controversy and, in July 1847, following instructions from Britain, Robe introduced a modified system in which the *per capita* aid was replaced by a more limited subsidy based on the actual amounts subscribed voluntarily by each congregation. This too was strenuously opposed but in 1848 the ordinance came into force, to take effect for three years, although most Dissenting churches refused to accept state aid. The debate rumbled on after Robe's departure in August 1848 and was a significant political issue in the contested elections for an enlarged Legislative Council in 1851. Here the voluntary principle triumphed and state aid was duly allowed to lapse, South Australia becoming the first Australian colony to break completely the link between church and state.[11]

Frederick Robe, it seems, had not enjoyed his time as Governor, and early in his term had asked to be relieved. He was a bachelor, which had sometimes made entertaining at Government House awkward, but he was not unsociable, regularly attending meets of the Adelaide Hunt Club and advocating (unsuccessfully) the establishment of an Adelaide Arts Society. Although he had many critics, most colonists appreciated his straightforward manner, and (notwithstanding hindsight's judgement) some were indeed sad to see him go. Having been promoted Lieutenant-Colonel in 1847, Robe went on to become Deputy Quartermaster-General of Mauritius, and was appointed full Colonel in 1854. By 1862, he had made Major General. He died in London on 4 April 1871.

Henry Fox Young
(2 August 1848 – 20 December 1854)

In contrast to the untried and inexperienced Frederick Robe, Henry Edward Fox Young was an accomplished colonial administrator who had demonstrated his credentials and worth long before his inauguration as Governor of South Australia on 2 August 1848. Seen as part of the Whig tradition (as his 'Fox' name intimated), his liberal reputation stood him in good stead in the colony, at least initially, although his neutrality over state aid to religion caused much annoyance among the Dissenters.[12] Henry Young was born on 23 April 1803 in Bradborne, Kent, the third son of Aretas William Young, a colonial administrator in the West Indies and later Governor of Prince Edward Island, and Sarah Cox of County Wexford.[13] He received his early education in Bromley, also in Kent, before joining his father in Trinidad. Subsequently, he enjoyed a number of prominent positions in the British Caribbean, being involved, among other things, in the emancipation of slaves, both before and after the formal abolition of slavery in the British Empire in 1834. By 1830, Young was in Demerara in British Guiana, where he became a clerk in the Colonial Secretary's office and aide-de-camp to the Governor, deputising for his father during the following year as Protector of Slaves, where his task was to ameliorate the treatment of slave workers and hear their grievances.[14] In November 1833, he was appointed Treasurer of St Lucia, also serving as Council member and acting Colonial Secretary as well as a junior judge. In 1835, Young was promoted Government Secretary in British Guiana. He returned to Britain during 1846, where he was knighted for his services to colonial administration.

In 1847, Sir Henry Young was appointed Lieutenant Governor of the recently annexed eastern districts of Cape Colony but in the June he was recalled to take up the governorship of South Australia. He returned to England and, on 15 April 1848, married Augusta Sophia Marryat, daughter of the former slave owner Charles Marryat, who had been a major recipient of compensation as a result of emancipation in Trinidad and St Lucia.[15] (She was thus also granddaughter of Joseph Marryat, the staunch anti-abolitionist who published his critical *Thoughts on the Abolition of the Slave Trade* in 1816.)[16] The newlyweds set sail in the *Forfarshire*, bound for South Australia, and arrived in Adelaide on 1 August 1848 to a rather indifferent welcome – just two policeman and a rudimentary coach were sent to meet them, only half-a-dozen bargemen were on hand at the Port to cheer, and no officials were present at Government House to proffer greetings.[17]

Governor Young faced his first major crisis after barely a month in office. This was the so-called 'Revolution at the Burra Burra Mines'.[18] Trouble had been brewing for some time, centred on a dispute as to the value of the copper ore won by the miners, and thus the appropriate level of their remuneration.[19] Henry Ayers, Secretary of the South Australian Mining Association, which ran the mine, arrived there on 13 September 1848 with a delegation from the directors to find the men on strike. In his estimation, the workers had effectively taken over the mine. He sent a strongly worded despatch to Governor Young, requesting immediate action if a popular revolt was to be avoided in the colony:

> acts of the most violent character and actual force having taken men up from the shafts tied together and carried from the mine . . . [warrants were issued] against two of the ringleaders but the police were prevented from making the capture by the mob of about one hundred and sixty men. The total number now in revolt is about three hundred. The men have virtual possession of the Mine and have prevented ore from being carted away . . . This being the first time that anything like this has occurred in the province the Delegation feel that it is necessary to act with energy and decision or otherwise we should be entirely in the hands of the people.[20]

The *South Australian* newspaper echoed Ayers' alarmist tone. 'On Saturday', it announced, 'the good citizens of Adelaide were astounded with the information that three hundred of the Burra miners had taken possession of the mine . . . There had been some rioting.'[21] The *Register*, meanwhile, reminded readers that 1848 had been the Year of European Revolution, and wondered whether the revolutionary impulse that had convulsed the European continent had now found its way to the Antipodes.[22] That the strike's ringleaders had adopted the rhetoric of political radicalism also caused unease among observers. The strikers had condemned the 'aggression on the part of the *monied* capitalists on their subservients', advocating instead a 'reciprocal return' to redress the balance, and they invited other 'fellow sufferers' to 'give language to their opinions in this . . . all-important subject'.[23] This was a call to arms, perhaps, that reminded Ayers and others that Cornish miners, such as those now on strike at the Burra, had only recently been the perpetrators of the extensive food riots across Cornwall during the 'Hungry Forties'.[24]

Governor Young, thoroughly unsettled by Ayers' request and the subsequent press reports, despatched a force of twenty-six armed troopers under the command of Commissioner of Police G.S. Dashwood. Dashwood, on his arrival at the Burra, found that Ayers had exaggerated the situation, and Dashwood himself acted as an intermediary between the strikers and the delegates. His negotiations had appeared to resolve the conflict, although Ayers later provoked a renewal of the strike, which at its height involved 600 men, the affair lasting until January 1849 when the miners grudgingly drifted back to work. It was hardly the revolution the Governor had been led to expect, but it was the first inkling of the emergence of organised labour in South Australia.[25]

Mining of a different sort led to Governor Young's next crisis, this time on an altogether more significant scale. During 1851, gold had been discovered in various parts of Victoria, and by October 1851 the *Register* was proclaiming 'Gold in Abundance' in the neighbouring colony.[26] The news had a major impact in South Australia. Houses were boarded up in Adelaide as their occupants went to try their luck on the diggings and, in December 1851, it was noted that a hundred Burra miners had arrived at the Port to join ships bound for Victoria, with others joining them in January and February 1852. Before long the Burra Burra mine was at a standstill, as was the Kapunda and other mines across the colony; the South Australian economy was in a parlous condition. Money as well as people flowed from the colony, as would-be diggers took their savings with them to cover their expenses.

Governor Young was under pressure to do something. He consulted financial experts in the colony, and at his prompting the Legislative Council in January 1852 passed the *Gold Bullion Act*, which allowed the South Australian Government to receive gold for refining into ingots, which in turn enabled banks to support the issue of notes as legal tender.[27] Police Inspector Alexander Tolmer was sent to Mount Alexander in Victoria, where there were known to be many South Australian diggers (presumably sympathetic to South Australia's plight). He bid for gold at £3/11/- per ounce, much higher than the going rate in Melbourne. Tolmer returned to Adelaide in triumph in March 1852, and by December 1853 gold worth £1,000,000 had been brought across in eighteen such 'gold escorts'. Gradually, the South Australian economy recovered. Business confidence was restored, and the rapidly expanding population of the Victorian goldfields stimulated demand for all kinds of goods produced in the colony, while wheat and flour production soared.

In 1850, Young had explored the lower reaches of the Murray River and, in 1853, encouraged by the growing possibilities of Victorian trade, he undertook an extended tour of the Murray in the paddle-steamer *Lady Augusta*. He departed Goolwa on 25 August, travelling as far as Gannawarra Station on the Gunbower Creek in Victoria – a distance of 1500 miles – before returning with a barge full of wool bales, demonstrating the commercial potential of such river traffic.[28] The Governor was similarly interested in railway development, and although he left the colony before the advent of steam locomotives, he had been supportive of the horse-drawn tramway at Port Elliot, and endorsed schemes for railways to Port Adelaide and northwards from Adelaide to Gawler.

Governor Young had shown himself innovative and progressive in supporting commercial and infrastructural expansion. But he was more cautious and conservative in responding to the persistent calls in the colony for responsible self-government. In February 1850, early in his appointment, an Australian Government Bill had been introduced into the British Parliament, designed to allow New South Wales, Victoria, Tasmania and South Australia to establish bicameral legislatures, should they so desire. Initially, these colonies were authorised to inaugurate Legislative Councils of no more than twenty-four members, of whom two-thirds would be elected and one-third appointed. On this basis, and with a restrictive property qualification in place, South Australia's first popular elections for a reconstituted Legislative Council were held in July 1851.[29]

A principal task of this new Legislative Council was to decide what form of responsible government it wished to adopt for the colony. In 1853, Governor Young presented a conservative draft constitution to the Council, which made provision for an entirely appointed upper house. Most councillors wanted an elected bicameral parliament, and a period of sometimes acrimonious debate ensued, with various appeals made to the Secretary of State in Britain, a process which dragged on after Young was moved on to become Governor of Tasmania.[30] Governor Young was relieved on 20 December 1854, arriving in Hobart on 6 January 1855 to discover a very similar debate in full cry. In the following year, Tasmania achieved responsible government, in the process formally changing the colony's name from Van Diemen's Land to indicate a break from its convict past.

Sir Henry Young, as Governor of Tasmania, found, perhaps to his surprise, that he enjoyed the redefined position of Governor, now that it was no longer a day-to-day, hands-on executive role and was generally removed from routine political controversy. He put his energies instead into the completion of Government House in Hobart. In South Australia, despite his clashes with political opponents over responsible government, he was acknowledged by many as an efficient and approachable administrator, not least for his firm action during the Victorian goldrush and his keen support for infrastructural development. Augusta Sophia, Sir Henry's 'spirited wife', had also enhanced Young's governorship in South Australia, with her popularity and reputation as 'a woman of wit'.[31] Together, the Youngs and their family left Tasmania in December 1861, returning to England where they lived in retirement in London until Sir Henry's death on 18 September 1870. Augusta Sophia outlived her husband by forty-three years, expiring in Christchurch, Hampshire, in 1913.

Richard Graves MacDonnell
(8 June 1855 – 4 March 1862)

Frederick Robe's term as Governor had not been entirely successful; his replacement, Sir Henry Young, had been an experienced colonial administrator from a non-military background, thought to be a more appropriate balance. The same formula was repeated with Richard Graves MacDonnell. Born in Dublin on 3 September 1814, he was the eldest son of Dr Richard MacDonnell, Fellow and later Provost of Trinity College, and Jane, second daughter of Richard Graves, the Church of Ireland Dean of Ardagh.[32] Richard MacDonnell junior studied Law at Trinity, and subsequently practised in London until appointed Chief Justice of Gambia in July 1843, becoming Governor of the protectorate in 1847. In 1852 he was transferred to St Lucia as an administrator, and from there was appointed to St Vincent in the following year.

Governor Young had departed South Australia just before Christmas 1854, leaving Boyle Travers Finniss as interim administrator until Richard Graves MacDonnell (only recently dubbed 'Sir Richard' by the Queen) arrived over five months later to take over the gubernatorial reins on 8 June 1855. Although his experience and background ostensibly stood him in good stead, MacDonnell was in some ways a curious appointment. He had a reputation for sternness and severity, acquired in his earlier colonial positions, and appeared to have few of the diplomatic qualities necessary to steer South Australia towards the achievement of responsible government. He shared Young's conservative objections to a bicameral system, preferring, he explained, a single-chamber Legislative Council made up of thirty-six elected and four nominated members. He also worried that too 'democratic' a solution would reduce the Governor's power and influence, something he did not relish.

The latter point was not lost on the *Register*, which in December 1855 observed that the 'constitutional history of England is the history of a continuous effort on the part of the people to win the right of self-government'. This struggle had now been extended to British possessions overseas, the newspaper argued, not least because the 'peculiar plan by which Great Britain has governed its colonies in their earlier stages has placed them all under a very arbitrary form of government'. The role of Governor was the personification of such arbitrary government, it was claimed, but all this would change with the achievement of responsible government. Thereafter:

> On all points touching imperial interests, the Governor is still retained as the Queen's agent, and is bound to care for the royal prerogatives. But on all points of local interest the Queen resigns all power or right to interfere . . . All matters of purely internal policy are left to be settled by colonists themselves, and with respect to them the Governor stands in the same position as the Sovereign does to the policy of the English Parliament, and he has no right or authority to interfere at all with the wish of the people.[33]

As well as stating plainly the aim of responsible government, the *Register* also criticised Governor MacDonnell personally, reminding him: 'We have been longer in the colony than His Excellency, and know more of men and things here than he does.'[34] For his part, Governor MacDonnell worried that the longer the responsible government debate was allowed to drag on, the more it would result in 'a democratic spirit, likely to bear its fruits in a constitution to which notwithstanding the intelligence and orderly character of South Australians as a people, many would consider it perilous to entrust the future destinies of this Province'.[35] He also complained to Lord Russell, Secretary of State in London, that such a constitution would have the effect of 'destroying almost all that has been hitherto useful or respected in the functions of the Queen's representative'. Moreover, despite all the evidence to the contrary, MacDonnell could still blindly insist that 'the desire, almost universal, as represented to me, for a single Chamber in preference to two, might lead to the acceptance of a safer and more conservative constitution in that shape'.[36]

The Colonial Office, however, was inclined to side with the colonists, informing Governor MacDonnell that his proposals for a single chamber were 'inconsistent with the establishment of Responsible government', and that there was 'no reason why South Australia should remain exempted from the operation of a system conceded to the neighbouring colonies of New South Wales, Victoria and Tasmania'.[37] In a last-ditch attempt to force the issue, MacDonnell dissolved the Legislative Council, necessitating a fresh election. But those members returned were of the same liberal disposition as before, and the Governor bowed to the inevitable. Accordingly, *An Act to Establish a Constitution for South Australia 1856* received Royal Assent on 24 June 1856, having been passed in both Houses of British Parliament. On the same day that Governor MacDonnell received notice of the Assent (24 October 1856), he proclaimed the Act in the colony, and South Australia thus achieved responsible government. The *Register* was jubilant:

> Responsible government, in application to this colony, may therefore be defined as a Government exercising *enlarged powers upon a popular basis*. Until Saturday last the powers of the Governor were real rather than nominal; the Governor was the Government . . . The people had no constitutional check upon the Executive, the whole administrative force

residing in the Governor, who not only possessed the power of appointing to office, but was under no necessity of appealing to the wishes of the public.[38]

'The source of power was in the vice-regal office', the *Register* continued, 'now it is in the constituencies'. Moreover:

> The promptitude and freedom with which Sir Richard MacDonnell has hastened to put the colony in possession of responsible government is a sure guarantee that His Excellency wishes to govern in South Australia upon those principles which the community shall constitutionally adopt. The people, in fact, rule themselves, instead of being ruled, the Governor presiding over the two estates of the realm as a constitutional representative of the British Crown.[39]

The 'two estates' was a reference to the bicameral system that had been established. The upper house, the Legislative Council, comprised eighteen members, six of whom had to face re-election every four years, and there were property qualifications for both electors and candidates (£50 of freehold property or an annual value of £20). The lower house, the House of Assembly, was elected by universal male suffrage. The first election to both houses was on Monday 9 March 1857.

Sir Richard MacDonnell served for another five years as Governor of South Australia, adapting to his changed constitutional role. He never quite attuned to the democratic nature of the colony (he opposed charity, for example, claiming it encouraged indolence and pauperism), and had often been at loggerheads with officials. But he developed more than a passing affection for South Australia. He supported various artistic and literary groups, and was an enthusiastic advocate of the volunteer defence movement. He also took a keen interest in pastoral and agricultural development, and was especially appreciative of the colony's hardworking German community, predicting a fine future for the wine industry. He was similarly supportive of the rise of copper mining on northern Yorke Peninsula. As Governor, MacDonnell also visited remote outback areas of the colony, revelling in his role as 'explorer', and urged South

Australians to back John McDouall Stuart in his quest to cross the continent, an event which led ultimately to the annexation of the Northern Territory by South Australia.

MacDonnell left South Australia on 4 March 1862, travelling by way of his native Ireland to Nova Scotia to take up the role of Lieutenant-Governor. He remained for little more than a year, being adamantly opposed to the Confederation of Canada, in which he believed he would become subordinate to the new post of Governor-General. In October 1865, MacDonnell was appointed Governor of Hong Kong, serving in the colony until 1872. He retired to London, where, among other things, he became involved in the Aborigines Protection Society. He was predeceased by his wife Blanche, whom he had married in 1847, and died in February 1881.

Dominick Daly
(4 March 1862 – 19 February 1868)

Inevitably, the achievement of responsible government in 1856 altered the nature of governance profoundly. One particular aspect, a function of the 'democracy' that Governor MacDonnell had feared, was the rapid change of administrations. In the lengthy era before firm party affiliations emerged in South Australia, parliamentary politics revolved around factions and personalities and shifting alliances. In the first twenty years of responsible government, therefore, there were no fewer than twenty-eight different governments.[40] Successive Governors were kept busy swearing in Premiers and Ministers, and attending to other constitutional obligations, as governments came and went. Sir Dominick Daly, the first Governor to be appointed since the achievement of responsible government, had to deal with nine changes of administration during his almost-six years in office. Fortunately, he was scrupulously impartial and loyally supported each Premier in turn. Although P.A. Howell considered that he 'carried out his duties perfunctorily', Daly set an important standard for gubernatorial behaviour in the new parliamentary system.[41] Indeed, as Eric Richards noted, some observers considered Daly to be the best of South Australia's early Governors.[42] As the *South Australian Advertiser* put it: 'We never had a wiser, better, or more popular governor.'[43]

Dominick Daly was born on 11 August 1798 at Ardfry, County Galway, Ireland, the third son of Dominick Daly senior and Joanna Harriet Blake.[44] He was educated at Oscott College in Birmingham, England, and in 1823 he was appointed Secretary to the Lieutenant-Governor of Lower Canada. Three years later, he married Caroline Maria, the daughter of Robert Gore of Barrowmount, County Kilkenny. Daly had proved popular in Canada and, after a spell as Lieutenant-Governor of Tobago in 1851–1854, was appointed to the same gubernatorial position in Prince Edward Island in 1854, where he remained until 1859. He was knighted in 1856, in recognition of his services to colonial administration.

Sir Dominick Daly was appointed Governor of South Australia in October 1861, and arrived in Adelaide, with his wife and two daughters, on 4 March 1862, the day before his predecessor, Sir Richard MacDonnell, was due to leave the colony. In many ways, his was an ideal appointment. Like MacDonnell and Young before him, Daly was an experienced colonial administrator, without a military background, which may or may not have been an advantage. However, unlike MacDonnell and Young, he was a democrat and an ardent supporter of colonial self-government. MacDonnell was an Irishman, but in the Anglo–Irish Protestant tradition. Daly, by contrast, was both Irishman and Roman Catholic, something that might have been expected to raise eyebrows in largely Protestant South Australia, but his religious affiliation proved no impediment in practice. On the contrary, the *Register* commented approvingly that Daly's appointment was the 'first practical recognition by the Downing-street authorities of the fundamental principle of religious equality upon which this colony is founded'.[45]

As in Canada, Governor Daly proved a popular choice in South Australia. But he was already over sixty-three years of age when he arrived in the colony, and his health and that of his wife was failing. He was, as P.A. Howell put it, 'too far past his prime'. According to Howell: 'Gout made him short-tempered, and incapacitated him for days at a time. For years he had lived beyond his means, and now his wife became so crippled by paralysis that she needed constant nursing and could take no part in public or social occasions.'[46] Daly worried constantly that he could not afford to retire but, alas, he died in office on 19 February 1868.[47] His state funeral was on one of the hottest days of the year but large crowds lined the streets to watch the procession and pay their last respects. He was buried in the Catholic section of West Terrace Cemetery in Adelaide. His wife, Caroline Maria, died at Glenelg on 18 July 1872, aged seventy-one.

James Fergusson
(16 February 1869 – 18 April 1873)

James Fergusson (1869–1873) arrived in South Australia as Dominick Daly's successor on 15 February 1869. He had briefly served as a soldier (in the Grenadier Guards from 1851 until 1859, and wounded in the Crimea), and a British MP (member for Ayrshire in 1855–1857 and again in 1859–1868). His administrative experience, gained as Under-Secretary for India in the British Government in 1866–1867 and for the Home Office in 1867–1868, set him up for what would be a long and varied colonial career. He was born in Edinburgh on 14 March 1832, the eldest son of Sir Charles Dalrymple Fergusson, 6th baronet of Kilkerran in Ayrshire, and Helen Boyle. Fergusson was educated at Rugby, succeeding to the baronetcy on the death of his father in 1849, and attended the University of Oxford, although leaving without taking a degree, before joining the Army.

In the yearlong gap between Daly's death and Fergusson's arrival, Lieutenant-Colonel F.G. Hamley, senior officer in command of Her Majesty's Forces in the colony (50th Queen's Own Regiment), had been temporary Acting Governor. It was a short term of office but not an easy one, Hamley having to cope with changing administrations and the shifting nature of parliamentary alliances.[48] It was a situation inherited by Sir James Fergusson, who was used to the clear party lines of the British Parliament and was nonplussed by the apparent inconsistencies and complexities of South Australia's system. The first real crisis was in January 1870, when Premier Henry Strangways advised Governor Fergusson to dissolve parliament. This was Strangways' way out of the difficulties he was experiencing in passing his Budget, and the tactic was met with howls of disapproval in the press and among some parliamentarians. However, Fergusson felt compelled to accept the advice. When the new parliament met, Strangways promptly resigned, and John Hart, commanding a majority in the House of Assembly, was asked to form a government. On Hart's resignation in November 1871, the main contenders, Henry Ayers and Arthur Blyth, both failed to form ministries, and a bemused Fergusson again agreed to dissolve parliament. The new parliament met in January 1872. Blyth was unable to form a ministry, so the task fell to Ayers. Ayers' ministry lasted for little more than a month, when it succumbed to a 'vote of dissatisfaction', whereupon Governor Fergusson asked him to form a new administration, which Ayers did, with an entirely new set of ministerial appointments. And so on it went.[49]

The *Register* considered that the uncritical readiness with which Fergusson acceded to requests for dissolution was the 'gravest error[s]' of his governorship, and he was accused of mistaking the changing opinions of members for institutional dysfunction, not realising that in colonial parliaments alliances altered with every issue.[50] He was also thought to be aloof, his social events at Government House rather austere affairs. Yet in other respects, his governorship was deemed a success. When Fergusson arrived in 1868, the colony was in the grip of a depression but by 1871 the economic situation was already much improved. This was hardly attributable to the Governor, of course, but he reflected the growing sense of optimism, encouraging trade with India and supporting the expansion of the agricultural frontier. He was especially enthusiastic about the Overland Telegraph, and played a not insignificant part in securing the route from Port Augusta through the Northern Territory, which would require the submarine cable linking Adelaide to the rest of the world being landed at Darwin. Risking the potential disapproval of the Colonial Office, Governor Fergusson liaised directly with South Australia's Agent-General in London to ensure that the British Australian Telegraph Co. won the contract for the project. Likewise, he was prominent in the formation of the University Association, which led directly to the foundation of the University of Adelaide.

Despite these successes, Sir James Fergusson's time in Adelaide was marred by his wife's ill-health and her death on October 1871, aged only thirty-two. Fergusson had married Edith Ramsay in August 1859, and in their dozen years together they had produced two sons and two daughters.

In November 1872, Fergusson was appointed Governor of New Zealand, and it was in that colony in 1873 that he married Olive, daughter of John Richman of Warnbunga, South Australia. Alas, she was to die of cholera in Bombay less than a decade later, Fergusson marrying for a third time in 1883, to Isabel Hoare, a widow.

During his time in New Zealand, James Fergusson decided to return to his former political career, and resigned his governorship in 1875, journeying to Britain where in 1876 and 1878 he tried without success to enter the House of Commons. In March 1880 he accepted instead the governorship of Bombay, where he remained until March 1885. In that year, he successfully re-entered the British Parliament at last, representing Manchester until 1906 and serving as Under-Secretary in the Foreign Office (1886–1891) and Postmaster-General (1891–1892). Along with other MPs with Australian experience or interests, he formed an 'Australian party', and with his own background in communications became director of the Royal Mail Steam Packet Co. and the National Telephone Co. In 1907, Sir James Fergusson was attending a conference in Jamaica when, on 14 January, he was caught in a violent earthquake and tragically killed.

Anthony Musgrave
(9 June 1873 – 29 January 1877)

Dominick Daly had calmly negotiated the often turbulent waters of responsible government in South Australia. James Fergusson, with his experience of the British party-political system, found the colony's parliamentary politics bewildering, and was castigated for his lack of understanding. Anthony Musgrave, who succeeded Fergusson as Governor on 6 March 1873, thought the system positively dangerous and said so, considering it a folly that stood in the way of stable and thus good government.[51] South Australia, he thundered, possessed 'the most thoroughly irresponsible system of administration with which I am acquainted'.[52] Yet he protested in vain, the *Australasian* as late as 1889 explaining, tongue-in-cheek but with a modicum of truth, that in South Australia governments were made and broken for harmless fun. 'The simple fact', it reported, 'is that after a ministry has been two years in office, everybody falls to yawning, and wants a change. Political crises cause no disturbance in South Australia, which is a placid country. They take place in order that politicians and writers may have material for moderate excitement'.[53] Others thought Musgrave 'a little bit behind the times in his conception of popular government', yet he was an early advocate of Australian Federation and, far from being reactionary on progressive matters, took a keen interest in the protection of Indigenous people in Australia and across the Empire.[54]

Anthony Musgrave was born on 17 November 1828 in Antigua, son of Dr Anthony Musgrave, a member of the island's House of Assembly, and Mary Sherriff.[55] The Musgraves were a slave-owning family, and Anthony Musgrave senior made his money from the trade, or rather from the compensation he received when slavery was abolished. Anthony Musgrave junior was educated locally in the West Indies, at the age of twenty-one becoming Secretary to the Governor of the Leeward Islands. He served as Treasury Accountant in Antigua in 1852–1853 and was the island's Colonial Secretary in 1854–1860. He was administrator of Nevis from October 1860 to April 1861, then moved to St Vincent where he became Lieutenant-Governor in May 1862. From 1864 to 1869 Musgrave was Governor of Newfoundland, which he hoped would join the imminent Canadian Confederation. In this he was disappointed, although in his next post, British Columbia, he was altogether more successful, persuading the colony to join the Canadian union by negotiating the construction of the Canadian Pacific Railway to link west with east.[56]

Following this triumph, Anthony Musgrave was posted to Natal in 1872, and from there was appointed Governor of South Australia in the following year. In 1875 he was knighted for his services to colonial administration. Much of his career had been devoted to sorting out colonial finances, which were often in turmoil when he took over his appointments, and to encouraging international trade and economic development. Early during his posting to Adelaide, Musgrave, finding himself with time on his hands (or so he said), turned his attention to writing, compiling a book entitled *Studies in Political Economy*, which he completed in August 1874 and was published in the following year in London. The title page proclaimed proudly 'Governor of South Australia', and the wisdom gained from his wide experience of colonial administration purportedly underpinned his many scholarly judgements and recommendations. As in his commentary on South Australian politics, he confessed that in economic analysis 'it is difficult to evade the necessity of appearing controversial'. He took issue, for example, with the 'inconsistent statements and opinions of Adam Smith', and was likewise critical of John Stuart Mill.[57] His contributions to economic debate also extended to various pamphlets and articles in learned journals, although apparently without lasting impact.

Despite his glittering public career, Musgrave's private life was tinged with tragedy. In 1853, in Antigua, he had married Christiana Byam, but she died five years later, leaving him with two small boys. Later, en route to British Columbia, he married Jeannie Lucinda Field, the daughter of a prominent New York lawyer with connections to Abraham Lincoln. Her American 'good-natured liveliness' charmed South Australians during the Musgraves' time in Adelaide, and together she and Anthony had three sons and a daughter.[58] Sadly, their little girl, Joyce, then just over three years old, died in a tragic accident in Government House. On the evening of 20 October 1874, her nurse had been preparing hot water for bath-time, when somehow Joyce slipped into the tub. She was badly scalded by the still-boiling water, and died from her injuries a few days later.[59]

After South Australia, Sir Anthony Musgrave served as Governor of Jamaica for six years, returning to Australia to become Governor of Queensland in July 1883. When Samuel Griffith became Premier in November of that year, he found that he and Governor Musgrave had much in common, including an enthusiasm for the cause of Australian Federation. Although he discounted the threat of German colonialism in the Pacific region, Musgrave threw his weight behind the establishment of a protectorate in southern New Guinea in 1884. Following a visit to Britain in 1886, he planned to retire from his colonial career, but deferred his decision in 1888 when Sir Thomas McIlwraith (whom he disliked intensely) became Premier of Queensland. Soon McIlwraith and Musgrave were at daggers-drawn, the former opposing the Governor's unrestricted exercise of the prerogative of mercy. The heated clashes were a cause of much anxiety for Sir Anthony Musgrave, and he died a few weeks later on 9 October 1888, apparently from a heart attack.[60]

William Francis Drummond Jervois
(2 October 1877 – 9 January 1883)

Musgrave's successor as Governor of South Australia was Sir William Francis Drummond Jervois (pronounced Jarvis). This was ostensibly a return to military appointments, but Jervois was a military man with a difference, his Army career having been devoted to the infrastructural defence of the Empire through fortification. In this way, he had acquired a broad if unconventional knowledge of the diversity of British colonial possessions. Jervois was born on 10 September 1821 at Cowes on the Isle of Wight, the eldest son of General William Jervois and Elizabeth Maitland.[61] Following early education in Gosport, Hampshire, he attended the Royal Military Academy at Woolwich and, in 1839, was commissioned as a Second Lieutenant in the Royal Engineers before studying military engineering at Chatham for a further two years. He was noted for his excellent draughtsmanship, and in 1841 was appointed to the Cape, seeing action in the 7th Xhosa War (1846–1847), during which time he drew military sketches of 'British Kaffaria' (also known as Queen Adelaide's Province), the eastern Xhosa lands annexed in 1847 and which later became part of Cape Colony.

Returning to Britain in 1848, Jervois commanded a company of sappers and miners at Woolwich, before being posted to Alderney in the Channel Islands to enhance local fortifications to thwart any attempted French invasion. By now an acknowledged expert on the art and science of fortification he was promoted Major and, in 1855, became Commanding Royal Engineer for the London District, with an appointment as Assistant Inspector-General of Fortifications in April of the following year. As relations with France again deteriorated, William Jervois was made Secretary of a Royal Commission established in August 1859 to examine the preparedness of Britain's land-based defences for repelling naval attack. The Commission reported in 1860 and recommended that England's southern naval dockyards be ringed with a series of new fortifications. As the international situation changed and existing technologies became obsolete, these new forts where soon dubbed 'Palmerston's Follies', after the Prime Minister Lord Palmerston.[62] But for the moment they were state of the art, and William Jervois had an important role in their design and construction.

During the American Civil War, Jervois travelled to the United States to examine the latest in fortification techniques (including the use of iron), and he also reported on the (apparently poor) state of military fortification in Canada. These were politically sensitive activities and it is said that, disguised as an artist, he surreptitiously sketched the harbour defences of Portland and Boston from a rowing boat. Subsequently, he was tasked with inspecting British colonial fortifications in locations as diverse as Gibraltar and the Andaman Islands. He was knighted for his services in 1874.

Sir William Jervois' career acquired a new dimension when, in April 1875, he was appointed Governor of the Straits Settlements. He did not take to the Indigenous Malay population but warmed to the Chinese of Singapore, admiring their work ethic, so much so that he later advocated the migration of Asian labour to Australia and New Zealand. In early 1877, Jervois was asked to assist in a survey of the defences of Australasia, but while in Melbourne in the June he learned that he had been appointed Governor of South Australia. Arriving in HMS *Sapphire*, he commenced his duties in Adelaide on 2 October 1877, serving until 9 January 1883. From the beginning, he expressed his concern about the state of South Australia's maritime defences, prompting Attorney-General William Bundey to compose his parody of the well-known ditty of the day:

> *We don't want to fight,*
> *But by Jingo if we do*
> *We've got no ships, we've got no men,*
> *We want the money too.*[63]

But a more immediate issue requiring Governor Jervois' attention was the latest in South Australia's periodic political upheavals, such as those that had sorely tried his predecessors. On 6 June 1876, John Colton had become Premier, with a ministry that would last all of one year and 152 days. On 17 October 1877, just a fortnight after Governor Jervois had been sworn in, a motion of no confidence in Colton's Government was carried on the casting vote of the Speaker. The resolution that led to this fall from grace had expressed disapproval of the Government's recent decision on a site for a new House of Assembly, a move made without first seeking the sanction of both Houses of Parliament. The Legislative Council simultaneously voiced its dissatisfaction with the allegedly premature decision, considering that Colton's actions had been unconstitutional. Colton duly submitted his resignation to Governor Jervois, who in turn asked James Penn Boucaut, mover of the no-confidence motion, to form an administration instead. This was to be Boucaut's fourth term as Premier in the kaleidoscopic politics of the South Australian Parliament.[64]

Eventually, a Select Committee of both Houses was set up for the purpose of agreeing the site for what would become initially the west wing of a new Houses of Parliament. With his background in large-scale construction, Jervois took a keen interest in the plans as they emerged, but the periodic delays meant the building was not completed and opened until June 1889, more than half-a-dozen years after his departure as Governor.[65] More expeditious was the planning and erection of Marble Hill, the Governor's summer residence (see pp. 16–18), in which Jervois again showed intense interest, although uncharacteristically he chose a poor site, susceptible as it was to bushfires.

Jervois was on surer ground when in 1880 he published his booklet *Defences of Great Britain and Her Dependencies*, based on a lecture he had given in Adelaide. It began by reviewing the threats posed throughout history by the Vikings, the Spanish Armada and the French, bringing the story up to date with his exhaustive account of the measures in place to protect the sea lanes and maritime commerce of Empire. The title page announced that he was 'Governor of South Australia', as well being now a Major General, and he spent some time detailing his own role in the fortification of Britain and the colonies. He alluded to the 'Palmerston's Follies' (while avoiding the phrase), insisting that 'Portsmouth and Plymouth are now the finest maritime fortresses in the world', although admitting that 'owing to the rapid and constant changes that took place in matters relating to ships, fortifications and artillery – a period of transition in the science of war which has no equal in history – the designing of the defences was conducted under circumstances of unprecedented difficulty'.[66]

Turning to the defences of the Australian colonies, Jervois expressed some satisfaction that his earlier recommendations were now being acted upon – albeit 'it must be admitted without any undue haste' – and he recorded that his 'good fortune in occupying the position which I now hold is originally due to the circumstance that I came to Australia to advise respecting the defence of this and the other colonies'.[67] Jervois made it clear that he took an Australia-wide perspective when it came to defence, and declared himself a supporter of Federation. As he put it, the 'consideration of this matter leads me to observe that the federation of these colonies would amongst many other benefits be of immense advantage in dealing with the subject of defence'.[68] Indeed, he went on:

> It is, I know, urged by some that the several colonies if federated would be deprived of their individual freedom and power of self-development. This, however, would not be so. Whilst each one would unite with the others in matters of common interest to all, the individual freedom of action which now exists would continue to prevail in all matters of local concern. As regards defences, each colony is now engaged in gradually carrying out a plan for its own protection; but there are matters which can only be dealt with by combined action. Unity of military organization, and measures required for general naval protection, including the defence of naval stations in Australian waters, which are common to the whole of these colonies, can only be carried out under federal arrangement.[69]

Sir William Jervois was an early advocate of Federation, his booklet appearing a full decade before the Melbourne Constitutional Conference in 1890. But his detailed concern, of course, was South Australia. For most of his period as Governor, the colony enjoyed good times. The agricultural frontier was pushed to its limits (and beyond, as it turned out) and new railways penetrated the far-flung corners of the colony. Excellent rainfall appeared to give credence to the old adage that 'rain follows the plough'. Jervois visited the extremities of this new settlement, enthusing over South Australia's triumphant expansion. He laid the foundation stones of the University of Adelaide and the new Institute and Art Gallery, and was active in the Bible Society, the City Mission, and the Young Men's Christian

Association. His wife, Lucy Northsworthy, whom Jervois had married in March 1850, was similarly busy in the colony's voluntary and philanthropic societies, including the foundation of a Young Women's Institute.

By the eve of Governor Jervois' departure, however, prospects in the colony appeared less roseate. Rainfall declined, prelude to a drought that would see a contraction of the only recently expanded wheat frontier, as far-northern properties returned to scrub and semi-desert. Jervois warned of the problems of mounting debt, and he wondered aloud whether there should be increases in taxation.[70] But he left with South Australia's warm wishes, the *Register* concluding that he was 'not only one of the ablest and most judicious but also one of the most deservedly popular of our Governors'.[71]

Departing South Australia, Jervois served as Governor of New Zealand from 1883 to 1888, where he was similarly active in colonial life, from advising on harbour defences to officiating at the opening of Auckland University College. By 1889, he was back in Britain, serving on the Stanhope Commission as it reviewed Britain's fortifications. He managed a brief visit to South Australia and New Zealand in 1892, before becoming honorary Colonel Commandant of the Royal Engineers in the following year. He settled into retirement but in 1895 his wife Lucy, with whom he had had three daughters and two sons, died. Jervois followed her two years later on 17 August 1897, dying, at the age of seventy-five, as a result of injuries sustained in a carriage accident. He was buried in Virginia Water, Surrey.

William Cleaver Francis Robinson
(19 February 1883 – 5 March 1889)

In December 1882, the Sydney *Bulletin* proffered an enigmatic – but accurate – summing up of William Cleaver Francis Robinson, Jervois' successor as Governor of South Australia. Robinson was, said the *Bulletin*, 'tall and slight, with an intellectual cast . . . by no means an enthusiast in sporting matters . . . a thorough red-tape ruler . . . He has a genius for music'.[72] William Robinson was born in Rosmead, County Westmeath, Ireland, on 14 January 1834, the fourth son of Admiral Hercules Robinson and Frances Elizabeth Wood.[73] He was educated at the Royal Naval School at New Cross in Surrey and, in 1855, aged twenty-one, he began a career in colonial service that was to become a life-long passion. His initial appointment was as Private Secretary to his elder brother Hercules, then Lieutenant-Governor of St Kitts, and in 1859 he followed Hercules to Hong Kong when he was appointed Governor. In 1862, William Robinson was elevated to his first vice-regal position, as President of Montserrat, in April of that year marrying Olivia Edith Dean, daughter of the bishop of Meath. By 1865 he was in Dominica, and a year later appointed Governor of the Falkland Islands. In July 1870 he became Governor of Prince Edward Island, steering the colony towards its inclusion in the new Canadian Confederation, the Dominion of Canada. The next posting in his already hectic career was to the Leeward Islands and, in January 1875, he was appointed Governor of Western Australia, with instructions from the Colonial Office to discourage local aspirations for responsible government.

By now, Robinson had acquired a reputation as an efficient administrator, if sometimes a pedantic stickler for detail (the 'thorough red-tape ruler'), although he was considered somewhat aloof and reserved by the officials who worked with him. He was, nonetheless, a good public speaker and a powerful advocate of causes he embraced. From Western Australia, he went to the Straits Settlements as Governor in 1877, in the same year receiving a knighthood, and in the following year led a British diplomatic mission to neighbouring Siam. Robinson was then selected for Natal but before he could take up the appointment, he was sent back to Western Australia in April 1880. Next, it was on to South Australia, where he became Governor on 19 February 1883. His arrival was marked by a public performance of 'Unfurl the Flag', a composition he had written especially to accompany the patriotic words of Francis Hart. As well as establishing him in the public mind as a gifted musician ('a genius for music'), his endorsement of Hart's words indicated his enthusiasm for the elevation of Australia within the panoply of Empire, its proto-nationalist sentiments shortly adopted as one of the songs of Federation:

> *Australia's sons your flag unfurl*
> *And proudly wave the banner high*
> *That every nation may behold*

Our glorious stand and in the sky
Unfold the flag that all may see
Our proudest boast is liberty.[74]

Notwithstanding such patriotic fervour, Sir William Robinson had arrived in South Australia in the midst of drought and economic downturn. Labour was increasingly organised, and clamour for the eight-hour day became ever louder. In 1886, one demonstration marched on Government House, where the protesters were met graciously by Governor Robinson.[75] On another occasion, he attended eight-hour celebrations at the Exhibition Grounds in Adelaide. One cynic saw his apparent support as mere tokenism:

His Excellency the Governor, and several members of Parliament were present on the grounds by invitation; they came because they were bound to; they went into a room because they were asked; sat down and drank a few toasts because it is the custom; made some 'speeches' because they were expected to, and then cleared off because – thank heaven – it was all over.[76]

Unlike his recent predecessors, however, Governor Robinson had no major parliamentary political upheavals to contend with, and he settled into the social and symbolic dimensions of his role with considerable enthusiasm. He was reputed to have entertained more people at Government House than any earlier Governor, and was intimately involved in Adelaide's musical, literary and educational life. He sang, played the piano and violin, and his compositions such as 'Remember Me No More' and 'I Love Thee So' were well received. He assisted the celebration of the colony's jubilee in 1886, and that of Queen Victoria in 1887. He championed the funding of the university's chair in music, and was a favourite speaker at meetings of the Young Men's Christian Association and other groups.

On one occasion he lectured on 'Duty in Many Lands', a masterful talk in the estimation of the *Register* newspaper, which explained that Robinson had 'seen distinguished service in many lands' and had observed 'the working of the British Constitution in so many colonies, at so great a distance, with such different races of people'. This incomparable experience, the *Register* opined, was especially relevant 'at the present time, when the subject of federation came within the range of practical politics'.[77] It was noted that the Governor had played an important role in the creation of the Dominion of Canada, the inference being that he could be similarly significant in the achievement of Australian Federation.

In fact, having declined the governorship of Hong Kong in 1887 (he hated the climate), Sir William Robinson was appointed Acting Governor of Victoria from March to November 1889, and then, having also turned down the governorship of Mauritius, was made Governor of Western Australia for a third time in October 1890. He brought with him from the Colonial Office a draft constitution Bill for responsible government, and was warmly welcomed in the colony as an administrator with a sympathetic and widespread knowledge of Western Australia. Robinson presided over the appointment of John Forrest as first Premier of Western Australia, and Forrest in turn offered him the position of the colony's first Agent-General in London. Robinson considered the position but, perhaps reluctantly, decided that it was time to retire. He died in South Kensington in London on 2 May 1897, survived by his wife Olivia and their three sons and two daughters.

Algernon Keith-Falconer, 9th Earl of Kintore
(11 April 1889 – 10 April 1895)

By the time of Sir William Robinson's departure from South Australia, the Colonial Office in London had reviewed its policy on vice-regal appointments. In recent decades, Governors had been chosen from the ranks of accomplished career colonial administrators, of which Robinson had been an exemplar, the rationale being that they would bring their extensive comparative experience to bear in each new post. Now, however, it was thought that this approach was no longer appropriate in mature settler societies that had achieved responsible government, and where the Governor's role had evolved accordingly. The plan now was to appoint members of the British nobility to such governorships, this being more redolent of constitutional monarchy as well as an implied compliment to the self-governing settler societies. The first such appointment in South

Australia was that of Algernon Keith-Falcolner, 9th Earl of Kintore, who served from April 1889 to April 1895.

Kintore fitted the new mould exactly. He was born on 12 August 1852 near Edinburgh, the eldest son of the 8th Earl of Kintore and Louisa Madeleine Hawkins. He was educated at Eton and Trinity College, Cambridge. In 1873 he married Lady Sydney Charlotte Montagu, second daughter of the 6th Duke of Manchester, and in 1880 he succeeded his father as Earl. Subsequently, Kintore was 'appointed to court and other offices appropriate to a member of the nobility'.[78] In 1885–1886, for example, he was Lord-in-Waiting to Queen Victoria, and held various posts in the House of Lords. In 1886 he was appointed Privy Councillor and Captain of the Yeomen of the Guard. Three years later he became Governor of South Australia. He and his wife and family arrived in the *Orient* on 11 April, met by Chief Justice Samuel Way, who had acted as administrator in the month since Governor Robinson's departure.

Samuel Way became a close friend and confidante of Governor Kintore, the cause of considerable discord when the current Premier, Thomas Playford, took offence at Way's appointment by Kintore as Lieutenant-Governor without reference to him. Thereafter, Playford's Government tried to minimise the amount of ministerial information provided to the Governor, an ostracism taken to new heights by one of Playford's Ministers, the radical liberal Charles Cameron Kingston, when he became Premier himself in 1893. In many ways the apogee of the nineteenth-century responsible government era in South Australia, Kingston was Premier for all of six years, in marked contrast to the often much shorter terms of his predecessors. He was a formidable character with voracious appetites (he was rumoured to have fathered at least six illegitimate children, on one occasion reputedly being discovered *in flagrante delicto* with a maid in Parliament House), and was an unfailing supporter of radical and progressive causes. He encouraged the formation of trade unions, promoted the establishment of a Trades Hall in Adelaide, and was persuaded to support votes for women. He established a state bank, introduced new factory legislation, enacted a progressive system of land and income tax, and was responsible for the very first conciliation and arbitration legislation in Australia, designed to settle industrial disputes.[79]

Kingston was also an implacable foe of privilege, especially in the form of the conservative Legislative Council, with its restricted voting qualifications. He tried unsuccessfully to reform the Legislative Council (which had watered down his Arbitration Bill) but had more luck in making life difficult for the aristocratic Governor Kintore. Kingston decided to simply ignore Kintore as much as possible, keeping him out of the loop in important discussions, and communicating directly with the Colonial Office via the South Australian Agent-General in London. Papers submitted for approval by meetings of the Executive Council often arrived so late that Kintore had no time to read them beforehand. In 1893, Kingston requested a long interregnum after Kintore's departure, so the South Australian Government could both save money and participate in discussions about the nomination of future Governors. He was, therefore, outraged when the Colonial Office reacted by extending Kintore's appointment. Kingston, in turn, responded by abolishing the vice-regal expenses allowance of £2670 a year, so that future Governors would have to fund their staff appointments out of their own pockets, and he also insisted that they should pay income tax, postal, telegraph and stationery bills, and the insurance premiums for the contents of Government House.[80]

Kintore was no more popular with the general public, especially the working class, and was said to be too interested in speculating in Broken Hill mining shares.[81] At public meetings he adopted his 'usual listless attitude', assumed by observers to be symptomatic of aristocratic foppishness, and on one such occasion a voice from the crowd demanded: 'Take your hands out of your pocket, Kintore.'[82] It appeared that Kintore's gubernatorial appointment had not been taken as the compliment that was intended; nor did it auger well for future Governors drawn likewise from the nobility.

Yet Kintore himself was enthusiastic about South Australia. He had had to deal with five changes of Government before Kingston's emergence as Premier, a duty he had accepted with equanimity. A keen Mason, he became Grand Master of the United Grand Lodge of South Australia, Samuel Way having resigned the position in his favour. Kintore was also intensely interested in outback Australia and its possibilities, travelling from Adelaide to Melbourne and then Brisbane by train before journeying by sea to Darwin. From there, he and his small party made their way south via the Overland Telegraph route through Katherine, Daly Waters, Tennant Creek, Alice Springs and on to Oodnadatta in South Australia, before completing the remainder of the journey to Adelaide by rail.

Following his departure from South Australia, Kintore returned to his previous life in London, resuming his post as Lord-in-Waiting, serving first Queen Victoria and then, after her death, Edward VII until 1905. He was also showered with honours by the crowned heads of Europe, and in 1913 became Deputy Speaker of the House of Lords. He died on 3 March 1930, survived by his wife and two sons and two daughters. His time in South Australia had not been entirely successful, soured as it was by the animosity of Charles Cameron Kingston. Yet curiously, both men, Kintore and Kingston, had been united by their commitment to the cause of Australian Federation. Kintore had enthusiastically attended the Melbourne Constitutional Conference in 1890 and only missed the next Conference in Sydney because he was engaged in his Darwin expedition. Kingston, meanwhile, earned distinction as a founding father of the Australian Federal Constitution, and was one of the first South Australian members of the new Commonwealth Parliament when it met in 1901.

Chapter 4

FEDERATION

Governors Jervois (1877–1883), Robinson (1883–1889) and Kintore (1889–1895) had each, in their different ways, expressed their support for the Federation of the Australian colonies. In this they reflected a growing South Australian interest in the prospects of Federation, echoing and supporting politicians such as Thomas Playford and Charles Cameron Kingston. Although, for Kingston and others like him, the status of colonial Governors was irksome, the office allegedly a drain on the public purse, vice-regal influence was actually a distinct asset in the Federation debate as it emerged.

Thomas Fowell Buxton
(29 October 1895 – 29 March 1899)

This was especially so in the case of Sir Thomas Fowell Buxton, Governor of South Australia from 1895 until 1899, when the focus on Federation was at its height. Initially, Kingston had not relished Buxton's arrival. He had earlier crossed swords with Kintore, abolishing the Governor's expense allowance (see p. 74), and had not been amused when he learned of Buxton's appointment the day before Kintore's extended term expired. Buxton's selection by the Colonial Office in Britain had been the result of a lengthy search for a suitable aristocrat willing to take up the position and with the means to sustain himself financially in the face of colonial parsimony. Kingston's reaction to the news of Buxton's appointment was to introduce legislation to reduce the Governor's salary from £5000 to £4000 per annum, and to further restrict the Governor's entitlements. He advised the Police Commissioner that he should not provide the Governor with the use of a horse or trap, and he slapped twenty-five per cent customs duty on the imported carriage especially adapted by Buxton to accommodate his invalid wife, Lady Victoria.[1]

However, despite this unpromising beginning, Buxton and Kingston, no doubt to their mutual surprise, found they had much in common. Buxton did not exhibit the aristocratic airs and graces of his predecessor and, despite his strict evangelical Christian morality, was prepared to overlook Kingston's extramarital indiscretions. As P.A. Howell put it, 'the government welcomed the change from Kintore's condescending manner, and Buxton's gentle courtesy and unassuming friendliness disarmed all radical criticism'.[2] Moreover, Kingston found to his evident pleasure that Governor Buxton shared his commitment to political and social reform. According to the Sydney *Bulletin*, 'Kingston declares Governor Buxton and his flock to be the most genial, sociable and common sense family who have ever inhabited the Adelaide vice-regal mansion'.[3]

This understanding reached its high point in the movement to achieve Federation. A Federal Convention, with the task of drafting a Constitution for the new Commonwealth of Australia, was held in Adelaide in March 1897, with a second in Sydney in the September and a third in Melbourne in March 1898. The proposed Bill was formally adopted at the Melbourne Convention, and was subsequently put to the vote. It failed initially because New South Wales, although narrowly in support, did not achieve the requisite margin. Slight amendments were made to accommodate the concerns of New South Wales, and in the referendum of 1899 all five participating colonies now voted unequivocally for Federation (the vote in Western Australia, which was also in favour, was held the following year). In 1898, South Australians had voted 'yes' by a margin of two to one; this was increased to four to one in 1899. On 1 January 1901, the Commonwealth of Australia came into being, with South Australia a constituent State.[4]

As historian (and former Premier) John Bannon observed, Kingston had played a pivotal role in keeping the negotiations going, 'always pushing for progress and action, chiding and appealing to colleagues, demanding deadlines, seizing initiatives, and generally refusing to let go of the concept of a united nation.'[5] Behind the scenes, he had been ably supported by Governor Buxton, who (at his own expense) attended each of the Federation Conventions as an observer. Buxton engaged in not a little discreet lobbying and bridge-building between delegates, and he hosted private dinner parties where differences could be aired and resolved.[6] Contrary to the received opinion that Governors had minimal influence in the era of responsible government, Buxton had demonstrated how vice-regal guidance might subtly be deployed to achieve desired ends. As he explained in a letter from Government House to his eldest son in April 1897:

> We are now getting well embarked on the work of the [Federation] Convention. The Western Australian Delegates have come. Those ... for the other four Colonies began work on March 22 and what with our Garden Party that day, the dinner on the 25th, the party on the 3rd April at Marble Hill, and other entertainments, have had every opportunity of getting to know each other – and to all appearances have been friendly and happy together. It is certainly the case that the opposing opinions have been expressed with clearness and some asperity.[7]

Politically adroit, Buxton was also careful to send a telegram to Queen Victoria, announcing the opening of the Convention. The Queen replied immediately, and Buxton made sure her response found its way into the hands of Kingston, who was to chair the Convention, before he made his opening remarks. As Buxton recalled, 'the proceedings began by his saying he had a message to read from the Queen. At once Delegates, visitors, all stood up, and he read it and proposed three cheers'.[8]

The paradoxical relationship of Governor Buxton and Premier Kingston reflected a wider set of paradoxes. As Howell explained, Buxton himself 'was a bundle of curious paradoxes'. He was:

> a brewer who supported the temperance movement; an Evangelical who commissioned a crucifix for his favourite church; a superb horseman,

who often galloped around the Adelaide parklands before breakfast, but who could only twice be persuaded to attend a race meeting; and though a grandson of that immensely wealthy financier, Samuel Gurney (who was known as 'the bankers' banker'), he gave away most of his fortune.[9]

Resolution of these paradoxes lay partly in Buxton's apparently unwavering commitment to profound moral principles, which was only to be modified when situations demanded. In such cases, he was not above using his common sense and indulging in a good deal of pragmatism. But his sometimes paradoxical behaviour was also explained by the fact that he saw himself as heir to the tradition of public service established by his paternal grandfather and namesake, Sir Thomas Fowell Buxton (1786–1845), the great Whig reformer and slave trade abolitionist, who, among other things, had chaired a Select Committee in 1835 to examine the condition of Indigenous peoples in British possessions (see pp. 22–23). The younger Thomas Fowell Buxton wished to follow in his footsteps unerringly, although on occasion practical circumstance might necessitate temporary deviation. As one contemporary observer put it, commenting on Buxton's time at Trinity College, Cambridge:

> His career as an undergraduate was blameless; sober and devout, but not the least austere. He rowed in moderation, and hunted regularly, not disdaining a hard-mouthed bus-horse when no better mount was available . . . It is to be remarked that, unlike most men of Evangelical antecedents, he sometimes played whist, and deliberately justified the practice in after-life. 'It is a pleasant way of meeting others, and it is good training for some departments of the mind. It only becomes evil if men play for money so as to care for their gains or losses. It may be easier not to play at all than to draw a line. I did not play except very little whist my last year, and I think my not doing so helped to break down some habits of high play that prevailed.'[10]

Thomas Fowell Buxton was born on 26 January 1837 at West Ham in Essex, England, eldest son of Sir Edward North Buxton, second baronet, and Catherine Gurney.[11] He was educated at Harrow and Trinity College,

Cambridge, and in 1858 succeeded to the baronetcy, together with various landed estates and a principal partnership in the brewing firm Truman, Hanbury & Buxton. In 1862 he married Lady Victoria Noel, a goddaughter of Queen Victoria. Although suffering from a debilitating spinal condition (probably osteoarthritis) by 1869, Lady Victoria had thirteen children with her husband, of whom ten survived into adulthood. Conception, pregnancy and childbirth must each have been extremely trying, and perhaps we see here, for all his empathy and insights, Buxton as a paternalistic Victorian sure of his conjugal role and rights.

Yet despite her affliction, Lady Victoria remained intensely active in a wide range of religious and philanthropic causes. She was also philosophical, even resigned, about her ailment. As she wrote to one daughter:

> I am wonderfully well though so crippled . . . Pain and illness are a mystery, but *to me* one comfort is that, if the perfect and Divine Man suffered as He did and was 'a Man of sorrows acquainted with grief', is it wonderful that some of us should have to suffer in a lower sense, we who are so unworthy and imperfect? Surely there must be some wise and loving reasons why we are allowed to do so, as we 'pass through the body' in this short life?[12]

Thomas Fowell Buxton had become a prominent speaker at Exeter Hall, an impressive building situated on the Strand in London, the venue for religious, progressive and philanthropic debate, a home too of the anti-slave trade movement. He served for many years in senior positions in both the Church Missionary Society and the British and Foreign Bible Society. He played a major role in organising relief for former slaves freed by the American Civil War, and successfully brought the Aborigines Protection Society and the Anti-Slave Society into a single body. Buxton also became a major benefactor for the London Hospital (situated near his brewery), the Consumption Hospital at Hampstead, and the Home for Freed Women Slaves in Cairo. Other public activities included support for home defence (he became Colonel of the 2nd Tower Hamlets Rifle Volunteer Corps) and the saving of open spaces for enjoyment by all, donating parts of his own oak and beech woods to enlarge Epping Forest.

Following in his grandfather's Whig tradition, Buxton became Liberal MP for King's Lynn in the British House of Commons in 1865, although his principled support for the disestablishment of the Church of Ireland cost him his seat three years later, when it fell to his Tory rival. He became a member of Essex County Council from its inauguration, and chairman of school boards in Essex and the East End of London. He toured Canada and the United States in 1874 to see how public education worked in those two countries, and while in North America developed an interest in federalism. This led him to support the Imperial Federation League, advocating the creation of a federal union of the United Kingdom and her self-governing settler societies overseas, and later translating into his enthusiasm for Australian Federation.

Gladstone, the British Prime Minister, offered Buxton a peerage in 1880 but he declined the honour, mainly because he was proud to bear the same style and name as his illustrious grandfather. Perhaps, as Howell observed, it was as well, because he became increasingly critical of Gladstone's interventionist Imperial policy in Egypt and elsewhere.[13] In the end, he severed his links with the Liberal Party over Home Rule for Ireland, part of Gladstone's grand plan for dealing with the 'Irish question', which (paradoxically) Buxton had decided to oppose. Like other anti-Home Rule Liberals he was attracted to the ranks of the breakaway Liberal Unionists, although he declined to stand as a parliamentary candidate.[14]

In March 1895, Buxton was offered the governorship of South Australia. After much 'anxious and prayerful reflection' he accepted.[15] As well as his concerns for his business interests and religious and philanthropic responsibilities in Britain, he also worried about his wife, Lady Victoria. As ever, she put on a brave face. 'I hope', she wrote, 'that my physical weaknesses and infirmities will be no hindrance to Father. I am so afraid they may be. I shall certainly give some amusement to the Colonists with my couches and Bath chairs and water-beds!'.[16]

In fact, the Buxtons' life together in the colony was to continue much as before, both immersing themselves in good works and worthy causes. Governor Buxton, as he now was, regularly visited the inmates of the Adelaide and Yatala gaols, the Home for Incurables, the lunatic asylum, and various refuges for the destitute. As in Britain, his concern was for the 'downtrodden and the outcast . . . [but they] were never to him mere objects of pity, but individuals with lives and interests of their own'.[17] The sympathy he had shown for 'the natives of Africa', including those from British colonies whom he had invited to weekends at his country house in England, was seamlessly extended to the Aborigines of South Australia.[18] He went out of his way (it seems with limited success) to explain to white settler society Indigenous concepts of land tenure, urging all who would listen that they should atone for past injustices. He was possibly the first Governor since Hindmarsh to invite Aborigines to Government House, although he did so, as Howell noted, 'to honour them, not to amuse other guests'.[19]

More generally, the *Register* thought that Buxton and Lady Victoria had 'brought Government House nearer to the people than it ever was before'.[20] According to one report, Government House became 'the centre of much literary work', while Lady Victoria in particular 'took the greatest interest in a series of Shakespeare Readings in the more general Reading Circles held at Government House'.[21] She also helped orchestrate some of the Governor's social activities, later recalling these as 'things, certainly, I look back on with satisfaction':

One is that the good Christian people 'had their turn' at Government House, and that we were privileged to entertain many there who had not been received within its walls before. Our Garden Parties for State school-teachers, for the police and their wives, the hospital nurses, the market-gardeners and their families (in the hills), the Anglican Sunday-School teachers, and such like, one looks back upon with *real pleasure*, and also the parties of the Y.M.C.A. and the Y.W.C.A., the G.F.S. [Girls Friendly Society], and the Ministering Children's Leagues, the Home Reading Circles, the Missionary meetings etc, these gatherings were all most pleasant to ourselves and others.[22]

Governor Buxton's generosity was legendary. He had only been in office for a month, when the *Quiz and the Lantern* noted that he had 'given away more in a fortnight than Kintore did in a year'.[23] It was reputed that in three years his gifts to the community had exceeded his salary by £38,000.[24] He was also keen to explore the country beyond Adelaide and the Hills and, like some of his predecessors, sailed along the Murray to see something of the interior. Lady Victoria gamely accompanied him. First, she wrote, there was the rail journey to Morgan 'over desolate burnt-up plains and then over sort of heaths – but covered with the Mallee scrub (a small eucalyptus) and the salt bush, a low, round flowering bush with a ghastly white flower'.[25] At Morgan, they joined the *Nellie*, a flat-bottomed boat, and from there visited the Murray 'Settlements', self-help communities established along the river by Kingston (who now styled himself a 'State Socialist') with the support of the fledgling United Labor Party (ULP) to give farming land to Adelaide's unemployed and homeless.[26] It was a scheme calculated to win the heart of the Governor. As Lady Victoria explained:

> We started at about 6 p.m. on our voyage up the river and soon stopped at a 'Settlement' where all the people were assembled on the shore . . . Father and the girls walked up to see some of their houses with lanterns, and then before we steamed away they sang to us. It was a pretty sight that evening with the moon shining . . . There was something rather touching to me steaming away from each of these places, sometimes by day and sometimes by moonlight, leaving the little crowd on the banks, cheering father [*sic*] and the women waving their handkerchiefs. Sometimes they sang songs (['Song of'] 'Australia' among them). Sometimes Sankey's, sometimes 'God Save the Queen' – and *often* 'God be with you till we meet again'.[27]

Moreover, Lady Victoria continued, the 'Settlements' folk were 'such particularly nice-looking and pleasant people, the women so pleased to see us and squeezing our hands, and the men had such good manners and were apparently far more intelligent than our average [British] working-man'. Pausing for reflection, she added: 'But then their wits have been sharpened by all they have had, and have still, to do.'[28]

The Buxtons' affection for South Australia was further heightened in 1896, when their third daughter, Constance Victoria, wed the Revd Bertram Robert Hawker of Bungaree. Two years later, the Buxtons visited England on leave. It was designed to be a temporary sojourn but while they were there their eldest son became gravely ill, and Lady Victoria's health declined markedly. Sadly, Buxton decided that he could not return to South Australia, and tendered his resignation as Governor. He and Lady Victoria had not had an opportunity to say goodbye properly to the colony and its people, a source of regret to the Buxtons as well as to South Australians, but the *Advertiser* spoke for many when it said of their erstwhile Governor that 'no one could have more completely identified himself with the aspirations of the people over whom he ruled'.[29]

Back in Britain, Buxton determined to 'stick up for South Australia'.[30] He was as good as his word, not least in tackling Joseph Chamberlain, then Secretary of State for the Colonies. Although he had earlier supported Chamberlain's Liberal Unionists, Buxton vigorously opposed Joseph Chamberlain's attempts to meddle with the Constitution of the Commonwealth of Australia. He also returned to his philanthropic work. During the First World War he turned Colne House, his home at Cromer in Norfolk, into a hospital for wounded soldiers, while his other big property, Warlies, became a Dr Barnado's home for orphaned children. When Buxton died on 28 October 1915, it was in a modest cottage on the Colne estate.[31]

Lady Victoria survived her husband for less than a year, expiring in the same Norfolk cottage on 9 August 1916, aged seventy-seven. To the last, she had retained her fond memories of South Australia: 'Long will the picture of her green hills, sweet yellow Wattle blossoms, blue seas and skies, and wealth of fruit and roses live in our memories. Still longer will her kind, friendly faces and loving words and deeds live in our *hearts*. "Advance, Australia!"'[32]

Hallam Tennyson
(10 April 1899 – 17 July 1902)

If Sir Thomas Fowell Buxton had done much to advance the cause of Australian Federation, then his successor, Hallam Tennyson, earned a reputation as its staunch defender. As Alexandra Hasluck, editor of Audrey, Lady Tennyson's letters, has put it: 'Hallam's chief contribution to Australia was to try to harmonise Commonwealth and State relations in the critical early days of Federation, and his calm, pleasant and benign personality must have soothed the savage breasts of politicians contending for their State's rights.'[33]

Not surprisingly, perhaps, after the heady days of conventions and referenda, of such excitement, optimism and anticipation, and of the lofty aspirations of nation-building, life after Federation seemed an anti-climax. All the expected advantages appeared to be dwarfed by apparent disadvantages, and the newly united States bickered as though still separate colonies, while jointly pouring scorn on the new Commonwealth Government. As Lady Tennyson observed in April 1902, describing the mood of disillusion: 'Federation seems daily to become more & more the despair of everybody, and you don't mention the subject to a single man or woman of any class that is not disgusted with the whole thing. One can only hope that it will turn out better than now appears.'[34]

It was this sense of disappointment with which Hallam Tennyson, in his short tenure as Governor-General, would eventually have to contend. But he had been an advocate of Federation long before. Tennyson's father, the poet laureate Alfred Lord Tennyson, had been an enthusiastic supporter of Imperial Federation, the romantic notion (also embraced by Thomas Fowell Buxton) that Britain might one day be joined in a Federal union with its overseas self-governing settler societies, and it was an enthusiasm that Hallam had inherited. He had also acquired from his father an interest in the possibility of Australian Federation, prompted by visits from Henry Parkes, the New South Wales politician (later Premier), when he was in England in 1881 and 1883. Taking leave of the Tennyson household in June 1883, Parkes wrote to Alfred, expressing the view that the 'future of Australia in which you take so deep an interest will in a few short years surprise the world'. As he explained, 'Federation in some form or other, of the now existing colonies will come by natural processes. There is no real abiding principle of conflict between them'.[35]

This was an outlook Hallam Tennyson was happy to adopt, and which he adhered to, first as Governor of South Australia, and then in his brief tenure as Governor-General of the Commonwealth of Australia (1902–1903).[36] When appointed to the latter position, Hallam Tennyson could reflect with satisfaction: 'This will be *especially* interesting work to me as my father was one of the first to speak of and for an Australian Federation, and he and my mother would have thanked God that their son was 2nd Governor-General of the consummated Commonwealth.'[37]

Hallam Tennyson was born on 11 August 1852 at Twickenham in Middlesex, the eldest son of Alfred (later Lord) Tennyson and his wife, Emily Sarah Sellwood. He was educated at Marlborough College and Trinity College, Cambridge. He trained as a barrister but never practised. In June 1884, Hallam Tennyson married Audrey Georgiana Florence Boyle. Like his father, the younger Tennyson had literary leanings, acting as his amanuensis until succeeding to his father's title on his death in 1892. He produced a two-volume biography of his father entitled *Alfred Lord Tennyson: A Memoir by His Son*, published in London in 1897, and also wrote a children's book, *Jack and the Beanstalk*.[38]

Looking for a role to suit his interests, Hallam Tennyson had let it be known that he would be interested in a governorship in one of the Australian colonies. Eventually, after further enquiries, Joseph Chamberlain issued a formal invitation; the position in South Australia was shortly to become available. Tennyson turned it over in his mind for a month, before expressing misgivings, now that Federation seemed inevitable. Paradoxically, despite his enthusiasm for Federation, he wondered whether the creation of the proposed new post of Governor-General might make State Governors redundant, or at the least reduce them to inferior status (see p. 4), perhaps as Lieutenant-Governors. He was told not to worry, that he would be in the post as Governor for at least a year before the Commonwealth came into being and, in any case, the status quo was likely to endure after Federation. Although not entirely reassured, Tennyson decided to accept.[39]

Hallam Tennyson arrived in Adelaide in time for him to assume the governorship on 10 April 1899. The late nineteenth century was the highpoint of Empire enthusiasm, in Australia as elsewhere, and the name Tennyson was revered throughout the Anglophone world, the late Alfred Lord Tennyson's poetic works, including the heroic 'The Charge of The Light Brigade' and the Arthurian romances 'Idylls of the King' and 'The Lady of Shalott', finding a place in nearly every home. Hallam Tennyson and his wife Audrey, Lady Tennyson, received hearty greetings, which contrasted with the indifferent, even grudging, welcomes experienced by some of their predecessors. As Lady Tennyson recorded:

> we were warmly cheered by the vessels & the work-people on the wharves. At Port Adelaide there was a triumphal arch with WELCOME, & thousands of people packed close where they had been standing in the sun for 2 hours . . . After the addresses 1500 children all massed together sang God Save the Queen, & the Australian National Song ['Song of Australia'] accompanied by the local band. Then the special train came up, our own splendid saloon carriage, & when we got in we went to the windows & the children beamed and the hundreds of hands were put up to wave to us, along the line we now again had fresh cheering till we arrived at Adelaide where the station was beautifully decorated with plants & red drugget and heaps of people who bowed as we passed . . . and we drove quite a short distance to Government House.[40]

Despite the deferential welcome, the new Governor and his wife had a taste of democratic Australian humour a few days later when they attended a 'Play' at the Theatre. Lady Tennyson, writing to her mother, explained that (fortunately) she and her husband were greatly amused by the not entirely respectful reference:

> I forgot to tell you a funny joke at the Play the other night which made us & the House laugh very much: one of the characters, an old woman – a regular ragged tramp – on being asked where she lived, said 'Marble Hill is my summer residence'. And later a sort of street beggar came backing on to the stage and in the distance one heard shouts of hurrah & clapping – the man, as I say, backed on the stage saying 'No! No! You are quite mistaken, I am *not* the new Governor'. You may imagine the roars of laughter there were.[41]

Thus the Governor and Lady Tennyson were introduced to the varieties of South Australian life. There was more hilarity when they paid a courtesy visit to the Fire Brigade, and they 'went up to examine the steam engine pumping water, & one of the horses suddenly turned by mistake & gave me, the boys & the Captain a shower bath, much to the amusement of the large crowd'.[42] Soon after their arrival, the Governor and his wife were taken to view *their* summer residence, Marble Hill, Lady Tennyson writing that the 'dust & heat were terrible at first till we got out of the town & then had a lovely drive up hills with sheep, green hills with gum trees, & wild roses'. This was the Tennysons' first experience of the colony beyond the confines of the city, and they found Marble Hill enchanting, with 'a white-painted gate at the entrance to a wide drive through woods with a very wide tall clipped laurel hedge on one side . . . It is a very nice comfortable house . . . We shall get on very comfortably in large airy lofty rooms . . . Lovely views of wooded hills all round'.[43]

A more chastening task for Lady Tennyson was her duty visit to the workhouse, 'which is just across the road outside Government House garden wall'. She was amazed to find the number of elderly inmates – 105 women, and three times that number of men – but she added that the provision was for the entire colony, not just the city. Nonetheless, she admitted that 'I had no idea that there could be so many destitute people here where labour is so scarce & wages so high'.[44] In the previous year, she said, the authorities had given outdoor relief to no fewer than 4460 people. Lady Tennyson was also surprised by the diversity of backgrounds she encountered:

I came across an old German to whom I spoke in German & he told me he had been in Australia 16 years, & in Adelaide, three, & could not speak a word of English – also a Frenchman from Bayeux to whom I spoke in French, another poor young German, from Hamburg, & a dear old Scotchwoman who still talks her Gaelic tho' she has been there in bed paralysed for 30 years and is always cheerful and happy and bright. The superintendent and & the matron seemed extremely nice with them & the old people all looked well and happy either in bed or sitting in their rooms or in the verandahs all round the buildings . . . I received a good many 'God Bless You's' as I shook hands with them & they had very pretty respectful manners, most of them.[45]

More harrowing still was a visit to the adjoining building, a home for

29. Left: Governor Sir William Cleaver Francis Robinson (courtesy SLSA B5960).

30. Right: Governor Algernon Keith-Falconer, 9th Earl of Kintore, c.1890 (courtesy SLSA B5986).

31. Above: Governor Sir Thomas Fowell Buxton, c.1895 (courtesy SLSA B3710)

32. Right: Lady Victoria Noel, later wife of Governor Buxton, as a young woman (courtesy Royal Collection Trust).

33. Above: Sir Thomas Fowell Buxton and Lady Victoria Buxton at their family home, Warlies, Essex, England, as depicted in a supplement to the Adelaide *Advertiser*, Monday 28 October 1895 (courtesy SLSA B1445).

34. Right: 'Afternoon Tea at Oodnadatta'. A cartoon in *Quiz and the Lantern*, 9 July 1896, depicting Governor Buxton, Chief Justice Way and two Aboriginal Australians.

35. Above: Governor Hallam Lord Tennyson and
Audrey, Lady Tennyson at Government House
c.1900 (courtesy SLSA B71638).

36. Right: Audrey, Lady Tennyson, from a portrait by
Briton Riviere (courtesy Tennyson Research Centre,
Lincoln City Libraries).

37. Left: Governor Sir George Ruthven Le Hunte, c.1903 (courtesy SLSA B3690).

38. Below: Governor Sir George Le Hunte and Caroline, Lady Le Hunte greeting guests at a garden party at Government House, c.1903 (courtesy SLSA PRG 280/1/13/490).

39. Left: Governor Admiral Sir Day Hort Bosanquet, c.1910 (courtesy SLSA B5340).

40. Below: Governor Admiral Sir Day Hort Bosanquet with Caroline, Lady Bosanquet and their two daughters at Government House, c.1910 (courtesy SLSA B10990).

41. Above: Governor Lieutenant Colonel Sir Henry Lionel Galway, 1919 (courtesy SLSA B12400)

42. Right: Marie Carola, Lady Galway (courtesy National Portrait Gallery, London).

43. Governor Galway as 'The Supercilious Ornament' in the *Australian Worker*, 30 December 1915.

44. Lady Galway, in her role as President of the Red Cross Society of South Australia, at her desk in Government House in 1917 (courtesy SLSA SRG 770/40/294).

45. Governor Sir Henry Gawler with his wife, Marie Carola, Lady Galway, sitting at his left, and his step-daughter 'Miss d'Erlanger' on his right, 1914 (courtesy SLSA PRG 280/1/21/9).

46. Governor Sir William Ernest Archibald Weigall, 1922 (courtesy SLSA B17110).

47. Left: Grace Emily, Lady Weigall, c.1920 (courtesy SLSA B45285).

48. Right: Priscilla, daughter of Governor and Lady Weigall, with her doll, c.1922 (courtesy SLSA PRG 2801/1/34/193).

49. Governor Lieutenant General Sir George Tom Molesworth Bridges, from the frontis-piece of his *Alarms and Excursions: Reminiscences of a Soldier*, first published in 1938.

50. Left: Governor Sir Tom Bridges in full dress uniform outside Government House, 1923 (courtesy SLSA 280/1/45/70).

51. Below: Governor Sir Tom Bridges and Janet Florence, Lady Bridges, sitting on his left, with guests in the grounds of Government House (courtesy PRG 280/1/40/195).

52. Left: Governor Brigadier the Honourable Sir Alexander Gore Arkwright Hore-Ruthven and Zara Eileen, Lady Hore-Ruthven at Government House in 1928 (courtesy SLSA B5029).

53. Below: Zara Eileen, Lady Hore-Ruthven planting a gum tree at Angorichina Hostel, a tuberculosis sanitorium in the Flinders Ranges, c.1933 (courtesy SLSA SRG 488/18/129).

54. Right: Governor Major-General Sir Winston Joseph Dugan, c.1934 (courtesy SLSA B6495).

55. Below: Governor Dugan and Ruby, Lady Dugan with the nurses at Port Augusta Hospital during an official visit in 1938 (courtesy SLSA B7798/443).

GOVERNMENT HOUSE.
ADELAIDE.

7th Jan 7 1936.

My dear Wrottesley.

Splendid hearing from you again.
We are still afloat. The temperature
has been over the century mark once
or twice of late. But no matter;
we are off tomorrow to our funk
hole in the hills, 15 miles away.
As they say...

England

ADELAIDE
10 PM
7 JAN
1936
S.A.

SOUTH AUSTRALIA
CENTENARY
CELEBRATIONS
1936

Captain R. Wrottesley D.S.O.
R.N.
Wick Cottage
Downton
Wiltshire

56. Envelope containing Governor Dugan's entertaining letter, with its affectionate descriptions of South Australia, sent to his friend Captain R. Wrottesley Royal Navy in England in January 1936 (courtesy SLSA D8718/1[L]).

57. Above: Governor Sir Charles Malcolm Barclay-Harvey in 1939 (courtesy SLSA B9101).

58. Right: Lady Muriel Barclay-Harvey, wife of Governor Barclay-Harvey (courtesy Vintage Edition).

single mothers, 'where no one else is ever allowed except the clergy, doctor, or relations, so that no one may know the girls have been there'.[46] As Lady Tennyson explained:

> This is only for the first time of falling. I was horrified to find 19 there either with their babies or waiting for them, one a girl of *14* ... Nearly all the babies were boys. They keep them with their babies for 6 months until they are both strong & well & they feel that the babies will have every chance of being properly cared for; of course the mothers have to do work of different kinds. If they offend a second time they go to the general lying-in ward & sometimes they have them there 4 or 5 times. It is all paid for by the government.[47]

The following year, in June 1900, Lady Tennyson again visited the single mother annex, finding that 'immorality among the young girls is terrible & I am told very much on the increase. The other day there were 18 babies in the workhouse, all for the *first* offence & heaps more coming on, varying from 15 but generally about 16'. The 'charming Matron' explained that most of the girls under her care were well-behaved. But, to Lady Tennyson's evident horror, Matron described a recent 'case of The Cenci' (an allusion to a verse play by Shelley about incest) where 'after the 6 months the girl was only 16½ & they came to fetch her away to the Reformatory for 18 months, & the poor girl clung to and fought for her baby & begged & entreated not to be separated from it'. It was a scene 'too heartrending for words', and eventually it was decided that the girl's mother would be allowed to care for the baby instead of it being 'boarded out with strangers', a solution 'which somewhat consoled' the young girl.[48]

Lady Tennyson's first encounter with an Aboriginal Australian proved equally startling, her mixed reaction reflecting both her alarm at unexpectedly meeting 'a very old native woman' and an instinctive and discomforting sense that such people were routinely oppressed and maltreated. This Aboriginal woman had 'very black skin' but 'white hair', Lady Tennyson observed with surprise, 'with a shawl over her head and a bundle on her back'. As the vice-regal party had made to enter the city's Exhibition Building to attend an official function, so the woman had suddenly appeared, and 'made a low bow to Hallam & me touching her head'. Later, on leaving the event, 'the first person we met coming out was the old thing again but this time she insisted on walking alongside the Governor . . . upon which a policeman was called and the poor old thing was taken by the shoulders & pushed out of the way as if she were the bundle on her back'.[49]

Two months later, on a vice-regal visit to the railhead town of Oodnadatta in outback South Australia, there was a more formal introduction to the Indigenous population. The Tennysons were guests of honour at a corroboree, Lady Tennyson recording her vivid impressions in a letter to her mother. They had arrived at the location after dark, and found a hundred or so Aboriginal women and girls seated around a large fire. There were several men placed in front of these women, 'sitting with wooden instruments in their hands'.[50] Then, she explained:

> At the words of command these men began to hit them together & a low monotonous sort of chant was moaned out by them & then taken up by the women & then we saw about 50 or 60 naked natives (I was told there was one woman among them but I did not make her out) all dressed with their war-paint & head-dresses, & the gypsum or white clay mixed with human blood [sic] in patterns all over their faces like masks & in patterns over their bodies and feathers – and all holding a bunch of emu's feathers in each hand. They all suddenly appeared in a sort of rush towards us from their wherleys [huts] where they had been hiding till our arrival, then they went thro' all sorts of weird gestures supposed to be representative of tracking an enemy or emu-hunting.[51]

When the Tennysons felt they had seen enough, 'Hallam said so & thanked them in two or three simple words' and then announced 'there were lots of lollies & apples and baccy & flour for them & pipes, all of which he gave them, & tea & sugar, and the government had also sent up some shirts and blankets'.[52] Although Lady Tennyson did not say so explicitly, it was if the spell had been broken, the window onto a fast fading traditional way of life replaced immediately by the more prosaic practicalities of the

Aborigines' increasing reliance upon Government handouts and white society's demands. Lady Tennyson knew that Indigenous Australians 'have been treated brutally by white men, but thank God, Government is taking up their cause very strictly this session & ill treatment will be most severely punished'. Sadly, however, she thought that the Aborigines 'are dying out fast ... & our making them wear clothes near white people & giving them blankets, alas helps to kill them for they throw off the clothes when they go on their hunting grounds for lizards & kangaroos, emus & their eggs, rabbits and rats, & if fancy takes them, give away or leave behind their blankets'.[53] In yielding even temporarily to white society's ways, she thought, the Aborigines had become more uncertain and vulnerable in their own environment. It was a telling insight.

Lady Tennyson's pity for the unfortunate in society – the elderly German at the workhouse who knew no English, the paralysed Gaelic-speaking Scotswoman, the fourteen-, fifteen- and sixteen-year-old girls who had children when they themselves were still children, the Aborigines with their proud but seemingly doomed ceremonies – was translated into her attempts to affect Government policy. She had taken a keen interest in the 'sweating system', as she called it, where young girls from the ages of fourteen to nineteen were paid a pittance for the manufacture of men's shirts and linen aprons, and she confronted Charles Cameron Kingston, the radical liberal Premier, demanding that something be done. 'I have been talking to the Premier, Mr Kingston', she wrote, 'about the terrible sweating system that alas is going on here, & he asked me to allow him to send a lady inspector of factories to talk to me about it'. Kingston shared Lady Tennyson's concern for social justice. But as Premier, and being a politician, he had competing priorities and pressures, which he tried to explain to Lady Tennyson. She noted that Kingston had 'promised to try & bring it before Parliament last session, but with Federation there was no time'. Now, however, she was assured that in the next session 'something will be done'.[54]

Governor Tennyson's relationship with Kingston was by no means as cordial as his wife's, and the rapport established between Governor Buxton and his Premier was not replicated during Tennyson's appointment. As Howell has put it, the 'tension which had characterized Kingston's dealings with the Earl of Kintore reappeared after the arrival of Buxton's successor, Lord Tennyson'.[55] Indeed, Kingston's long premiership (over six years) came abruptly to a halt on November 1899, when his ministry was defeated in the House of Assembly by twenty-six votes to twenty-five.

Kingston advised Governor Tennyson to dissolve the Assembly so that the Government might appeal to the electorate to reverse the vote of no confidence. However, Tennyson decided to ignore this counsel and sent instead for Thomas Burgoyne, the member who had moved the fatal motion. Burgoyne declined and the task of forming a new ministry fell to Vaiben Louis Solomon. His Government lasted just one day, succumbing to an adjournment motion moved by Frederick William Holder (who had been encouraged by Kingston). Controversially, Solomon advised Governor Tennyson to send for Thomas Playford, one of Solomon's supporters, rather than Holder, the mover of the adverse motion. Sensibly, Playford declined to form a Government, and so the Governor sent for Holder, who accepted and whose premiership endured until May 1901 when he entered the new Federal Parliament. Kingston, meanwhile, was likewise elected to the fledgling Commonwealth Parliament, becoming Minister of Trade and Customs in the first Federal Government.[56] For Governor Tennyson, it had been a taste of the sometimes byzantine nature of South Australian politics, to which the House of Assembly appeared to have returned after the lengthy Kingston ministry.

The one area where Governor Tennyson and Kingston were generally in agreement was that of Federation. Tennyson, like Kingston, was a strong supporter, although, as we have seen, he worried that State Governors might be sidelined or even abolished altogether in the new system. This partly reflected concern for his own status as Governor of South Australia but it was also based on his increasingly firm belief that, if Federation was to work, the States – with Governors as their symbolic heads – should in no way be subordinated to the new Commonwealth authority. Instead, he argued for partnership and parity of esteem.

Speculation about the future roles of State Governors was constant during the Tennysons' time in Adelaide. In early June 1899, for example, Lady Tennyson confided to her mother that after Federation 'there is no doubt it seems that there will only be Lieutenant-Governors, & some people go so far as to say we may all be sent back by January 1901'. The overwhelming result of the 1899 referendum served only to stimulate such anxieties. On 20 June, in another letter to her mother, Lady Tennyson expressed her joy at the outcome. 'Well, the great day has arrived', she exclaimed, '& Federation of Australasia is no longer a dream but a fact, & a grand thing it is'. She and the Governor had been out for the evening when the votes were counted, '& Hallam desired that he should be kept acquainted by telephone there of the votes recorded from NSW. Just as we went into dinner a majority of five thousand – then later, on 10 – and this morning 21,000. The papers say there was great rejoicing at Melbourne and Sydney'. Nonetheless, she added cautiously, 'of course everybody is at sea as to what will happen & whether the Governors remain on as they are'.[57]

To defend the status of Governors, Tennyson organised what was effectively a boycott of the Commonwealth inauguration ceremony in Sydney on 1 January 1900, explaining in a cable to the Colonial Office in London that 'the States would resent any appearance of subordination of States to Governor-General'. Instead, Tennyson participated in his own local ceremony. At 12.30 pm, in Adelaide Town Hall, he was sworn in as Governor of the State of South Australia, a change of nomenclature which also brought with it a subtle change of status, as, somewhat ironically, in his capacity as senior State Governor, he would now fulfil the role of Administrator of the Commonwealth Government in the absence of the Governor-General.[58]

Their status assured, at least for the time being, the State Governors did attend the opening of the Federal Parliament (where, of course, the States were to be represented by constituencies in the House of Representatives and directly in the Senate), a recognition of sovereignty split formally between Commonwealth and States. There was some bad feeling, however, when Lord Hopetoun was selected as Australia's first Governor-General. As Lady Tennyson explained, 'I am afraid there is a good deal of disappointment over Lord Hopetoun's appointment . . . everyone feels that the position, a *very* difficult & unenviable one I should say, requires a much abler man, in fact, a *great statesman*'. Moreover, she continued, a major part of his role would be to 'keep the peace between all the petty jealousies of the different colonies [*sic*], especially Melbourne and Sydney – who have always hated each other'. Yet inter-State rivalry and mutual suspicion had been exacerbated by Hopetoun's appointment, as 'NSW is jealous of a former Governor of Victoria being chosen instead of one of their own, being the Mother Colony'.[59]

In fact, Hopetoun's period in office was a disappointment. Early in his governor-generalship, he committed what was to go down in history as the 'Hopetoun Blunder', when, failing to understand the complexities of Australian politics, he designated Sir William Lyne, Premier of New South Wales, as prospective Prime Minister. But Lyne could not form a ministry, and so it fell to Edmund Barton, who commanded majority support, to actually become the first Prime Minister of a unified Australia.[60] Other gaffes followed, and Hopetoun was also accused of lavish expenditure to maintain his lifestyle. He felt unable to continue in office, he said, without a firm commitment to a permanent allowance, and so tendered his resignation. Hearing the news, Governor Tennyson wrote to Joseph Chamberlain, subtly elucidating Hopetoun's various failings and stressing his own qualifications for such a post.[61] Accordingly, he was appointed Acting Governor-General on 4 July 1902, and was confirmed in the position in January 1903, at his request for one year only. This he saw as the culmination of his vice-regal career, and, as he had promised, he used the office to protect States' rights and promote good relations between States and Commonwealth.

The Tennysons' term in Government House in Adelaide had encompassed dramatic events. Federation had been the dominating political event, although the end of Kingston's long ministry also caused a sensation at the time. But there were other major happenings too – the Boer War, with all its attendant anxieties, including the death of Lady Tennyson's brother Cecil, killed in action in April 1900. 'It made me feel very sick & was a horrid blow', wrote Lady Tennyson on hearing the grim news.[62] The Boxer Rebellion in China, with the prospect of sending a colonial gunboat, caused much excitement, as did the Royal visit of the Duke of York and Duchess of Cornwall (the future King George V and Queen Mary). And then there was the death of Queen Victoria.[63] As the news of the Queen's last illness came through, Lady Tennyson had written 'one cannot for a moment realise England without Her', her reaction no doubt echoing that of countless other subjects throughout the Empire. When the dreaded telegram arrived – 'The Queen is dead God Save the King' – there was 'heartfelt grief all over the colony'.[64]

Governor Tennyson's time in office had also straddled the change from nineteenth to twentieth century, and on his return to Britain in 1904 he decided it was time for new directions. Accordingly, he refused the governorship of Madras in 1905, and returned to his earlier literary interests. He edited collections of his father's poems and in 1911 published *Tennyson and His Friends*, an eclectic volume, part anthology and part memoir, of pieces written for and by his father's acquaintances. He did accept the ceremonial position of Lieutenant-Governor of the Isle of Wight, in honour of his father's long association with the island, and was active in the Royal Literary Fund and the Folklore Society. Unfortunately, the Great War years brought their share of sorrows. The Tennysons' son Harold was killed when his ship HMS *Viking* struck a mine in January 1916, and a little over ten months later, on 7 December 1916, Audrey, Lady Tennyson, author of the spirited correspondence, also died. In March 1918, a second son, Aubrey, was killed in action on the Western Front. In the July, now lonely and bereft, Hallam Tennyson married again, this time to Mary Emily Hichens, a widow. He died at Freshwater on the Isle of Wight on 2 December 1928.

George Ruthven Le Hunte
(1 July 1903 – 18 February 1909)

The Tennysons would always be a hard act to follow (in 1978 Alexandra Hasluck wrote that they 'were perhaps the most interesting vice-regal couple Australia has ever seen'),[65] and this was certainly true in respect of Governor Tennyson's successor, George Ruthven Le Hunte. Joanna Barr Smith, member of a leading Adelaide family, wrote to Lady Tennyson to describe the new Governor soon after his accession: 'Personally, I find him a very stodgy man. He has no sense of humour at all. Ah, when I remember the twinkle in Lord Tennyson's eye I heave a sigh.'[66] Yet Lady Tennyson, who had first met Le Hunte in September 1899, thought him 'a delightful man', and in 1925, after Le Hunte's death, the *Register* remembered him fondly as 'a popular South Australian Governor'.[67] He was the first Governor of South

Australia to be appointed after Federation, and, perhaps awkwardly, his immediate predecessor was now Governor-General of the Commonwealth.

George Le Hunte was born in Ireland on 20 August 1852 at Artramon, County Wexford, of which his father (also George Le Hunte) was High Sheriff. His mother was Mary Pennefather, daughter of the Lord Chief Justice of Ireland.[68] The younger George was educated at Eton and Trinity College, Cambridge. He embarked on what would become a lengthy colonial career in 1875 when he became Private Secretary to Sir Arthur Gordon, who was vacating his gubernatorial appointment at Mauritius to become the first Governor of Fiji, which had just been ceded to the British Crown by the paramount chiefs of the archipelago. Le Hunte served as magistrate in Fiji and in the Western Pacific High Commission (whose jurisdiction included the Solomon Islands, among other territories). He showed himself adept at handling ethnic sensibilities, respecting the existing Fijian ranking system as well as protecting the Indigenous population against the competing interests of the European planters and the immigrant Indian labour force. In 1884, on leave from Fiji in England, he married Caroline Rachel Clowes.

When Gordon left Fiji to become Governor of New Zealand, he recommended Le Hunte for the post of President of Dominica, which he duly assumed in 1887. From there, he was promoted to Colonial Secretary of Barbados in 1894, where again he found himself having to moderate and adjudicate the conflicting interests of the Indigenous community and white settler society. It was a role he performed once more in Mauritius, where he was appointed Colonial Secretary in 1897, the settler society this time being of French origin. Two years later, he became Lieutenant-Governor of British New Guinea, to European eyes a forbidding and largely unknown territory, administered jointly by Britain and three Australian colonies, and soon to be taken over by the new Commonwealth of Australia. He spent much of his time lobbying for funds to support the changing arrangements but his most traumatic experience was in dealing with the Papuan inhabitants of Goaribari Island.

Two British missionaries, Revds James Chalmers and Oliver Tomkins, together with ten Papuan missionary students, had been captured in April 1901 by the head-hunters and cannibals of Goaribari Island, to whom they were attempting to minister. The prisoners were beheaded and eaten, their bones displayed about the local village. The London Missionary Society appealed for clemency but Le Hunte decided upon punitive action against the islanders, and three weeks later led an expedition which killed twenty-four Goaribari villagers, as well as burning the houses containing the skulls of victims and destroying Goaribari war-canoes. Le Hunte confessed that he 'deplored' having to conduct such an operation but considered 'the natives brought it upon themselves and I believe conscientiously that they deserved it'.[69] Not surprisingly, there was much criticism of his action in both Australia and Britain, and, partly in response, Le Hunte led a second, conciliatory expedition in March 1902 to try to establish good relations with the Goaribari Islanders.

From New Guinea, it was perhaps a natural step to Australia, in advance of which he received a knighthood. The Colonial Office, having seemingly abandoned its policy of replacing career colonial administrators with suitable aristocrats, selected Le Hunte as Governor of South Australia in succession to Tennyson. The appointment had the additional advantage that Le Hunte could continue to give informal advice to the Commonwealth Government on the administration of Papua. Despite (or perhaps because of) his experiences with the Goaribari Islanders, Le Hunte retained his sympathetic understanding of Indigenous peoples, and took a keen interest in the welfare of South Australia's Aboriginal communities. He also displayed a concern for the needs and aspirations of young people, earning him the affectionate title 'the children's governor', and he acquired a reputation as being an able administrator, if sometimes rather unassuming and self-effacing. He had been an Anglican lay preacher in Fiji, and tried to apply his Christian convictions to his role as Governor in South Australia, taking a particular interest in religious affairs. To many observers he seemed an amiable, humane 'gentle giant' (being 1.9 metres tall). He busied himself in all the usual vice-regal activities. In 1903, for instance, he became the first patron of the Royal Automobile Association of South Australia at its foundation. In the following year, with a 'handsome silver trowel and mallet' presented by the architect, he declared open the new Adelaide Fruit and Produce Exchange.[70]

As Le Hunte's term of office neared its end, in 1908 he accepted the governorship of Trinidad and Tobago. In 1915 he retired to Crowborough in Sussex, in the south of England, here he died on 29 January 1925. Assessing Le Hunte's career, the *Oxford Dictionary of National Biography* decided that 'he was a "safe pair of hands" as the governor of small, potentially difficult colonies'.[71] It was not quite damning with faint praise. Of course, when Le Hunte was Governor of South Australia, the State was neither a colony nor 'difficult' in the way that some of his predecessors had experienced.

Although there had been no major upheavals, political or otherwise, during Le Hunte's time in Government House, the United Labor Party (ULP) had been steadily growing in strength under the leadership of Tom Price, recovering from its poor showing in the 1902 State election to the point where in May 1905 it won fifteen seats in the House of Assembly, becoming the largest single party. Meanwhile, Archibald Peake had formed a group of liberal-minded members to form what would eventually become a new party, the Liberal and Democratic Union (LDU). Peake's liberals took five seats in the 1905 State election. Voting together, the ULP and Peake's liberals defeated the existing Government, and Le Hunte asked Price, as senior leader of the emergent coalition, to form a Government. Although his ministry was not a majority Labor Government, Tom Price was nonetheless South Australia's first Labor Premier.[72]

A priority for the new coalition was reform of the Legislative Council, something that Kingston had attempted to achieve but failed. In the eyes of the coalition, reform became ever more urgent. During the 1905 session in Parliament a small number of Acts were passed but the Council threw out Bills on factories, judicial appointments, land value assessment, taxation, and municipal tramways, and allowed others to lapse on the State Bank and an increase in the number of Government ministers.[73] In 1906, the Government presented a new Legislative Council reform Bill, which was promptly rejected by the Council. Price had little choice but to seek a double dissolution of both Houses, which Le Hunte duly granted. In the resultant November 1906 State election, the ULP achieved its best result so far, winning nineteen of the forty-two seats in the Assembly, with Peake's LDU – which had been given 'immunity' by the ULP – gaining ten. Conservatives, however, continued to dominate the Legislative Council, and let it be known that, far from accepting the election result as a mandate from the people, they would continue to oppose reform. In the encroaching impasse, Price threatened a further double dissolution.[74]

Faced with this prospect, the Legislative Council decided to compromise, offering a £17 property franchise (that is, a vote for any adult paying £17 rent). This remained a restricted franchise but Price saw it as a stepping-stone to greater things, and accepted the deal. It was the first time since 1856 that an expansion of the franchise for the Legislative Council had been achieved. Thereafter, the Price–Peake arrangement seemed set fair to continue. But beneath the surface there were already tensions, the ULP, sensing its growing popularity with the electorate, hinting that it might not grant immunity to LDU members in the forthcoming 1910 State election.[75]

Day Hort Bosanquet
(18 February 1909 – 22 March 1914)

By now Vice-Admiral Sir Day Hort Bosanquet had been appointed Governor of South Australia, having taken up the position in February 1909.[76] Born on 22 March 1843 at Alnwick, Northumberland, in the north-east of England, he was the third son of Revd Robert William Bosanquet and his wife Caroline MacDowell. Bosanquet entered the Royal Navy in 1857, and rose rapidly in the service. He was promoted Commander in 1874, Captain in 1883, and Rear Admiral in 1897. He was appointed Commander-in-Chief, East Indies, in 1899–1902, and in 1902 was promoted Vice-Admiral, subsequently becoming Commander-in-Chief of the North America and West Indies Station in 1904–1907, and finally appointed to Portsmouth before retirement in 1908. He received a knighthood in 1905. In 1881 he had married Mary Butt, with whom he had a son and two daughters.

Bosanquet's appointment as Governor had been motivated in part by the British Government's hope that he might prompt action to upgrade South Australia's port facilities, which were reckoned now to be among the worst in the Empire.[77] Arriving at Government House, he found to his dismay that the Legislative Council had blocked all plans for harbour improvements. Not surprisingly, therefore, he sympathised with plans to reform the

Legislative Council. However, Governor Bosanquet was presented with his first political crisis only months after taking office when the Premier, Tom Price, who had been ailing for some time, died on 31 May 1909. The ULP lost no time in electing John Verran, a Cornish miner from Moonta on northern Yorke Peninsula, as its new leader. Labor had made it clear that it would only continue in coalition with Peake's LDU if there was another ULP Premier to replace Price, the ULP being the dominant partner in the House of Assembly. But Peake, in his role as Acting Premier, clung to power, accepting a commission from Governor Bosanquet to form a Government.[78]

At the time this was seen as simply bad faith, although it emerged subsequently that Bosanquet had been in touch with Sir Francis Hopwood, the permanent head at the Colonial Office, to discuss the issue. It transpired that Bosanquet had been to see Price on his deathbed, and Price had advised that Verran should be made the next Premier. Bosanquet, however, with Hopwood's support, decided the premiership should go to Peake, who was already Acting Premier and had ministerial experience while Verran had none. Labor, however, had now decided that it would support F.W. Coneybeer – who had been Minister for Education for a few months – as Premier, a move that annoyed Bosanquet who stood firmly by his original choice.[79]

The ULP made much of Peake's apparent treachery, and in the ensuing State election on 1 April 1910, the party won twenty-two seats, gaining an overall majority in the House of Assembly and thus the ability to govern in its own right. Bosanquet asked Verran to form a ministry, and thus John Verran, as Premier, became leader of the very first majority Labor Government in the world. Verran's honeymoon period was short-lived. His first year in office was characterised by widespread industrial action, with more than half-a-dozen major incidents in Adelaide and disturbances as far away as Renmark, each one an embarrassment for Verran as a Labor man. There was a railway strike in September 1910, followed in the October by a strike of 'tarpavers' sealing Rundle Street in the city, and in December the Drivers' Union struck. The latter was especially damaging for Verran, as virtually all traffic in Adelaide came to a halt. There were those who considered Verran was losing his grip. John McConnell Black wrote that

'Jack Verran took a jovial interest in the strike and Gunn, the secretary of the union, used to stroll across Victoria Square from Trades Hall to consult the Premier, who sat smoking his short pipe with his legs up on the fence of his boarding house in Landrowna Terrace'.[80] Verran was summoned to Government House for a dressing down by Governor Bosanquet (including, it was rumoured, a threat of dismissal), together with a warning that he would summon a gunboat to Port Adelaide if things got worse. In the end, the strike was settled amicably enough, but the credibility of Verran and his Government had been severely dented.

Meanwhile, attempts to further reform the Legislative Council had steadily worked towards their climax.[81] The Council had thrown out an adult suffrage Bill in 1910, and in September 1911 it rejected what was known as the 'Council Veto Bill', an attempt by the Verran Government to emulate the new restrictions placed on the House of Lords in the United Kingdom. Verran turned to the Asquith Government in Britain for Imperial intervention, requesting assistance so 'the Constitution be so amended by an Imperial Act as to enable the matured will of the people of South Australia on these and other questions to become law'.[82] Having already rejected or allowed to lapse more than a dozen Bills, the Legislative Council turned the screw yet tighter, finding an excuse to defer the Government's Appropriation [Budget] Bill and thus block supply. The pretext was Verran's controversial practice of 'tacking', of attaching new, hitherto undiscussed, public works to the Appropriation Bill – in this case, provision for a State brickworks and timber yard.

On 23 December 1911, Governor Bosanquet (who actually deplored the 'tacking' device), sent a telegram on Verran's advice to the British Government, again requesting Imperial intervention. Three days later came the reply: 'interference of Imperial Parliament in internal affairs of self-governing State would not be justified under any circumstances until every constitutional remedy had been exhausted and then only in response to the overwhelming majority of the people, and if necessary to enable Government of the country to be carried on.'[83] In the face of such a rebuff, Verran had little choice but to seek a dissolution of the House of Assembly, which Governor Bosanquet duly granted on 16 January 1912. Not surprisingly, perhaps, the

ULP suffered a major defeat in the election of February 1910, only sixteen Labor members being returned against twenty-four for the recently formed Liberal Union, led by Archibald Peake.

Alongside these constitutional wrangles, Governor Bosanquet lent support to both Verran and Peake in their endeavours to promote South Australia's interests, including a border dispute with Victoria, the struggle for a fair share of River Murray water, and the building of a proposed Oodnadatta–Pine Creek railway link as a *quid pro quo* for the transfer of the Northern Territory from the State to the Commonwealth. He also travelled widely within the State, on one occasion in 1909, for example, going deep underground in the Wallaroo copper mine (ironically, in John Verran's constituency) in the care of the general superintendent, H. Lipson Hancock, and three venerable Cornish mine captains: James Pryor, Nicholas Opie, and Tom Tamblyn.[84] On the expiry of his governorship in March 1914, Day Bosanquet returned to Britain, where he retired to Bron-y-Clos, his estate at Llanwarne in the Welsh Marches of Herefordshire. After his son was killed in action in 1916, he sold up and moved to Newbury, Berkshire, where he died on 28 June 1923.

Despite the fears of Hallam Tennyson and others, Federation had not led to the diminution or disappearance of the role of State Governors in Australia. On the contrary, not only had the office survived intact but, as the experience of Governor Bosanquet had demonstrated, Governors retained considerable powers to guide and even influence the constitutional process. Put simply, State Governors had survived Federation.

Chapter 5

THE GREAT WAR
AND BEYOND

When Governor Bosanquet left South Australia in March 1914, war clouds were already on the horizon, for those who cared to see. One who did was Brevet-Major (as he was then) Tom Bridges, an officer in the British Army who would later become Governor of South Australia (1922–1927). In 1910, Bridges was appointed British Military Attaché in Brussels, the Hague, Copenhagen and Christiania (Oslo). As he explained, 'With four countries to visit our four years passed quickly', especially given his many opportunities to observe 'German preparations for war along the Belgian frontier. The Franco–German situation became quickly more and more tense, causing war scares in 1913 and 1914, and generally keeping Europe in a jumpy condition'.[1]

The possibility of German violation of Belgian neutrality became an increasing preoccupation, and Bridges devoted considerable time and effort to covertly viewing German preparations. 'We were continually making fresh discoveries in the Ardennes', he wrote later, 'new camps, detraining stations, railway sidings and new roads'. He added, in the inimitable impish style for which he would be so fondly remembered in South Australia: 'For the benefit of spy-craft in general I may disclose that an expensive high-powered car and a good-looking girl are the best passports to forbidden areas.' Thus equipped, he explained, he penetrated the out-of-bounds German camp near Elsenborn, on the German–Belgian border, where he 'drank beer in the officers' casino and sent off a postcard of it to the Director of Military Intelligence'.[2] Bridges knew that war was coming, and was preparing for it.

Henry Galway
(18 April 1914 – 30 April 1920)

However, eight long years of war and its hectic aftermath would pass before Tom Bridges, by then a Lieutenant-General with a knighthood but minus one leg, would arrive at Government House in Adelaide, to be met by 'a warm-hearted and hospitable people, whose chief desire seemed to be to make us feel at home'.[3] Before then, South Australia had had to endure the attentions of the two perhaps least successful individuals, certainly in the twentieth century, to fulfil the vice-regal role – Henry Galway and William Archibald Weigall.

'At his welcome in 1914', according to P.A. Howell, Galway 'upset people by praising the River Murray Waters Agreement, [then] awaiting parliamentary debate, and compulsory military training'. He also made known his 'support for gambling, and of minimal restrictions on liquor trading', thus alienating a sizeable proportion of the State's population, and criticised the enfranchisement of women and South Australia's progressive education system. He disapproved of Australia's egalitarian spirit, and as Governor resented the limits of his constitutional authority. Put simply, as Howell noted, Galway was 'ill-chosen'.[4]

Henry Lionel Galway was born on 25 September 1859 at Alverstoke, near Portsmouth, Hampshire, the son of Lieutenant-General Sir Lionel Gallwey and his second wife, Alicia Lorinda Lefanu.[5] Lionel Gallwey was a native of Killarney, a minor member of the Anglo–Irish Protestant Ascendancy, and, then a Major in the Royal Engineers, was resident at Alverstoke to oversee the construction of Fort Blockhouse at the western entrance of Portsmouth Harbour. Although born in England, Henry Galway was aware of his Irish heritage, and this may have influenced his change of surname in 1911 from 'Gallwey' to 'Galway', affecting perhaps Anglo–Irish aristocratic credentials (but not to be confused with the Viscounts Galway). Galway's wife, Baroness Marie Carola Franciska Roselyne d'Erlanger, a widow he married in August

1913, was herself a daughter of an Irish baronet, Sir Rowland Blennerhasset, sometime MP for Galway in the British Parliament.

Henry Galway was educated at Cheltenham and, joining the British Army, at the Royal Military College, Sandhurst. By 1881, he was a full Lieutenant and was posted to India. Shortly after, however, his father was appointed Governor of Bermuda, and Galway secured his release from duty in India to become his father's aide-de-camp and private secretary. The position must have suited father and son, for Galway occupied it for all of eight years, then staying on in Bermuda to fulfil the same role in 1888–1889 under the next Governor. In 1890, and by now a Captain, he was posted to Ireland, where perhaps he met family members and learned something of his late great-uncle's adventures in Zululand and the Transvaal. Whatever the cause, Galway suddenly exhibited a newfound enthusiasm for 'Darkest Africa', as he called it, and within the year had secured a position as Deputy Commissioner and Vice-consul in the Oil Rivers Protectorate, which became the Niger Coast Protectorate in 1893.[6]

This Protectorate covered the coastal districts of what was later Nigeria, and its authority was enforced by the gunboats of the Royal Navy's West Africa Squadron, the local chiefs being required to submit to British rule and remove obstacles to trade, including the practice of slavery. The latter was relinquished with great reluctance, and Galway was in his element exercising the use of force to ensure compliance and concessions, including new customs duties and licensing fees for trading canoes. He revelled in his 'annual punitive expeditions', as he described them, and on one occasion he could not believe his luck when the sudden appearance of a flotilla of war canoes allowed him 'some very pretty practice . . . with a quickfirer'. Another time, Galway enjoyed his 'merry' experimentation with a Maxim machine-gun, and took pleasure in burning towns and villages to extend 'the grand and inspiring work of Empire-building'. His use of rockets caused great consternation, one survivor of an attack reputedly exclaiming in wonder: 'Truly the white men are gods.'[7]

Galway's most appalling excess was the wanton destruction of Benin City, including the slaughter of vast numbers of its inhabitants and the now notorious looting of its exquisite bronzes and ebony and ivory carvings, widely considered to be among the finest examples of non-Western art.[8] Determined to end the 'fetish rule' of 'his Duskiness', king Ovonramwen, Galway 'negotiated' a sham treaty in which all sovereignty was ceded to 'Her Britannic Majesty' in return for her formal protection. All matters, from trade to legal jurisdiction, were to be referred to British consular officers, and henceforth the king was required to act exclusively on their advice.[9] In fact, Ovonramwen continued much as before, including restrictions on the export of some of his most important commodities, including palm kernels, peppers and rubber. He may not have fully understood the terms of the treaty forced upon him (something Galway later acknowledged), and from the time of signing in 1892 until Galway's sudden onslaught in 1897, he ruled uninterrupted and unmolested, Galway being pre-occupied with his punitive expeditions elsewhere.

However, Galway had not forgotten Ovonramwen, and during leave in Britain he presented a paper to the Royal Geographical Society in which he condemned Benin as 'the City of Blood' and 'that city of skulls', a 'theocracy of fetish priests' which conducted human sacrifices and deserved to be overthrown because its 'rule is one of terror'.[10] His moment came in January 1897, when he was appointed Acting Commissioner and Consul General for the Niger Coast. Exercising his new authority, he mustered all available troops in the region and requested further reinforcements, which duly arrived in February, comprising 1200 Marines and sailors under the command of Admiral Harry Rawson (later Governor of New South Wales). Citing non-observance of the dubious treaty of March 1892, Galway sanctioned the destruction of Benin City and the exile of Ovonramwen. He delighted in the humiliation of the 'the dusky potentate', explaining that on 'more than one occasion, when I consented to see him at a certain hour and he turned up 10 minutes or so late, I refused to see him'. As he put it: 'My turn had come! He kept me waiting for three days in 1892 before he saw me, so I thought it quite fair not to see him at all unless he observed punctuality'.[11]

On the spurious basis that it had ended slavery and human sacrifice, the reduction of Benin City was deemed justifiable in the eyes of British authorities, although there was certainly some discomfort in high places.[12]

Yet it was a story that Galway was always happy to tell, and he no doubt dined out on it on numerous occasions. It was also an account that others were often inclined to accept uncritically. Early in Galway's appointment as Governor of South Australia, for example, at a function to welcome Dan Crawford, a visiting missionary from Africa, Chief Justice Way opined that Galway (who was presiding) was especially 'fitted to grace the occasion':

> His Excellency had . . . journeyed to Benin, bloody Benin, and persuaded the monarch of that great city and territory to place himself and his country under the protection of the British Crown. (Applause.) Unfortunately that monarch did not act well, and he was ultimately deposed. The very wise act of His Excellency the Governor, however – and he recalled the fact with pride – was the means of bringing a great territory into the benefits of British rule . . . On that occasion the Governor was the minister of righteousness to a much oppressed country. (Long applause.)[13]

Despite such adulation, Galway's extreme actions (and their much-protested justifications), may have had an adverse effect on his military career. He was pointedly not summoned with his regiment when it was ordered to South Africa in 1899, and although promoted Major in that year, his failure to participate in the Boer War further diminished his prospects. In April 1901 Galway was placed on half-pay and joined the Army's retired list, being accorded the courtesy rank of Lieutenant-Colonel on retirement, as was the custom in those days. Meanwhile, his colonial career had also languished, his wings clipped by the emergence of the new Protectorate of Southern Nigeria in 1899–1900, and prospects for further promotion in West Africa seemed remote. Accordingly, in 1902 he sought a transfer, and thought it prudent to accept what Howell has described as 'one of the humblest posts the Colonial Office had at its disposal' – Governor, Chief Justice and Colonial Secretary of St Helena.[14]

St Helena had flourished during the Boer War, the internment of 6000 Boers on the island stimulating high demand for local produce. But by the time Galway arrived the Boers had gone home and the economy was in deep depression. He embarked, therefore, on a series of innovations to revive commerce and trade. To make good the recent denudation of the island by the Boers' demand for firewood, Galway organised the importation of thousands of tree seeds from Kew Gardens in England. But no sooner had the saplings appeared, than they were eaten by feral goats. Similar experimentation with flax growing failed, as did a fish cannery, which was abandoned when the great shoals of mackerel suddenly disappeared from local waters. The population of St Helena declined by some forty per cent during Galway's governorship. Yet his strenuous, albeit unsuccessful, attempts to rebuild the local economy had not gone unnoticed, and in 1910 he received a knighthood. In 1911, Galway was appointed Governor of the Gambia, back in West Africa, but he remained there for just eighteen months before journeying to London where, in 1913, he married Lady Galway. He had been told discreetly that bachelors could no longer expect important gubernatorial appointments, so Galway's timely marriage opened the door to South Australia.

Howell's assessment that 'Galway was a poor choice for an Australian state' is surely correct.[15] Governor Galway despised typically Australian traits such as self-confidence, independence and love of liberty, and criticised the 'marked lack of discipline and want of respect' he had encountered. He was sure Australia would become 'the laughing stock of the Empire' due to the rise of trade unionism and the attendant 'wave of socialism' sweeping the country, adding that 'a bad year or two would be an excellent tonic' as it would give the workers 'the opportunity of practising self-denial and of learning what adversity really was'.[16]

The 'bad year or two' was already at hand, the outbreak of the Great War in August 1914 having an immediate impact on employment. Mining was a significant component of the South Australian economy on the eve of war, comprising the great copper mines of Wallaroo and Moonta on northern Yorke Peninsula and the silver-lead-zinc mines of Broken Hill just across the New South Wales border. By 1914, the base metal industry across Australia was controlled almost entirely by German interests, so that when war broke out its overseas markets were denied at a stroke.[17] At Broken Hill, almost all of the lead concentrate had hitherto been sold to German smelters, and Australian plants (including the smelters at Port Pirie in South Australia) had only limited capacity to cope with the sudden excess. Zinc too had been exported to Belgium and Germany, and again Port Pirie was capable of processing only a tiny fraction of this output. As a consequence, Broken Hill output was stockpiled, and jobs were shed.[18]

At Wallaroo and Moonta, the story was the same. In August 1914, H. Lipson Hancock, general superintendent of both mines, explained coyly that 'in consequence of the outbreak of war in Europe, and the inability of the contractors to take our delivery of copper, it has become imperative to at once curtail operations'.[19] Some 2000 workers lost their jobs, and thousands more in the local economy were put at risk, the shockwaves being felt throughout the State. Fortunately, the Federal Government soon stepped in, taking charge of strategic metals for the war effort, the copper being sold to Britain to assist in the manufacture of munitions.[20] But the dislocation had been profound, made worse by the drought – the worst for seventy-five years – that drove many farmers from their land, their crops destroyed and livestock decimated. The Mayor of Adelaide led an appeal for funds to help the distressed, raising $38,000 by the end of 1914. Yet Governor Galway was unmoved. He reported to the Colonial Office in London:

> The Australian worker demands his three meat meals a day, and indulges in many luxuries besides. The result is he is particularly hard hit when lean years have to be faced. The majority of labourers appear to me to live on a lavish scale, and even go to and from their work on bicycles. Those not possessing such machines use the tramways ... In an optimistic vein I would suggest that good may yet come out of evil, as the present crisis may be the means of strengthening the fibre of this prosperous community, and of teaching them, especially the labouring class thereof, to become, inter alia, less irresponsible and more self-sacrificing.[21]

Galway's superiors in London were appalled but, oblivious, the Governor continued in similar vein. Despite Australia's distinguished contribution to the war effort, Governor Galway singled out the so-called shirkers – those who would not volunteer for military service – for withering criticism. In October 1915, for example, he complained that 'there are a very large number of wastrels and loafers who count their own comfort and convenience as of more importance than the welfare of the Empire', opining that these 'undesirables can only be dealt with under either conscription or some other drastic measure'.[22] He was no less dismissive of those who did volunteer. By early 1916, there was a steady stream of servicemen returning to Australia, many of them having been severely incapacitated or otherwise rendered unfit for further service, and Australians clamoured to lend a hand, at first through voluntary organisations (not least the Red Cross), and then through an ambitious Commonwealth Government 'Repatriation' program.[23] Governor Galway, however, considered that:

> The average returned soldier is not an easy individual to handle. His disinclination to take up regular work is most marked ... He is easily discouraged, whilst being very difficult to please ... the majority of these men appear to demand all that is done for them as a right. Their complaints are many, whilst any sign of gratitude on their part is not often distinguishable.[24]

Deciding to play on his mother's Scottish birth, Galway cultivated a Scots persona to complement his Anglo–Irish identity, and used the State's Caledonian Society as a platform for some of his more extreme public pronouncements. When ironworkers at the Islington railway works went on strike, for example, he denounced them violently, declaring they should be put in uniform and sent to the front to fight. The *Daily Herald* thought this outburst 'a gross violation of vice-regal duty', while one speaker at a specially convened meeting of the Trades and Labor Council reckoned 'the Governor should be put in his place. He got £80 a week to keep his mouth shut and he could not do it ... The Governor should go to the front. If in no other capacity, he could go as a private. He could be spared from here, where he had nothing to do but malign men'.[25]

By now, it was clear that Galway had all but abandoned his gubernatorial commitment to apolitical neutrality and impartiality, and in doing so had diminished his own vice-regal standing as well as that of the office of Governor. He had also brought the Imperial connection into disrepute, at the very moment the Empire was fighting for its life. Elements of the Adelaide Establishment may privately have welcomed his tough line on shirkers and strikers but his divisive rhetoric had alienated a large proportion of the population, not least in the Labor movement. The Premier, Crawford Vaughan, leader of the Labor Party in Parliament, demanded an apology from Galway – and got it – while others decided it was time to petition the British Government to seek Galway's recall. Later, after the Great War, Labor members of the House of Assembly, so incensed by Galway's behaviour, argued for the abolition of the office of Governor, and although this move was unsuccessful, it was a prelude to persistent Labor demands throughout the 1920s and 1930s that Governors should be Australian-born, rather than Imperial appointments.

Predictably, Galway supported the 'Yes' votes in the conscription referenda during the Great War, and after the 'No' vote in the first referendum he claimed that German influence in the State had fatally undermined the campaign. He viewed South Australia's sizeable 'German' community with increasing suspicion and contempt, and led demands that German place names be erased from the map – an obsession that even extended to Petersburg (now Peterborough), which, like Johnsburg (renamed Johnburgh), had actually been named after Governor Jervois' sons. Similarly, he wished to root out Irish nationalism, claiming that Melbourne's Catholic Archbishop, Daniel Mannix, 'hardly ever opens his mouth without sowing the seeds of dissension . . . I am quite unable to understand why the gentleman referred to is able to scatter his infamous doctrine broadcast without being placed in . . . custody'.[26] The Colonial Office was disturbed by Governor Galway's attempts to fan the flames of hatred and unreason, and would later be incensed by his flouting of constitutional convention and even the ignoring of Imperial instructions. As Howell has suggested, Galway survived for as long as he did because, despite everything, he was an effective recruiting-sergeant, touring the country to cajole and embarrass young men into joining the colours.[27]

However, with the end of the war in sight in October 1918, Galway became concerned that he had heard nothing about future gubernatorial appointments, and was worried that he was about to be passed over.

Subsequently, he was granted a one-year extension in South Australia but his request for at least four months leave on half-pay was refused, being offered instead a mere two months. In December 1919, the Colonial Office instructed Galway to inform his Premier that Sir Archibald Wiegall had been selected to succeed him as Governor. Thereafter, Galway refused to submit his required quarterly reports to London, and this sealed his fate – there were to be no further vice-regal or other official appointments.

Henry Galway's one saving grace was his wife, Marie Carola Franciska Roselyne d'Erlanger, Lady Galway.[28] Ironically, Lady Galway was part-German and also Roman Catholic, two 'defects' which her husband contrived not to notice. It is not difficult to appreciate what Galway saw in his prospective bride before their marriage – an accomplished and well-connected woman with aristocratic credentials and an Anglo–Irish heritage to boot. Also, Galway needed a wife if he was to be appointed to South Australia. It is less clear what she, a widow of independent means, saw in him. She did, however, concede that 'he had a way with him', a glimpse perhaps of a more agreeable personality behind the unattractive façade.[29] She knew the story of Benin City, but much later admitted that in those days she was an uncritical Imperialist. Nowadays, she explained in 1953, the word had 'fallen into disrepute and people are shy of using it'. But in earlier times, 'we were all Imperialists. If Africa was to be opened up by a great power, then let it be under the British Flag; we could see no flaw in this argument'.[30]

Sir Henry and Lady Galway were married in London on 26 August 1913. Six weeks later he was appointed Governor of South Australia, taking up his position in April 1914. On arrival in Adelaide, Lady Galway 'was much impressed. Government House, our home for the next five years, was like a pleasant country house standing in lovely grounds, sufficiently large but not unwieldy'.[31] As she observed, 'April is a glorious month in South Australia, the heat of the summer has gone and the sky is endlessly blue ... What struck me vividly was the translucence of the atmosphere: so incredibly light! Flowers seemed to bloom all year round'.[32]

In contrast to her reactionary second husband, Lady Galway was a broad-minded intellectual. Her first husband, Baron R. d'Erlanger (whom she had married at seventeen and who died on their third wedding anniversary, leaving her with two small children), had been a noted biologist, and she was enthralled by his work: 'these were the days of the beginnings of biology, and biology seemed to promise an answer to the very mystery of life.'[33] Lady Galway carried this enthusiasm to South Australia, delighting in its biodiversity, and on one occasion she and her new husband the Governor paid an official visit to the University of Adelaide. Shown some scientific slides projected on a screen, she exclaimed: 'Dear me, ascaris eggs.'[34] Needless to say, this caused a sensation. Lady Stanley, wife of the Governor of Victoria, was equally impressed by the range of Lady Galway's learning. After a visit to Adelaide in 1916, she declared:

> She [Lady Galway] is a *wonder* in the amount she knows. There is no political aspect of the modern history of Europe she cannot descant upon nor, I believe *any* subject – religious, philosophical, political, artistic or scientific that she has not a grasp of and cannot talk admirably upon. Her Italian, French and Spanish are all spoken with a perfection of accent and an accuracy which is really astounding.[35]

Inevitably, the outbreak of the Great War had an immediate and profound effect on Lady Galway's life. One of the many patriotic bodies in which she became involved was the Belgian Relief Fund, where she organised and then edited a remarkable anthology, the *Lady Galway Belgium Book*. Published in 1916 by the local Adelaide firm Hussey & Gillingham, the anthology included essays, short-stories, poetry and other material from leading figures in the State and across Australia, with gross proceeds of the sales given to the Belgian Relief Fund. Modestly, she explained that the fact the book 'bears my name is due solely to the kindly wish of my co-workers in a field where they are all equal'.[36] She wrote the introductory chapter, 'The Point of Honour', in which she pondered the human qualities that were necessary in dealing with armed conflict and its resolution: 'Neither pride nor fear; neither the lust of conquest nor the desire for revenge, is the most exacting task-maker. The thing supremely difficult is to obey the dictates of the voice within, to satisfy the claims of conscience and to approach the lofty ideal of the point of honour.'[37]

Lady Galway maintained a life-long interest in the fate of Belgium, and after the country was overrun by the Germans for a second time in 1940, she penned a heart-felt review of Roger Motz's *Belgium Unvanquished*, a 'grim and moving tale', as she described it.[38] But even more significant in the Great War years was her commitment to the Red Cross.[39] As she admitted:

> We soon woke up to the meaning of war. As far as I was concerned the process began when I received a wire from Lady Ferguson (afterwards Lady Novar), wife of the Governor General, telling me to start Red Cross work in South Australia. Except for Lady Helen herself there was, as far as I know, not a living soul in the country who knew anything about the Red Cross. Certainly I was ignorant to the degree of incompetence.[40]

As Lady Galway later explained, she called a meeting of prominent citizens – men and women – 'and in order to confront this embryo committee with something tangible, I asked my maid to cut a pattern from the pyjamas of the Private Secretary'. He was over six feet tall, and in 'presenting this pattern for acceptance I made the brilliant remark that you could always put a little man into big pyjamas, but never a big one into little ones. This passed as impeccable logic'. However, the unexpected consequence, as word was passed to the far-flung corners of the State, was the production of numerous pyjama trousers that 'would have fitted the hind legs of an elephant'.[41] Undeterred, Lady Galway persevered, with remarkable results:

> the ladies of South Australia built up a truly magnificent Red Cross unit. The generosity of Australians is proverbial. You can hardly illustrate this more convincingly than by stating that in South Australia funds raised in two years for the Red Cross and other patriotic efforts were thirty shillings per head of population. It continued so all through the years. Incidentally the cost of raising these vast sums was nominal, all the work being voluntary.[42]

Lady Galway was much impressed by the voluntary principle, so important to the people of Australia, and when her husband supported conscription to the armed forces, she took a rather different view. After conscription was rejected in two referenda, she reflected that 'I think the people were right. The response of volunteers was so splendid that, at best, the combing out could not have produced more than fifty thousand men and those were urgently needed for food supplies'.[43]

After the war, Lady Galway was appointed CBE for her efforts, and before her departure from South Australia in January 1919 (fifteen months ahead of her husband) she was presented with a diamond and opal necklace by the women war workers of the State. Her Red Cross work continued after her departure. For example, at Henley Beach, near Adelaide, in 1927–1928, the Lady Galway Convalescent Home was able to report that of 190 patients it had treated, sixty-eight were returned Army sisters whom the Red Cross had decided to assist. This was despite their not being referred by Repatriation Department, which had considered their conditions not sufficiently serious.[44] There were great outpourings of affection as Lady Galway prepared to leave the State. The *Register* considered that she had 'raised the whole status of women in public life'.[45] For her part, Lady Galway told the many women who had congregated at the Exhibition Building to farewell her, that 'it had been a great privilege to stand for the work of the women of South Australia, and they had done her the greatest honour she had known in the whole of her life'.[46]

Following their return to England, the Galways continued in public life. Sir Henry encouraged the emigration of British youths to Australia to work as farm labourers, and Lady Galway was involved in a variety of philanthropic and voluntary activities. Henry Galway died in London on 17 June 1949, survived by Lady Galway, who died at St Merryn in Cornwall on 29 June 1963.

William Ernest George Archibald Weigall
(9 June 1920 – 30 May 1922)

Arriving in the wake of Sir Henry and Lady Galway, Sir William Ernest George Archibald Weigall ('Archie' to his friends) and his wife, Grace Emily, Lady Weigall (formerly Baroness von Eckardstein), found it hard to settle in South Australia. Their predecessors had made a profound impact on the State's life, the consequences of which were still fresh in mind. Henry Galway was remembered for his often-foolish outbursts, which still rankled, not least in Labor circles, while the memory of his wife, Lady Galway, was cherished by those who recalled all her good works during the Great War. In their separate but opposing ways, they were difficult acts to follow, the role of Governor now regarded with suspicion in some quarters, while, paradoxically, much was expected of a Governor's spouse.

Archibald Weigall (as he was generally known) was born on 8 December 1874 in London. He was the fifth son of the portrait artist Henry Weigall (whose subjects included the Duke of Wellington and members of the Royal family) and the writer Lady Rose Sophia Mary Fane, author of a biography of Princess Charlotte, Queen Victoria's daughter, who had died in childbirth. Weigall was educated at the Royal Agricultural College in Cirencester, Gloucestershire, giving him a life-long interest in agricultural matters, and became an estate manager, specialising in animal husbandry.[47]

Like many rural gentlemen, Weigall joined the local militia – the 3rd (Northampton and Rutland Militia) Battalion of the Northamptonshire Regiment. In April 1902 the battalion was mobilised for service in South Africa but, with the end of the Boer War in June of that year, Weigall was soon on his way back to England from Cape Town. In the Great War, he served on the staff of the Northamptonshire Regiment, rising to the rank of Lieutenant-Colonel, and in June 1918 was appointed Surveyor of Food Consumption (with the aim of making savings in the Royal Navy, Army and other public services). Yet he stayed in this post for less than a year, resigning in protest against what he considered the unjust treatment of officials (by which he probably meant himself) at the hands of the Food Ministry.[48] He was Conservative and Unionist MP for the constituency of Horncastle from 1911 until 1920 but his inability to weather the storms of the Food Ministry did not bode well for the future – either for his developing commercial interests or, indeed, his governorship of South Australia. As Howell observed, Weigall 'had a genius for accepting directorships of companies which turned out to be shady and went bankrupt, so that towards the end of his life he lost his great houses in Mayfair and Lincolnshire'.[49]

Long after Weigell's departure from South Australia in 1922, the local press was still taking a keen interest in his misadventures, the *Register News-Pictorial* reporting in September 1929 that Weigall 'is concerned in the crisis' caused 'by the arrest of Clarence Hatry and his three associates'. Weigall, the newspaper revealed, was 'prominently associated' with one of the Hatry group businesses, Corporation & General Securities Ltd, whose difficulties meant that heavy 'losses are likely to be sustained by insurance companies'.[50] In fact, the collapse of the Hatry empire has been cited as one of the precipitatory factors in the Great Crash in September 1929.[51] Hatry himself was sentenced to fourteen years imprisonment for fraud. He was, as the economist J.K. Galbraith wrote, 'one of those curiously un-English figures with whom the English periodically find themselves unable to cope'.[52] Archibald Weigall was one such Englishman, drawn unwittingly into the web of Hatry's dodgy dealings and financial deceit.

Weigall's expertise in matters agricultural lay behind his appointment to a State in which primary produce was a significant element of the economy, and he was honoured with a knighthood before taking up the post. He was especially popular with the farming community, helped in the establishment of an agricultural high school, and assisted with the legislation requiring the registration and licensing of bulls. His stammer dissuaded him from making lengthy speeches but he was a witty and lively speaker. However, on arrival in Adelaide he was dismayed to learn that he would have to pay his staff's salaries (he had been wrongly advised on this by the Colonial Office), which he found a considerable strain on his private purse. He also had a low opinion of State politicians, criticising ministers for the twin practices of switching funds from one project to another without parliamentary approval and spending monies before supply had actually been granted. He concluded that the Federal system was unnecessary and unwieldy, and, likewise, that State Governors were an expensive anachronism. In December 1921, Weigall tendered his resignation for 'private and financial reasons', and left Adelaide on 24 April 1922, a month before the official expiry of his appointment.[53] He had been Governor for just one year and 355 days.

Prominent among these 'private' reasons for terminating his appointment was his wife's ill health. Howell noted that Grace Emily, the heiress of furniture magnate Sir John Blundell Maple, had always spent her annual allowance before the year was out, and argued that 'Weigall became so embarrassed by her outrageous extravagance and hypochondria (her personal staff included two resident doctors), that within a year of taking office in Adelaide he was compelled to beg leave to relinquish it'.[54] However, behind the façade of profligacy and the demand for constant medical attention, Grace Emily (Lady Weigall, as she had become on her husband's knighthood) was indeed often ill, suffering a series of miscarriages and possibly phantom pregnancies. Not surprisingly, she had a reputation for cancelling engagements at the last minute.[55] Nonetheless, she attended to her official duties as best she could, and was reckoned a good public speaker as well as a conscientious supporter of philanthropic causes. In the latter capacity, she toured the State to view local facilities.

After a visit to the Murray, for example, Lady Weigall wrote approvingly that 'the social amenities of Renmark are good and there is no need for outside assistance in this respect'. As might be expected, she took a particular interest in medical provision, explaining that at Renmark there 'is a good hospital, subsidised by the Government, as distinct from a purely Government hospital, or a purely private hospital'. Opened in 1915, the hospital was frequented, she added, 'by all classes of the community, a large section of which consists of soldier settlers, their wives and families. All general medical, surgical and maternity work is undertaken'.[56] Here was a genuine interest in the welfare of the community, especially given the recent influx of soldier settlers, struggling to turn the Mallee into farming country, and she demonstrated a commendable attention to detail in explaining the structure of the hospital and its functions.

A bohemian and in some ways mysterious woman, Grace Emily, Lady Weigall, was born in 1876, the only surviving daughter of Sir John Blundell Maple and Emily Harriet Merryweather. She counted Rudyard Kipling among her acquaintances and attracted a wide circle of male admirers.[57] She had two marriages, the second to Archibald Weigall, and had a succession of affairs, at least two of which produced a child each, discreetly placed in foster care. Her first marriage in 1896 was to Baron Hermann von Eckardstein, First Secretary (and later Ambassador to Britain) in the German Embassy in London. Presciently, Grace Emily's father had arranged that his fortune – which amounted to £2,153,000 at his death in 1903 – could not be accessed by his daughter's husband. Grace Emily, meanwhile, purchased forty acres near Woodhall Spa in Lincolnshire in 1905, where she built a spectacular country house, which she named Petwood. Her marriage appeared happy enough at first, with a daughter Kit born in 1898, and her 'society' progress was reported widely throughout the Anglophone world. In October 1906, for example, the *New Zealand Herald* explained that:

> Bright, kindly, and popular as ever is the Baroness von Eckardstein, only daughter of the late Sir Blundell Maple, who in her girlhood was one of the most petted and indulged young ladies in England . . . Baron von Eckardstein is a yachting man, and well known at Cowes. The baroness has no liking for the sea, but she is very keen on motoring, and owns a beautiful car. She dresses beautifully, is fond of society, entertains largely, and is at the present time greatly interested in the bungalow [*sic*] she is building at Woodhall Spa. She has a hobby for collecting old French furniture, so that her new house is sure to be as delightful as wealth and good taste can make it.[58]

Behind the gushing descriptions, however, was a hint of separate lives and conflicting interests, and Petwood increasingly became Grace Emily's retreat from what had become a distinctly unhappy marriage.[59] In 1906 she gave birth to a son, Reginald, whose father was Dr C.J. Williams, a family friend, and in 1907 began divorce proceedings against her husband on the grounds of cruelty. On 16 August 1910, Grace Emily, freed at last from her first marriage, wed Archibald Weigall at Metheringham parish church in Lincolnshire.[60] By then she was already three months pregnant, and the resultant daughter, Heather (whose father was Elidor Campbell, son of the Earl of Cawdor), was, like Reginald, quietly put away. Sadly, Kit, Grace Emily's first child, died during an operation in hospital in 1917 (no doubt fuelling her mother's hypochondria) but in 1914 another daughter, Priscilla, had already been born to Sir Archibald and Lady Weigall. Priscilla's parents doted on her, and her mother ensured her introductions to high society. 'Who will be the prettiest debutante of 1932?', asked the London *Daily Mail* gossip columnist in January 1932: 'My choice is Miss Priscilla Weigall, who will be 18 in April.'[61]

Remarkably, Elidor Campbell continued to be welcome at Petwood after the Weigalls were married. Years later, in 1975, Priscilla was able to describe Campbell to his daughter Heather, who, now in New Zealand, had embarked on the long and difficult task of identifying her biological parents. According to Priscilla, Campbell 'was a dear man, quiet but charming, someone I especially liked. Of all the hordes of people, he was my favourite. He was so gentle and patient, always the same, different as chalk and cheese to Mummy's temperament'.[62] Tellingly, perhaps, Priscilla's own daughter, Jenny Ponte, said much the same about her grandfather, Archibald Weigall, describing him as well-meaning but gullible, 'a complete charmer and a lovely man' to whom his wife 'was absolutely not faithful at all'.[63]

Despite the collapse of his business interests, Archibald Weigall remained active in public life in Britain. As chairman of the Royal Empire Society, he re-visited South Australia in 1935 and 1937, and was also chair of the Royal Veterinary College. By this time Petwood had been turned into a hotel, and the Weigalls had moved to more modest accommodation at Ascot in Berkshire. During the Second World War, Petwood was requisitioned by the Royal Air Force, becoming the officers' mess for the famous 617 'Dambusters' Squadron. Predeceased by Grace Emily in 1950, Archibald Weigall died at Ascot on 3 June 1952.

Tom Bridges
(4 December 1922 – 4 December 1927)

Between his spying on German preparations for the invasion of Belgium and his appointment as Governor of South Australia in December 1922, Tom Bridges had been extremely busy. Indeed, it was his daring exploits during the Great War of 1914–1918 that had commended Bridges to Winston S. Churchill, then Secretary of State for the Colonies and Dominions, for the governorship in succession to Archibald Weigall. As Churchill put it, Tom Bridges as 'His Majesty's representative had – as was proved – all the qualities and personality, all the comprehension and knowledge of men and affairs necessary for so important a task'.[64]

From the earliest days of the Great War, Bridges had been in action. He crossed to Boulogne on 9 August 1914, detrained at Hautmont, 'and marched north in triumphal possession, roses all the way, feted and cheered by the unfortunate inhabitants . . . The weather was so perfect and the country looked so peaceful and prosperous'.[65] Less than a fortnight later, on 22 August, he led 'the first action of the British Expeditionary Force' (BEF) in the war.[66] As Major in command of C Squadron, 4th Dragoon Guards, a cavalry regiment, Bridges ambushed a German mounted patrol ('Uhlans') on the Mons-Brussels road. Private Ted Worrell, one of his soldiers, described the encounter:

> The chase went on for a mile but we were better mounted and caught up with them on the outskirts of Soignies and there was a proper old melee. Captain Hornby ran his sword through one Jerry and Sgt. Major Sharpe got another. I got a poke at a man but I don't know what happened to him. There was a fair old noise what with the clatter of hooves and a lot of shouting. The Jerries couldn't manage their lances at close quarters and several threw them away and tried to surrender but we weren't in no mood to take prisoners and we downed a lot of them before they managed to break it off and gallop away . . . I suppose it was all over in five minutes but we certainly showed them that the 4th was hot stuff.[67]

Tom Bridges added his own account of the action in his memoir *Alarms and Excursions*, 'a tale told at a cavalry trot' as Churchill described it, a 'gay story of grim events, told with modesty and with feeling'.[68] Bridges recalled that C Squadron 'had just finished watering our horses at a cross-road when the first Uhlan scouts were sighted . . . I dismounted two troops for fire action and kept two mounted ready to charge'. Sensing a trap, the 'Uhlans, a squadron, took to their heels and the chase went merrily down the hard high road . . . the Uhlans were hampered by their long lances and a good many threw them away. Several were killed, Hornby for one running his man through'.[69] When C Squadron returned to their Division, complete with prisoners, captured Prussian horses, and 'a stack of lances', it was met by cheering. Captain Hornby, the hero of the hour, was awarded the

Distinguished Service Order (DSO), 'the Brigadier having announced that the first officer to kill a German with the new pattern cavalry sword would be recommended for this honour'.[70]

The second of Bridges' exploits was even more extraordinary. On 24 August 1914, two days after the skirmish with the Uhlans, the BEF fought its first major battle at Mons. In the subsequent retreat, elements of the British infantry reached St Quentin in a precarious state. 'Marched literally off their feet', as Bridges put it, 'they straggled into the town in a very demoralized condition'.[71] Bridges attempted to organise a rear-guard defence to hamper the German advance, and he found some 200 to 300 men lying about in the town's square – they 'were so jaded it was pathetic to see them':

If one only had a band, I thought! Why not? There was a toy-shop handy which provided my trumpeter and myself with a tin whistle and a drum and we marched round and round the fountain where the men were lying like the dead playing the British Grenadiers and Tipperary and beating the drum like mad. They sat up and began to laugh and even cheer. I stopped playing and made them a short exhortation and told them I was going to take them back to their regiments. They began to stand up and fall in, and eventually we moved slowly off into the night to the music of our improvised band, now reinforced with a couple of mouth organs.[72]

'The Toy Band' incident passed into the folklore of the Great War[73] – celebrated in the eponymous ballad by Sir Henry Newbolt, later set to music by Sir Richard Paget – and, according to Churchill, it was the 'story of the drum' which persuaded South Australian politicians to welcome Bridges so unreservedly as their new Governor. As he explained, it 'was compulsive upon their opinion'.[74]

George Tom Molesworth Bridges, always known as 'Tom', was born on 20 August 1871 at Eltham, Kent, in the south-east of England, the third son of Major Thomas Walker Bridges and his wife Mary Ann Phillips.[75] Tom's father had fought in the Indian Mutiny, and wrote a widely used scientific military manual, *Bridges' Gunner's Pocket Book*, which afforded him a certain reputation in Army circles. Unfortunately, he died while serving in the Garrison Artillery in Bermuda, leaving his wife Mary with 'a full quiver [of four young sons and a daughter] and a small income'.[76] She settled in Falmouth, Cornwall, and educated her children as best she could. Philippa, the daughter, eventually became a travel writer. Tom Bridges' eldest brother went into the Church and died at forty, the youngest brother died in childhood, but Tom and his second brother Edward were sent to Newton Abbot College in Devon. Edward graduated to Sandhurst as a Queen's India Cadet, and Tom, following in his late father's footsteps, joined the Artillery and went to the Royal Military Academy at Woolwich.

From Woolwich, Bridges was posted to Sha Jehan, the 'red fort' at Delhi, where the artillery consisted of 'archaic, old smooth bore 64-pounders looking through open embrasures and we actually did our occasional practices with round-shot down the Jumna Valley'.[77] Although the 'soldiering was stagnant', and mess life a bore, there were plenty of opportunities for shooting, hunting and polo, as well as learning Urdu from the *Moonshi* (teacher), and on balance he enjoyed his time in India before eventually yearning for pastures new.[78] In 1898, Bridges was sent to Africa to join a new formation, the Armed Forces of Central Africa, based in Nyassaland, the nucleus of what would become the famous King's African Rifles. He at once formed a bond with the troops drawn from the Yaos people of the Nyasa Highlands: 'Brave and hardy, intelligent and gay, they could march twenty-five miles in a day and build houses for their officers at the end of it.'[79] However, Bridges had learnt of the deteriorating situation in South Africa, with conflict with the Boers seeming increasingly likely, and, without waiting to secure formal permission, set off on a whim to join the fight.

It was in South Africa that Bridges first met Winston Churchill, later to be his friend and patron. 'My first impression' of Bridges, wrote Churchill, 'was gained a few days before the [battle of] Spion Kop'. This was when, 'in the first light of dawn I saw three or four horsemen swimming back to us across the Tugela River amid a rattle of Mauser fire. A few minutes later Tom Bridges, still dripping, joined us in the dip of ground from which we had watched his adventure'. Thereafter, continued Churchill, he and Bridges 'soldiered together in Dundonald's Brigade during the relief of Ladysmith, and ever since I have preserved a lively friendship and admiration for him'.[80] It was during the Boer War that Bridges also had his first taste of the Australians, when 'I took over a small column of the 5th and 6th West Australians to help clean up the "bush veldt". I found them excellent men . . . They had a particular swing in the saddle which even at a distance distinguished them from other mounted troops'. As he concluded: 'Their chief fault was a good one: over-eagerness to get at the enemy.'[81]

Subsequently, Bridges served in Somaliland, where he raised two regiments of Tribal Horse. He was wounded there in a desperate set-piece battle with the hostile Dervish forces, winning the DSO. 'The dervishes never reached the [British] square', he recorded, 'but fell in their hundreds in the high yellow grass, and although they rallied and led by their Hadjis [those who had made the pilgrimage to Mecca] made several brave attempts in a few minutes they were overwhelmed by our fire and broke and fled'.[82] Protesting that he was already recovering from his wound (he had hoped to join the expedition setting out for China), Bridges was frustrated when his local medical board took a different view and sent him back to England to recuperate. From there he joined the Army Staff College at Camberley, which gave him an opportunity to brush up on his several languages (he was a noted linguist and translator) and to travel to countries he had not visited before – Norway, Sweden, Denmark and the United States of America.

Bridges' accounts of colonial wars have a breathless *Boys' Own Paper* quality, popular in its day but uncomfortable reading now. But despite his obvious enthusiasm for soldiering, there is in his storytelling none of the bloodlust that characterises Henry Galway's reports. There is also a respectful regard for Indigenous warriors, whether friend or foe. Bridges was altogether more cerebral (he painted and wrote poetry; his uncle was the Poet Laureate, Robert Bridges). After the Staff College, where his talents were recognised, he was delighted to be sent to the War Office in London, 'in the capacity of "bottle-washer"' as he modestly described it, working in the German section of the Intelligence department.[83] This was the beginning of a diplomatic career that paralleled his military career, culminating in his appointment as Governor of South Australia in 1922.

In 1908, as he reported in *Alarms and Excursions*, Bridges married Janet Florence Marshall, a widow with 'a small boy at Eton' (we do not learn his name in Bridges' account; he was later killed in action).[84] Thereafter, Florence (as she was always known) makes only fleeting appearances in his book, and then merely described as 'my wife'. But despite this perfunctory treatment, she was clearly a formidable woman, certainly Bridges' equal. In the retreat from Mons in August 1914, for instance, Bridges had been kicked in the face by a horse (winning the first of his five wound stripes in the war) and rendered unconscious. According to Bridges, his wife:

> was then working in the Allied Hospital at Brussels, and hearing from the American Legation that I had been listed as 'wounded and missing', she set out for Mons in an ambulance flying the Turkish flag, and accompanied by a Turk with supplies for the hospital there. She had the laudable idea of finding me somewhere, but was disappointed. She drove from Brussels to Mons and back through marching German troops. She afterwards had a narrow escape of remaining in enemy hands as the hospital at Brussels was taken over by the Germans. But she eventually managed to escape by driving a market-cart to Ostend, and getting on the last boat to leave for England.[85]

Michael Bloch, the biographer, observed that 'Lady Bridges [as Florence became] was an impressive but imperious matron of the Lady Bracknell variety [the doughty dowager of Oscar Wilde's play, *The Importance of Being Ernest*]'.[86] The Bridges' daughter, their only child, was born in August 1909. According to Bloch, Florence, already pregnant, had discovered that her husband was pursuing a liaison with a Norwegian ballerina named Alvilde. When Florence and Tom's daughter was born, Florence insisted that she be named Alvilde, a reminder in perpetuity of Bridges' infidelity. As Bloch noted wryly: 'Whether true or not, the fact that this story gained currency gives some idea of Bridges' reputation and the personality of his wife.'[87] As Alvilde grew older, she became aware of her father's roving eye, responsible perhaps for her ambivalent attitude to men. But she was 'an attractive girl whose mother gave her a thorough schooling in the domestic arts, and she helped her father by charming the troublesome local politicians who came to dine at Government House [in Adelaide]'.[88]

Having survived Mons and numerous other encounters, including a diplomatic mission to America, fate finally caught up with Tom Bridges. Despite being safely ensconced in a dugout near Hill 60 at Passchendaele, he needed to return to his Corps Commander and, although 'it was raining old iron', he 'decided to chance it'. However, no sooner had he abandoned his shelter, than 'a big crump burst near me and shattered my right leg'. He was carried to a field dressing station, and from there was taken to a base hospital in Montreuil, near Boulogne, where he spent six weeks. He received numerous visitors, he said, and 'My wife came out for a time, but found me so bad tempered that she went home again'.[89]

Bridges conceded, possibly tongue-in-cheek, that he was a 'confirmed misogynist'.[90] The following story, told against himself, is certainly an insight into his extraordinary personality. As he lay desperately ill, before the operation to amputate his leg:

> A sister came in and peered gravely at me. I wondered if I looked as bad as I felt. She leant over me. Was this indeed to be the last woman I should see on earth? She should have been young, lovely and romantic but alas! in the dim light she had a face rather like a horse. What business had she here anyway, so near the front?
>
> 'Is there anything you would like done?' she asked, just in case . . .
>
> 'Things don't go all right?' I suggested.
>
> 'Yes.' Tactless female! She expected me to say, 'Give this ring to my mother.' Instead I beckoned her to come closer.
>
> 'What do you do with all the legs you cut off?'
>
> She looked shocked but said, 'Burn them.'
>
> 'Well', I said, 'don't burn mine. Give it to the lion mascot of the 19th Division. He hasn't had meat to-day and he'll know what to do with it. This is my last will and testament and if you don't I shall come back and haunt you.'[91]

The lion mascot was named Poilu, and had been won in a Red Cross raffle in 1916 when still a cub. Following Bridges' operation, the lion, now fully grown, was shipped to England, creating mayhem on the vessel when it broke loose from its cage and ran amok. Poilu ended his days in a private zoo in Maidstone, Kent.

In three years of war, Tom Bridges had risen from Major to Major General (and was later promoted Lieutenant-General). Despite his disability, he continued to play an important role. He was part of the delegation to the United States to make arrangements for American participation in the war, and later served with distinction in the Balkans, Russia and Asia Minor, for which he was knighted. He played an inspirational role in spiriting away the Habsburg royal family, almost certainly saving them from the grisly fate that overtook the Romanovs, and was responsible for evacuating 50,000 White Russians in the face of the advancing Red Army. However, it was gently put to Bridges that he was blocking promotion for those coming behind him, and there were only limited appointments available to him, given his disability. Accordingly, he retired from the British Army, and was offered the governorship of South Australia.

Although leaving the Army was a wrench, Bridges relished his new task. 'I had a strong desire to see those distant Antipodean Dominions', he said, 'whence had come such splendid contingents of citizen soldiers to help the Mother Country through two wars [the Boer War and the Great War]. Ever since my Light-Horse days, I have had a soft place for the Diggers'.[92] Before departing for South Australia, Bridges paid a courtesy visit to Marshal Foch in Paris. Foch had great admiration for the Australians and their disproportionate contribution to the Allied victory on the Western Front. 'Tell these doughty warriors of Australia', he instructed Bridges, 'that their memory will ever be green in France'.[93]

Arriving in Adelaide, Bridges was charmed by both the city's situation and 'its astonishing development'. As he explained, 'Adelaide, our home town, lies between the hills and the sea. It is a beautiful and delectable city sited and designed with inspiration that its houses and lovely gardens may spread towards the hills and the south coast, its factories towards the port and always leave a belt of green parkland around the city proper'.[94] The climate, he added, 'winter and summer, was as near perfect as any I know, though the summer was sometimes punctuated with a hot and violent dust-storm, the "Northerly Buster"'. His enthusiasm for South Australia extended to his interest in Australian flora and fauna, including the 'scrub fowl which leave their eggs to incubate in a heap of debris . . . The little Koala or Teddy-bear, which lives "on the tree-top", and on 'the north coast of Australia one finds the original mermaid in the shape of the Dugong, a vegetarian sea-cow of repulsive appearance'.[95]

Governor Bridges also took immediately to the Australian people. He decided that 'Australian women are great "sports"', and discovered that 'Australians are democratic and have no use for snobbery'. He enjoyed being hailed as a kindred spirit by returned servicemen: 'at some function which attracted Diggers, I would be greeted with a wave of the hand and shouts of "Ullo, Tom!". This to the King's representative might seem familiar, but I looked on at it as a compliment and a gesture that they were pleased to see me.' Likewise, at a boxing match 'the chairman opened the proceedings with "Please do not throw bottles as the Governor is here"'.[96]

The Governor and Lady Bridges threw themselves into South Australian life. He had a good baritone voice, and she was an accomplished pianist. The Governor played bridge at the Adelaide Club on evenings that he was free, and galloped in the parklands in the morning. Both Bridges were avid supporters of the Boy Scout and Girl Guide movements, which grew in strength and popularity during their time at Government House, and their daughter Alvilde, as well as being school captain, led the Guide company at Woodlands, the 'smart girls' school near Adelaide'.[97] In constant pain from his war wounds and a series of bad falls from horses, Bridges avoided sedentary activities that increased his discomfort (he hated watching cricket) and engaged instead in energetic pursuits such as riding, swimming, fishing and shooting. His evident enthusiasm for Australia was infectious, prompting a 'long enjoyable visit to my brother and sister-in-law at Adelaide' by Bridges' sister Philippa, which in turn resulted in her book *A Walk-About in Australia*.[98]

Bridges was also keen to see inland Australia and, like some previous Governors, took the train to Oodnadatta before proceeding by car. He was accompanied by the Premier, Sir Henry Barwell (who had raised the Governor's salary after Archibald Weigall's unfortunate experiences), as they ventured across the Northern Territory border to Alice Springs, the

Macdonnell Ranges and 'a couple of hundred miles beyond'. Here they 'met batches of Aborigines who had never seen white men . . . Three shy ladies we found one day hunting on their own, with dogs and spears, in the costume of Eve before she fell to the fig-leaf. One of these took a fancy to me and gave me a live lizard to eat, having first bitten off its head'.[99]

Privately, in his diary, Bridges' attitude to Indigenous Australians was less flippant and light-hearted. He feared for their future, and observed that:

> The natives of Central Australia form a rather pitiful study . . . they and the half-castes do nearly all the work. In fact . . . they have made the fortunes of several pastoralists. They are practically unpaid labour, and in a condition little removed from slavery. They are indeed free to wander, but wandering means starvation, as the game is disappearing, and the black is losing his skill at hunting.[100]

Bridges felt that Aborigines should be paid a minimum wage, and contrasted their hard work with 'most of the white men . . . in the Territory [who] appear to be wasters, and so unreliable that they cannot be trusted with a camel convoy. They hang about the stations and the bars, picking up a living with the aid of unpaid black labour, often living promiscuously with aboriginal [sic] women'.[101] Given his interest in native fauna, Bridges contrasted the fate of Australian birdlife – endangered, as he saw it, by the competing introduction of European species – with that of the Aborigines: 'the struggle between the aboriginal and the invader in which alas! in most cases the shy native birds, like man himself, have been defeated and driven from their immemorial haunts to the far north'.[102] He also visited New Zealand on two occasions, and found himself making comparisons with Australia: 'The Maoris, a fine and interesting people abound, but there seems to be no racial feeling and no colour problem, rather a spirit of democratic equality'.[103]

Publicly, Governor Bridges was complimentary about Australia's politicians: 'Whatever government might be in power, Liberal, Labour or Nationalist, they were able men who knew their work and who treated the King's Representative with every possible courtesy'.[104] In reality, however, relations were not always so cordial. He did not always see eye-to-eye with Labor Premier John Gunn (1924–1926). He was outraged when Gunn published a confidential memorandum from an earlier Premier to the Governor, and when one of Gunn's Ministers suggested incorrectly that the Imperial Government appointed retired Army officers to gubernatorial positions in order the avoid paying military pensions, Bridges was incensed when the Premier refused to correct the error.[105] But Bridges enjoyed his sparring matches with Gunn, and when the latter resigned the premiership to fill a Federal administrative appointment, the Governor did not take to his successor 'Lightning Lionel' Hill, finding that he had 'neither his [predecessor's] personality nor his brains'.[106]

Politically and socially conservative, Governor Bridges thought it would be a mistake to extend the franchise of the Legislative Council. He was a frequent speaker at RSL events, emphasising the threat of Bolshevism but also warning, as he did in his foreword to his sister Philippa's travel book, that Australia 'is an object of covetous interest to the teeming millions of the East'.[107] Presciently, Bridges thought that 'Australia is unlikely to be attacked unless the Mother Country is busy elsewhere', but he advocated extensive British immigration to swell the population and pressed for an integrated Imperial defence policy.[108] Yet he was no Colonel Blimp. He praised the German settlers 'who left their country for liberty of conscience and who have made very good colonists'.[109] And in contrast to Henry Galway, Bridges admired Archbishop Mannix's 'remarkable ability and strong character', as well as acknowledging his 'immense and enthusiastic following' in the Catholic Church and in the Labor Party. He thought Mannix would 'prove a great citizen of Australia ... I for one would not have minded seeing a [Cardinal's] Red Hat descend upon his head. As an influence on Labour, Rome would seem vastly to be preferred to Moscow'.[110]

Looking to the future, Bridges hoped for a closer co-operation between the British Empire and the United States of America, consolidating a felicitous Anglophone world of 'moderate and liberal-minded peoples who seek control without persecution and are determined to enjoy liberty without licence'.[111] He pondered what role he might have played in all this. 'Governors come and go in the Dominions and Colonies', he mused, 'and one sometimes wonders how they are remembered. The good men do, dies with them, and I have found that it was generally by some "gaffe" they had committed that they were recalled to mind'.[112]

Perhaps, he thought, he would be best remembered by an unwise speech he had made to a Licensed Victuallers dinner in Adelaide in praise of wine. He had told some funny stories about the Prohibition movement in America, and afterwards the (Labor) Premier and the Attorney-General had congratulated him: 'You *were* on good form', they said. Next day, however, they visited Government House 'with long faces', reporting that the speech had antagonised the supporters of Prohibition in the State, with the press indignant that he had 'insulted a great sister democracy', the newspapers opining: 'When the wine is in the wit is out.' There was quite a row but it subsided soon enough. As Bridges commented, it was a 'storm in a tankard'.[113]

Sir Tom and Lady Bridges declined the offer of an extension of their term in South Australia, the Governor again not wanting to stand in the way of new blood. They retired to Brighton in Sussex, on the south coast of England, where Bridges continued to paint and to write. Florence having already predeceased him, he died at his home in Dyke Road, Brighton, on 26 November 1939.

Chapter 6

DEPRESSION, WAR AND A NEW ELIZABETHAN AGE

'There were bad times coming for Australia', wrote Tom Bridges, looking back at his departure from Government House in 1927, 'and the signs were already ominous. Indeed the next decade was one of great difficulty'. However, he added, 'Australia tightened her belt and got down to it. Thanks to far-seeing and courageous legislation and the devaluation of the pound, but most of all to the fortitude and efficiency of the men and women on the land, the Commonwealth weathered the storm'. Moreover, he pointed out, 'the first state to record returning to prosperity was South Australia'.[1]

Alexander Gore Arkwright Hore-Ruthven
(14 May 1928 – 4 December 1934)

Bridges successor as Governor, Alexander Hore-Ruthven (later 1st Earl of Gowrie), had arrived in South Australia as the 'bad times' had begun to bite. As Bridges had noted, the warning signs had been there for all to see as he had prepared to leave for Britain. Unemployment was already beginning to grow as postwar prosperity faded, and the Labor Premier, Lionel 'Lightning' (an ironic sobriquet) or 'Slogger' Hill, proved a less effective leader than his predecessor, John Gunn. There had been unrest; on one occasion 250 unemployed workers had scuffled with the police as they confronted Hill, chanting 'Work! Work! What about Work!'.[2]

Not surprisingly, the increasingly unpopular Hill had lost the March 1927 State election, his Government replaced by that of Richard Butler, leader of the conservative Liberal Federation-Country Party alliance. However, Butler as Premier was faced with the same deteriorating economic conditions that had defeated Hill. There was further unrest – particularly among the wharf labourers – 'wharfies' – of Port Adelaide, Port Pirie and other South Australian ports. A long-anticipated improvement in their pay and conditions, dependent upon the deliberations of the Federal Arbitration Court in September 1928, came to nothing as the Court effectively dismissed the wharfies' claims. A strike ensued, with 200 wharfies locked out at Port Pirie and ten ships lying idle at Port Adelaide. At the same time, the automobile manufacturer, Holden, laid-off 3700 workers, providing a pool of desperate men from which 'volunteers' were recruited to act as strike-breakers at Port Adelaide.[3]

This was the situation that confronted Alexander Hore-Ruthven (pronounced 'Riven') as he settled into his role at Government House. Although the representative of a constitutional monarchy, dependent upon the advice of his Premier, Hore-Ruthven had a strong sense of duty and believed in firm leadership and decisive action. His was, as one South Australian newspaper put it, 'a popular appointment', the State looking forward to a steady hand in difficult times, and a cheery personality capable of spreading optimism among the people, especially as he was, like many of them, a keen sportsman.[4] Most of all, South Australians hoped that he would be from the same mould as his predecessor, Tom Bridges. As one newspaper explained:

> Although the exploit which earned for our new Governor the highest military award – the Victoria Cross – was performed 28 years ago, its daring placed it in the same category as that associated with the tin whistle and toy drum rally of Sir Tom Bridges. The promptness, high-mindedness and devotion to duty which inspired the then Capt. Hore-Ruthven to snatch a wounded brother officer almost from the grasp of bloodthirsty Dervishes and bear him, under hot fire, to safety showed that Major-Gen. the Hon Alexander Hore-Ruthven possesses the enthusiasm to 'do his job' for the Empire, which should make him a fit representative of His Majesty in Australia.[5]

Alexander Gore Arkwright Hore-Ruthven ('Sandie' to his friends) was born on 6 July 1872 at Windsor, in England, second son of Walter James Hore-Ruthven, 8th Baron Ruthven, and his wife Lady Caroline Annesley, nee Gore, daughter of the 4th Earl of Arran.[6] Although Hore-Ruthven was born well south of the border, his family was Scottish on both sides, a heritage of which he was especially proud. He was educated at Winchester and Eton, and in 1892 joined the 3rd Battalion Highland Light Infantry, a militia unit. By 1898 he was in Egypt, temporarily attached to the Egyptian Army, where he commanded a Camel Corps. In September that year he won the Victoria Cross (the first ever awarded to a militia officer) in the Sudan, an event which would bring him lasting fame. As the *London Gazette* reported:

> The Queen has been graciously pleased to signify Her intention to confer the decoration of the Victoria Cross on the undermentioned Officer . . . for his conspicuous bravery during the attack on the Baggage Guard at the action of Gedarif on 22 September 1898, as recorded against his name: Captain Hore-Ruthven, seeing an Egyptian officer lying wounded within 50 yards of the advancing Dervishes, who were firing and charging, picked him up and carried him towards the 16th Egyptian Battalion. He dropped the wounded officer two or three times and fired upon the Dervishes, who were following, to check their advance. Had the officer been left where he was first dropped, he must have been killed.[7]

Hore-Ruthven remained in Egypt – he was mentioned in dispatches three times – for the remainder of the campaign, before moving on to Somaliland in 1903–1904. In 1905 he returned to the United Kingdom, becoming aide-de-camp of Lord Dudley, the Lord-Lieutenant of Ireland. He married Zara Eileen Pollock in June 1908, her family fiercely opposing their union, as they considered Hore-Ruthven a poor catch with few prospects. In the same year, when Dudley was appointed Governor-General of Australia, Hore-Ruthven went with him as Military Secretary, gaining invaluable insight into the vice-regal role as well as the state of the country's defences. He returned to England in 1909 but within the year was back in Australia as part of Lord Kitchener's tour, conducted at the invitation of Prime Minister Alfred Deakin, to report on Australia's defence organisation and capability.[8] From there it was on to the Staff College at Quetta in India, and when war broke out in 1914 Hore-Ruthven accompanied an Indian Army unit to France, ostensibly as an Arabic interpreter. In fact, he was transferred to the Welsh Guards in April 1915, with the rank of Major, and was soon on the way to Gallipoli.

According to Malise Ruthven, Hore-Ruthven's grandson, his grandfather's enduring military reputation was made at Gallipoli.[9] Hore-Ruthven was appointed to the staff of Sir Ian Hamilton, the commander of British troops (including the Australian and New Zealand Army Corps) on the Gallipoli peninsula. His task was to report operational developments by submarine cable to Hamilton, based on Imbros island. On 7 August 1915, for example, he reported on the successful action at Lone Pine, on the following day forwarding the bad news that the attack on Chunuk Bair had failed. As the Gallipoli campaign began to stall, so Hamilton landed two fresh British divisions at Suvla Bay, the aim being to seize the heights above the Bay, link up with the ANZACs, and cut off the Turkish forces. However, once the British were ashore, local commanders gave priority to consolidating their positions. Hamilton feared that the element of surprise would be lost if they lingered too long, allowing the Turks to reinforce. He sent Hore-Ruthven with a personal note, urging immediate action. Alas, little notice was taken of Hore-Ruthven's entreaties, it being explained that the great difficulties in ensuring adequate water supplies, rations and ammunition precluded any movement at present.

All this Hore-Ruthven reported back to Hamilton. When an assault did take place, on Scimitar Hill on 21 August 2015, Hore-Ruthven was part of the attacking force. He was hit in the thigh, the bullet passing through his leg and lodging in his left testicle. It was a serious and extremely painful wound, and Hore-Ruthven was evacuated to England for treatment. He later testified to the Dardanelles Commission, set up to investigate the Gallipoli campaign, where he criticised the handling of the Suvla landings but insisted that the ANZACs were 'the finest soldiers in the world'.[10]

Hore-Ruthven's war was not yet over. By 1917 he was in France, and by the following year he was a Brigadier-General, serving initially in 7th Army

Corps and in July 1918 taking command of the Highland Brigade in the 8th Division. During his time in action on the Western Front, he was awarded the Distinguished Service Order (DSO) and Bar, and was mentioned in dispatches five times. The citation for the Bar to his DSO is an insight into his leadership style – leading from the front:

> He commanded his brigade with conspicuous gallantry and judgement throughout the operations east of Ypres from 28 September to 27 October 1918, inclusive. His presence and personal bearing at critical times during the fighting was of decisive value, especially during a strong enemy counter-attack. On 20 October, at St Louis, he went forward among the attacking troops at a critical juncture and inspired them to the final effort, whereby the high ground of great tactical value was captured.[11]

After the Great War, Hore-Ruthven remained in the British Army, retiring in 1928, when he received a knighthood. By the May he was in Adelaide, where 'much gratification was expressed throughout South Australia . . . at the appointment of another distinguished soldier as Governor of the State'.[12] Brave warrior he may have been, but Governor Hore-Ruthven was alive to the tragedy of war and the long-term suffering it caused. In 1919, the State Government had decided there should be a National War Memorial in Adelaide to commemorate the Great War, and it fell to Governor Hore-Ruthven to unveil the memorial before a crowd of 75,000 on 25 April 1931. His oft-quoted words are testament to his personal estimate of the nature of war:

> It is not only for ourselves that we have erected this visible remembrance of great deeds, but rather that those who come after us and have not experienced the horrors of war, or realised the wanton destruction and utter futility of it all, may be inspired to devise some better means to settle international disputes other than by international slaughter. This memorial is the seal of South Australia's homage to her sons, who in the ranks of brave company from all parts of the Empire, gave their lives during the Great War.[13]

Like Tom Bridges before him, Governor Hore-Ruthven was especially alert to the needs and aspirations of returned servicemen and women, and felt the industrial unrest he had encountered on his arrival in South Australia had aggravated the 'suffering hardship and deprivation' experienced by the returnees, a result of the 'misguided leadership of a few hot-headed irresponsible [strikers]'.[14] He was upbraided by the United Trades and Labor Council in Adelaide for expressing such opinions but the Governor's views chimed with those of many ex-servicemen, not least those of Arthur Blackburn, who had won a Victoria Cross at Pozieres, and was now leader of a group of volunteers formed to protect strike-breakers and 'Uphold constitutional government, maintain law and order and perform essential service'.[15] Years later, Blackburn's daughter, Margaret Forbes, explained that her father had been worried above all about the plight of returned servicemen, whose employment prospects, he believed, were being affected by strike action. She recalled that Blackburn 'was greatly concerned about the welfare of the ex-soldiers who were losing their jobs because of the action of the few'.[16]

Blackburn offered the service of his volunteers to Premier Butler who (no doubt with Hore-Ruthven's knowledge) gratefully accepted. In response, a group of unemployed workers formed their own Volunteer Labor Army to protect striking wharfies, the *Advertiser* noting gravely on its front page that 'Waterfront War Begins in Earnest'.[17] There were indeed scuffles, robust police interventions, and even the deployment of Blackburn's armed 'Black and Tans' (as they were known to their detractors, in an unflattering reference to the auxiliaries active in Ireland earlier in the decade). Lionel Hill, leader of the Labor Opposition, interceded to broker a deal, and grudgingly the wharfies returned to work in early October, although the scene had been set for years of unrest and bitterness.

Butler became increasingly unpopular, and in the 1930 State election Hill's Labor Party won a comfortable majority, Hill's election promises including expansionary measures to deal with unemployment. However, once in office, Hill found it difficult to implement these policies, and turned instead to local and national business leaders for advice on the way ahead. As a result, he adopted a severe deflationary policy, reducing the salaries of all State Government employees, cutting back on expenditure, and increasing taxation. Among those whose opinion he sought, was Governor Hore-Ruthven. Years later, Hill recalled:

> To start the necessary big reduction in the State Budget, Sir Alexander Hore-Ruthven, a man I always admired, took a reduction of £1,000 a year in his allowance as Governor. That was followed by Sir George Murray and all his judges. Then I as Premier took a 15 per cent reduction in salary and other Ministers a 12.5 per cent reduction. The reduction we placed on all wages and salaries was 10 per cent and for this we were called 'wage-slashers'.[18]

In London, J.H. Thomas, Secretary of State for the Dominions, observing these developments, considered that Hill's 'firm attitude' had been 'largely due to the Governor's influence'.[19] Be that as it may, Lionel Hill's approach was mirrored more generally across Australia in the so-called Premiers' Plan, where Prime Minister Jim Scullin sought to construct a similar deflationary plan in consultation with State Premiers. One Premier who signed-up reluctantly to the Plan, and later repudiated it, was Jack Lang of New South Wales. Lang launched a vigorous campaign against the Plan, proposing his own alternative policy, which would include (controversially, and possibly unconstitutionally, according to his critics) a suspension of interest payments on debts to the British Government. Hore-Ruthven took a dim view of Lang's suggestions, and privately advised his opposite number in New South Wales, Governor Sir Philip Game, to sack Lang – which he did, in May 1932.[20]

The British Government thought that Governor Sir Hore-Ruthven had done rather well in South Australia, and his term was extended until April 1934. On leave in England in 1933, Hore-Ruthven, a keen cricketer, helped to mediate during the Adelaide Oval 'body-line' Test dispute, which had threatened to damage Anglo–Australian relations. As well as affirming Hore-Ruthven's authority in the world of cricket, it demonstrated his diplomatic skills, leadership, and, perhaps above all, affection for Australia. As Governor, he had visited remote corners of South Australia, courtesy of the de Havilland 'Moth' biplane owned by his aide-de-camp, Captain Hugh Grosvenor, getting to know the State well. He and Zara, Lady Hore-Ruthven, were both keen supporters of the Boy Scouts and Girl Guides, and she was president of the State Red Cross Society.

On expiry of his extension, Hore-Ruthven was appointed Governor of New South Wales, arriving in Sydney in February 1935. However, moves were already afoot to appoint him Governor-General of Australia in succession to Sir Isaac Isaacs, a position he took up less than a year later on 23 January 1936. At the prompting of the Prime Minister, Joseph Lyons, Hore-Ruthven was created Baron Gowrie of Canberra and Dirleton (a title which combined his Australian and Scottish affiliations). Gowrie (as he now was) had planned to relinquish the governor-generalship in September 1939, to make way for the Duke of Kent, but with the outbreak of the Second World War he stayed on officially until 30 January 1945, although departing for Britain in the previous September. During the war years he formed a close working relationship with John Curtin (having initially been apprehensive of his appointment as Prime Minister), supporting the war effort in numerous ways. Lady Gowrie was equally busy, involving herself in fundraising and the establishment of a soldiers' club in Canberra, as well as assisting in the foundation of what became the Lady Gowrie kindergartens.

Sadly, during the war, the Gowries lost their only son, Patrick Hore-Ruthven, when he was serving in the Special Air Service (SAS) in Libya.[21] He was wounded in a raid near Tripoli in September 1942, and later died in the Misurata Italian Hospital. Patrick was a poet of some note, and several of his compositions (including a selection of war poems) were published posthumously in Australia in 1943 as *The Happy Warrior* (a Wordsworthian allusion), with a preface written by his mother, Lady Gowrie. A British edition, entitled *The Desert Warrior*, a title poignantly redolent of his father's exploits, appeared in 1944. A ruthless SAS officer, Patrick Hore-Ruthven was also a sensitive and cultured man:

> *Come, join the deathless priesthood of our band*
> *Renouncing all the dear things we know;*
> *Forgo the peaceful tilling of your land,*
>   *Leave sheep unborn,*
>   *Unbyred the kine,*

Unweaned the calves,
Untrained the vine,
Unhampered by the wheel the mill-race flow;
And in these ranks come proudly take your stand,
For to the laughing gods the young men go.[22]

On his return to Britain, Gowrie was created an Earl. He was president of Marylebone Cricket Club in 1948, and was Constable and Lieutenant-Governor of Windsor Castle until 1953. He died in Gloucestershire on 2 May 1955, survived by his wife Zara who died on 19 July 1965.

Winston Joseph Dugan
(28 July 1934 – 23 February 1939)

By the time Hore-Ruthven had departed South Australia in 1934, the State's economic prospects had begun to improve. The devaluation of the Australian pound helped, as Tom Bridges had noted, and there had been slow recovery of the primary export markets, especially Britain, as increased demand and higher prices stimulated growth.[23] Moreover, by the mid-1930s there was a decisive strategic shift towards industrialisation, a policy associated with the long thirty-two-year regime of the Liberal and Country League under the successive leaderships of Richard Butler and Tom Playford. Following the defeat of Lionel Hill's second government in 1933, Butler had again become Premier in 1933 (his earlier ministry had lasted from 1927–1930). Playford entered State Parliament in 1933, becoming Premier in 1938 and remaining in power until 1965. Both men supported industrialisation but its real architect was the State's Auditor-General, J.W. Wainwright, who was in post from 1934 until 1945. He advocated State intervention in the economy to promote manufacturing, a policy which received further stimulus during the Second World War, when South Australia was thought especially suited for arms and munitions production. The *Industrial Development Act 1941*, a key feature of the Wainwright–Playford plan as it developed, made public finance available for any project the State Government deemed worthy of support.[24]

By 1942 coal was being mined at Leigh Creek to enable a massive expansion of electricity supply in the State, and steel production had been established at Whyalla, with the Morgan–Whyalla pipeline completed by 1944. There was a vigorous expansion of State-sponsored housing and the construction of factories, the increased demand for goods and services leading to a marked rise in employment. This was, of course, a complete repudiation and reversal of the retrenchment policy pursued earlier by Lionel Hill with the active encouragement, even connivance, of the former Governor, Hore-Ruthven.

Hore-Ruthven successor as Governor, Winston Joseph Dugan (pronounced 'Duggan') took up his appointment in South Australia on 28 July 1934, and departed in February 1939, on the eve of war. There was already an air of renewed optimism in the State, the *Chronicle* newspaper excitedly devoting several illustrated pages to the new Governor, reporting that 'Sir Winston and Lady Dugan arrived in Adelaide on Saturday morning and were afforded an enthusiastic reception as they drove through the streets, first to Government House, and then to the Town Hall, where His Excellency was sworn in with the customary ceremonial'. There were photographs of him, resplendent in full uniform, descending the gangway from the SS *Orama* (which would have the misfortune to be sunk by the German cruiser *Admiral Hipper* in 1940), the Governor 'about to take his first step on South Australian soil'. As the *Chronicle* observed, Governor Dugan 'created a splendid impression'.[25]

The feeling was mutual, and over the coming months the Governor journeyed widely in South Australia to see for himself the improving economic conditions. In January 1936, he wrote to Captain R. Wrottesley Royal Navy, a friend in Wiltshire, England. 'I did a good deal of travelling last year', he explained, 'right into the "outback" – where I stayed with Station owners and hob-nobbed with Boundary riders and Kangaroos. Since our arrival I have done about 30,000 miles up and down the State but there is still a lot to see for we cover an area more than three times that of the British Isles'. Wryly, he added that 'some of the sheep paddocks are about the size of Jersey'. South Australia was 'certainly a land of wide open spaces', he said, admitting that 'it grows on one into the bargain. Good rains have recently improved pastures everywhere'.[26] As the Governor emphasised:

Rain is the main topic of conversation – everything depends on it out here. Horses and sheep smell it coming and make for the old waterholes, travelling miles in the day and then return to their pastures with bellies swollen. Twenty-four hours after a good fall a grey brown desert is converted into a green carpet of fresh herbage and the reserve feed in the shape of the salt bush gets a chance to recover against the next drought.[27]

Governor Dugan's travels were both an education – he had quickly learned so much about his new home – and an important morale boost for the country people, who were delighted to see their Governor taking such an informed interest in their often harsh and lonely lives:

At the moment everything is smiling. Wool and wheat are getting good prices – optimism prevails and our Centenary Year is upon is with the usual festivities and functions. Great people, these, with big hearts and wonderful grit in the face of difficulties. A bad year makes them hope all the harder for a good one. And they have just come through some pretty bad ones . . . but now the rains have come . . . stock is fattening well and the eagle hawk, the blow fly and the dingo are forgotten.[28]

He added that in Adelaide the 'temperature has been over the century mark once or twice of late. But no matter: we are off tomorrow to our funk hole [Marble Hill] in the hills, 15 miles away. As they say out here we are going "Bush".[29]

Winston Joseph Dugan was born on 3 September 1876 at Parsonstown, King's County (now County Offaly), Ireland, son of Charles Winston Dugan, an inspector of schools, and Esther Elizabeth Rogers. He was educated at Lurgan College, County Armagh, and joined the British Army in 1896, being commissioned in 1900 in the Lincolnshire Regiment.[30] He saw active service in South Africa in 1899–1902, and was promoted Captain in the Worcestershire Regiment in 1904. In December 1911, he married Ruby Lilian Applewhaite-Abbot, and from 1910–1914 was adjutant in the Irish Command.

In the Great War, Dugan was in action from the first. The 2nd Battalion Royal Irish Regiment was almost completely annihilated at the Battle of La Bassee in October 1914, it being reported that hardly an unwounded man survived, with several hundred dead found huddled together in their trench.[31] The battalion was reformed almost immediately, with Dugan in command, and he was awarded the Distinguished Service Order (DSO) in 1915. Promoted Temporary Brigadier-General in July 1916, at the beginning of the Somme campaign, Dugan commanded the 184th Infantry Brigade until badly wounded in the September. Recovering from his injuries, he led the 73rd Brigade from December 1916 until July 1918.

Field Marshal Sir Douglas Haig, Commander-in-Chief of British forces on the Western Front, visited Dugan's 73rd Brigade on 17 July 1917 as it prepared for the impending Third Battle of Ypres. Haig witnessed a rehearsal for the Brigade's planned assault against its objectives, Shrewsbury Forest and Tower Hamlets Ridge. 'It gave me great confidence as to the result of the attack', Haig recorded, 'to talk to the officers and men . . . Looking round the faces opposite to me, I felt what fine, hard looking, determined men the war had brought to the front'.[32] Dugan was mentioned in dispatches six times, but the Third Battle of Ypres did not bring about the victory Haig had hoped for, the operation becoming quite literally bogged down in the mud of an unseasonably wet summer, even by Flanders standards.

After the Great War, Dugan commanded the 10th Brigade in 1919–1923, being placed on half-pay until returning to duty (1926–1930) as assistant adjutant Southern Command, and then appointed to command the 56th (1st London) Division, Territorial Army in 1931–1934. Made aide-de-camp to King George V in 1928, he was promoted Major General in 1930. Dugan came to wide public attention in 1933 when he presided over the court martial at Chelsea Barracks in London of Lieutenant Norman Baillie-Stewart, winning applause for the exemplary way in which he ensured a fair trial for the accused. Baillie-Stewart was a Nazi sympathiser, who in 1931 fell in love with a German woman when on leave in Germany. Subsequently, he made contact with the German authorities, and was recruited as a spy. Under the pretext of studying for his forthcoming Staff College examinations, Baillie-Stewart borrowed from the Aldershot Military Library photographs of a prototype for a new tank, together with details of a new automatic rifle, all of which he duly passed on to his Nazi handler. When found out, Baillie-Steward was faced with the prospect of a maximum 140-year gaol sentence (the death penalty was not appropriate, as Britain was not then at war) but, pleading guilty, he was imprisoned for five years by Dugan.

Early in 1934, Dugan was chosen as the next Governor of South Australia. He retired formally from the British Army and arrived in Adelaide in the July, as we have seen, to great acclaim, it being said that he and his wife Ruby, Lady Dugan, were the 'most handsome couple ever to occupy Government House'.[33] They were both good public speakers, as well as good listeners, identifying problems that they brought to the attention of Ministers, and giving financial and other support to a wide range of deserving causes. Lady Dugan, 'known for her glamourous style', as it was reported, also travelled widely, involving herself in a variety of sometimes unusual activities. At Parafield on 18 June 1935, for example, as part of the Empire Air Day festivities, she christened the new Miles 2 Hawk VH-UA1 trainer, breaking a bottle of champagne across the aircraft.[34]

Evidence of the new mood of optimism, and also fruit of the State's industrialisation policy, was an ambitious program of locomotive construction begun at the South Australian Railways' works at Islington, with the more ancient classes being progressively supplanted by new designs exhibiting the latest best practices, often American. Among these was a new class of streamlined steam locomotives for the State's broad gauge lines, the first, number 620, named *Sir Winston Dugan*.[35] This ultra-modern machine was unveiled in 1936, which, as Dugan had reported to Captain Wrottesley, was South Australia's Centenary Year, an opportunity to look back over the first hundred years of European settlement but also to face the future with renewed confidence as economic prospects improved.

For Governor Dugan, the climax of the Centenary Year festivities was his unveiling of the Pioneer Memorial on the west side of Moseley Square at Glenelg on Sunday 27 December 1836, almost a hundred years to the day since Captain John Hindmarsh had made his Proclamation at much the same spot. Designed by G. Beaumont Smith, the memorial on its south and north faces displayed bronze tablets listing the names of those prominently associated with the European 'discovery' and settlement of South Australia. Those on the south were the 'explorers': Nuyts, Flinders, Baudin, Sturt, Barker, Light, and the first settlers. Those on the north were the 'founders':

Wakefield, Gouger, Torrens, George Fife Angas, and others. Above the panels were depictions of Wakefield, Hindmarsh, Gouger and Angas, and at the very top of the over forty-foot-high structure was placed a bronze replica of Hindmarsh's ship, HMS *Buffalo*.[36] The mayor of Glenelg, Mr Fisk, explained to the press that the unveiling would take place at 8.30 in the evening, and that 'following the opening, a divine service will be conducted appropriate to the occasion'. Mayor Fisk also expected 'a large influx of old colonists for the unveiling'.[37] He was not disappointed.

Politicians of all hues combined to lobby for an extension of Sir Winston and Lady Dugan's term of office in South Australia, but unfortunately Dugan had already agreed to succeed Lord Huntingfield as Governor of Victoria. He arrived in Melbourne in July 1939, where he and Lady Dugan were shocked by the run-down state of Victoria's Government House, which contrasted strongly with the comfortable and well-appointed vice-regal residence in Adelaide. Government House in Melbourne was an imposing Italianate building, reputedly modelled on Queen Victoria's Osborne House on the Isle of Wight, but it had fallen into dilapidation during the Depression years, the Victorian Government loath to spend money on its restoration.[38] As Stuart Sayers, the biographer, wrote:

The main structure, untouched and unpainted for probably thirty years, was crazed with cracks through which moisture seeped to the inner walls. The ballroom ceiling, flaking and apt to drop pieces of plaster at any moment on whoever happened to be below, was described in newspaper accounts at the time as a menace to public safety. The servants' wing . . . had no fire escape. Many guest bedrooms retained gaslight fittings of the previous century . . . Inadequate heating ensured that Government House in the winter was one of the coldest dwellings in Melbourne.[39]

The Dugans improvised as best they could, concealing stains and damp patches on walls by the judicious placing of their own pictures, and putting their own rugs over threadbare areas of the carpets. They used their private silver collection to augment Government House stock, ensuring complete table settings for formal dinners. The kitchens were similarly inadequate, with food cooked on an ancient range and then wheeled in hot boxes for an extraordinary eighty yards before being served at table. The Dugans largely concealed these shortcomings, which were not fully apparent until after their departure, when an embarrassed Victorian Government belatedly voted funding for refurbishment.[40]

Early in his term in Victoria, Governor Dugan ruffled feathers when, thinking perhaps of recent efforts in South Australia, he told members of the Victorian Chamber of Manufactures that they looked well fed and should be doing more to tackle unemployment. Lady Dugan, meanwhile, criticised the conditions she encountered when touring country hospitals, and after the outbreak of the Second World War set up a workroom in Government House for the Australian Red Cross, of which she was now national president. But, despite these initial frictions, Governor Dugan soon won the respect of Victorians with his adept handling of constitutional matters, which helped stabilise State politics in the 1940s. P.A. Howell has provided a concise summary of this complex period:

When the [Albert] Dunstan Country Party government disintegrated in September 1943, he [Dugan] commissioned the Labor leader John Cain as premier; four days later Dunstan cemented a coalition with the United Australia Party. On the collapse of that ministry in September 1945, Dugan invited in turn Dunstan, T.T. Holloway and Cain to form a stopgap ministry until elections could be held, but none of them was able to guarantee supply. Dugan then sent for the Liberals' deputy-leader, Ian Macfarlan. As soon as a supply bill was passed, Dugan dissolved parliament. After a general election in November left the Independents holding the balance of power, he commissioned Cain to form a ministry.[41]

Such was Dugan's popularity with Victorian politicians that his term was extended on five occasions. On 6 September 1944 he was appointed Acting Governor-General of Australia, serving until 29 February 1945, and he again occupied the position from 19 January to 10 March 1947.[42] Dugan was raised to the peerage in January 1941, and he and Lady Dugan retired to England in the February. Lord Dugan died in Marylebone, London, on 17

August 1951, and was interred in the Applewhaite family vault at Pickerham Hall, Swaffam, Norfolk. His widow, Ruby, died in 1985, leaving almost all her estate to charity.

Charles Malcolm Barclay-Harvey
(12 August 1939 – 26 April 1944)

Winston Dugan's successor as Governor of South Australia was Charles Malcolm Barclay-Harvey, a Scottish landowner and Conservative politician in the United Kingdom Parliament. He was born on 2 March 1890 at Kensington, London, son of James Charles Barclay-Harvey and Ellen Marianne Hills. Known usually by his second name, Malcolm, he was educated at Eton and Christ Church, Oxford, and was commissioned into the 7th (Territorial) Battalion of the Gordon Highlanders in 1909. On 7 February 1912, he married Joan Heywood, who died in 1935. They had one daughter. Barclay-Harvey was invalided out of the British Army in 1915, and was attached to the British Ministry of Munitions for the duration of the Great War.[43]

Malcolm Barclay-Harvey was elected as member for Kincardinshire and West Aberdeenshire in the House of Commons in 1923, serving from 1924 as Parliamentary Private Secretary to the Secretary of State for Scotland until his defeat in 1929. He regained his seat in 1931, and was again Private Secretary from 1932 to 1936. He was knighted in 1936. On 23 March 1938 he married a widow, Lady Muriel Felicia Vere Liddell-Grainger, daughter of the 12th Earl of Lindsey. On his appointment as Governor of South Australia in March 1939, Barclay-Harvey resigned his parliamentary seat, arriving in Adelaide in the P&O liner *Strathnaver* and taking office on 12 August 1939.

Alongside the usual welcomes, there was particular interest in Lady Muriel because, as the Adelaide *Mail* reported, her mother – Millicent Cox, late of Sydney – was Australian. Lady Muriel was interviewed by the *Mail's* 'Special Woman Writer' in Government House just after her arrival: 'Tall and slim, with brown hair, and a smile that puts her visitors at ease at once, she speaks softly and gives the impression that she is entirely feminine and extremely capable.' Lady Muriel confessed herself perfectly satisfied with Government House, pronouncing it 'comfortable and convenient', and adding 'I think I should be very happy here . . . It is most important to be happy and contented if you want to do your very best'.[44]

As well as being partly Australian, Lady Muriel was also interested in horseracing, another source of her local popularity. She was spotted at Morphettville Racecourse, comparing notes with W.B. Carr, chairman of the South Australian Jockey Club. 'I think the course is very pretty', she told the *Mail*, 'and I thoroughly enjoyed the racing – although I had no luck. I lost 2/6. I would back a horse which they all advised me not to, and it not only came in last, but fell over'.[45] Having spoken to her new trainer at Morphettville, she had also decided, she explained, not to bring her horses from Scotland, but to acquire new racehorses here in Australia, probably in Sydney or Melbourne.

Of course, the elephant in the room – in Government House and on the racecourse at Morphettville – was the threat of war, which now seemed increasingly likely. Lady Muriel admitted that she and her husband were very lucky to have been appointed to distant South Australia at this time. In Britain, she said, 'the people have been living in a state of uncertainty since last September. And it is difficult to be normal and happy when the mind is unsettled. All day long one hears aeroplanes and the trenches seem to have become permanent'.[46] However, the sense of safety and remoteness from conflict would not last long, and just as Britain felt that it stood alone in 1940, so Australia would soon seem vulnerable and isolated, the capture of the Empire's bastion at Singapore a stunning blow, the Japanese bombing of Darwin bringing the war to the country's doorstep. In these dangerous days, the role of the Governor became all the more vital, and Sir Malcolm and Lady Muriel Barclay-Harvey were tireless in their support of the war effort, visiting disparate parts of the State to boost morale and encourage the various voluntary patriotic organisations that had been swiftly mobilised.

Adding to Lady Muriel's early popularity was her growing reputation as 'formidable and energetic'.[47] She founded the Lady Muriel Nurses' Club for servicewomen, and visited every Red Cross branch in the State, often as part of her husband's official engagements in far-flung settlements.[48] Vice-regal visits caused much excitement but sometimes anxiety too, especially in small or remote communities not used to welcoming such distinguished guests. In 1986, for example, the older residents of Avenue Range, in the South East, could still recall vividly the events of November 1941, when the Governor called. Barclay-Harvey was scheduled to visit the local school but he arrived early. The teacher, Miss McLean, had gone home for lunch, and on her return was mortified to find all the children crowding around the Governor's car, with Barclay-Harvey still inside. There was worse embarrassment for a young girl called Rosemary Smith. All the children set off for school that day in their best clothes, but when Rosemary climbed down from her horse and gig, she stood on the hem of her dress, which ripped from neck to knee. When the Governor arrived, he asked to meet any girl called Rosemary (he had a daughter of the same name), and poor Rosemary Smith was pushed forward, 'with her dress hanging half off and pinned up with safety pins'.[49]

At Millicent, also in the South East, and in the same month, the Governor and Lady Muriel stayed at the principal local hotel. An official dinner was held for His Excellency, while Lady Muriel invited women from local voluntary and patriotic organisations to attend a reception. After dinner, the Governor met members of the Millicent sub-branch of the RSL, and later attended a meeting of the local Masonic lodge. Lady Muriel, meanwhile, having 'intimated that she will be wearing evening dress' but hoping that others will 'wear whatever is most convenient', received members of the Country Women's Association, the Red Cross, the Mothers and Babies Health Association, the Guides Parents Association, the Salvation Army war fund, and the Fighting Forces Comfort Fund. It was explained that 'Ladies whose surnames begin with A to M inclusive are asked to bring a plate of sandwiches for supper, and those who surnames begin with N to W inclusive a plate of cake'. Additionally: 'Mothers who are in the habit of taking their babies to the baby health centre are invited to being their babies to the supper room of the Institute at 8.15 as Lady Muriel will meet them there before going into the hall for the reception.'[50]

The evening's events were a template for hundreds of similar visits across the State during the Second World War years. The Governor was back in Millicent in March 1944, when he attended the St Patrick's Day Races, which raised over £230 for patriotic funds, being divided between the Red Cross, the Country Women's Association, and the Catholic Soldiers' Guild.[51] At Clare in the Mid North, the Governor and Lady Muriel inspected the local hospital, meeting the matron, sisters and nurses, and viewing facilities, which included the operating theatre, private and general wards, the 'splendid kitchen', nurses' quarters, and laundry. It was explained that there were only eighteen inpatients at the time, including 'an aborigine from Queensland who had been indisposed while shearing at Bungaree'. As was customary, 'the visitors expressed their delight with everything that they saw'.[52]

During their visit to Clare, the Governor and Lady Muriel also planted an oak tree each at the Soldiers' Memorial Park, and visited local schools, including the primary school, where the School's Patriotic Fund had collected £250 for war savings certificates, £200 in cash and £200 in 'waste products'. The Governor declared the pupils 'such a fine lot of children', and in one classroom 'a remarkable display of wildflowers and orchids was favourably commented on'. He also inspected the Scouts and Cubs, exclaiming, 'Well done, Cubs – awfully well done!', while Lady Muriel met the Guides and Brownies, telling the young girls that her daughter Rosemary, also a Brownie, was 'an ardent collector of toothpaste tubes so badly wanted for the war effort'.[53]

At nearby Burra, there was a similar visit, complete with tree planting and an inspection of the hospital, with Lady Muriel as usual meeting members of the Red Cross, Countrywomen's Association and the Fighting Forces Comfort Fund. In the evening there was a reception and ball, 'under Vice-Regal Patronage'.[54] Additionally, the Burra sub-branch of the RSL asked: 'Would all Diggers who can possibly do so please assemble at Burra Institute as under – Guard of Honor 10am; Personal Talk with His Excellency, in the Mayor's Parlor, 8.45 pm. Medals to be worn'.[55] A similar program was followed when the Governor and Lady Muriel visited Quorn in the Flinders Ranges, although on this occasion it was noted that Sir Malcolm would also 'inspect the Railway Running Sheds'.[56] Quorn locomotive depot was an important maintenance facility on the Ghan route from Port Augusta through the Pichi Richi pass and then on from Quorn to Alice Springs, a railway of great strategic significance in transporting troops and equipment to northern Australia during the war.[57]

As well as being keen to support the war effort, Barclay-Harvey was also a railway enthusiast, who relished the prospects of visiting engine-sheds and riding on the footplates of steam locomotives. At Marble Hill he had installed a miniature garden railway and, in 1940, while Governor of South Australia, published *A History of the Great North of Scotland Railway*, which remained the standard work for many years.[58] Unfortunately, most of the stock of this first edition was destroyed in the Blitz, and he had to wait until 1949 for a second edition to appear.[59] Barclay-Harvey's railway enthusiasm was well known across the State, not least within the South Australian Railways (SAR) hierarchy. He had struck up a particular friendship with F.H. 'Frank' Harrison, the railways' Chief Mechanical Engineer, who was busy building a new class of steam locomotive.

Inspired by the latest streamlined designs of the Pennsylvania Railroad in the United States, Harrison's state-of-the-art Class '520' were stylish engines, making clever use of modern materials and techniques to achieve maximum power for a minimum of weight. This efficiency was complemented by the locomotives' wide route availability, allowing them to work over lightly laid branches as well as heavy-duty main routes. The Governor was much excited by these innovations, and was delighted when the first of the class (there were twelve altogether), completed at Islington Works in 1943, was named *Sir Malcolm Barclay-Harvey* in his honour. Railway historian O.S. Nock tells a mildly amusing story of the confusion that ensued:

> One day Frank Harrison called in his clerk and said, 'Find out for me where Barclay-Harvey is.' The clerk replied, 'Yes, Sir,' and returned to his office. About an hour later he returned to Harrison's office and said, 'Sir. I have rung up Government House and Parliament House and made other enquiries but nobody seems to know where Sir Malcolm is.' 'Stone the lizards, Jack,' replied Harrison, 'I meant the b_____ engine *Sir Malcolm Barclay-Harvey*.'[60]

Not surprisingly, such tales abounded, Sir Malcolm and Lady Muriel having become such familiar figures during the war years. A rather startling story was that told about the Premier himself, Tom Playford, and the

Government House butler, nicknamed 'Jeeves' (no doubt to ensure his anonymity) after the P.G. Wodehouse character. 'Jeeves', apparently, was on friendly terms with the Premier. Narrated by Stewart Cockburn in his Playford biography, the tale explains how Lady Muriel came to summarily dismiss her butler, who then appealed to the Premier for help:

> 'I've been sacked!' announced the overwrought butler, 'It's that little bitch [sic] of a housemaid Nora who started it. She gave me cheek in my own kitchen. Of course I couldn't stand for that.' 'Of course not,' responded the intrigued Premier. 'So what happened?' Jeeves continued: 'I put the girl across my knee and gave her a few hard slaps on the bottom. Lady Muriel heard the noise and came in to investigate. I'd lost my temper by this stage and told her: 'You keep out of this or I'll give you the same treatment!' So I got the sack.[61]

Today, the butler's behaviour, with its undisguised misogyny and intimations of domestic and sexual violence, would elicit little sympathy. In the mid-1940s, however, reactions were liable to be different. In an effort to retrieve something from the unfortunate situation, the Premier telephoned Louisa O'Brien, the famous proprietor of the South Australian Hotel. As well as owning and managing a chain of hotels in Adelaide, O'Brien was active in the Red Cross and other voluntary organisations, and in the 1940s the South Australian Hotel on North Terrace was home to, first, Dutch refugees, and then American servicemen.[62] Playford asked whether she could use 'an experienced butler', adding quickly: 'It's the butler from Government House. He's just threatened to assault Lady Muriel and she sacked him.'[63] Louisa O'Brien could see no problem, and the butler was duly employed at the South Australian Hotel.

Harold Guard, a top newspaper journalist, also had a wartime story about Lady Muriel. Guard had arrived in Sydney in March 1942, having narrowly escaped from invading Japanese forces in the Far East. He had earlier served in the Royal Navy but now worked for an American news agency, and was reckoned by the Australian press to be one of the leading four newsmen covering the war in the Pacific. Arriving in Adelaide, he was staying at the

59. Governor Sir Charles Malcolm Barclay-Harvey and Lady Muriel Barclay-Harvey with David and Rosemary Liddell-Grainger, Lady Muriel's children from her first marriage (courtesy SLSA B11127).

60. Governor Lieutenant General Sir Charles Willoughby Moke Norrie (right) with Ben Chifley (left), Prime Minister of Australia, and Thomas Playford (centre), Premier of South Australia (courtesy SLSA B48482/6).

61. Patricia, Lady Norrie with children at Bowden Kindergarten, Adelaide, April 1945 (courtesy SLSA B74160).

62. Left: Governor Air Vice Marshall
Sir Robert Allingham George
and Sybil, Lady George, in 1954
(courtesy SLSA B62971).

63. Right: Governor Sir Robert
George visiting the Holden car
manufacturing plant at Woodville,
Adelaide, in 1953 (courtesy SLSA
BRG 213/77/53/VOL3/21).

64. Above: Governor Sir Edric Bastyan (standing, centre) at an Army parade in the South Parklands, Adelaide, in 1962 (courtesy SLSA B15063).

65. Right: South Australian Governor, Sir Edric Bastyan and the Lord Mayor of Adelaide, Walter Bridgland, at Government House on 18 July 1966. (courtesy SLSA B55806).

66. Right: Sir James Harrison was the first Australian born Governor of South Australia from 1968 to 1971 (courtesy Old Geelong Collegians' Association Notables Gallery).

67. Governor Major General Sir James William Harrison arrives at Parliament House in Adelaide for the opening of Parliament in 1971 (courtesy SLSA PRG 830/20/137).

68. Left: A youthful Mark Oliphant, already a nuclear physicist with an international reputation (courtesy Australian Government).

69. Right: Professor Ernest Lord Rutherford (seated, left), with Rosa (later Lady) Oliphant at his feet (from Mark Oliphant's *Rutherford – Recollections of the Cambridge Days*, published in 1972).

70. Governor Sir Mark Laurence Elwin Oliphant inspects the Guard at the opening of Parliament in Adelaide, 1972 (courtesy SLSA PRG 830/20/152).

71. Above: The swearing-in of Sir Douglas Ralph
Nicholls as Governor of South Australia (courtesy
National Archives of Australia).

72. Right: Governor Sir Douglas Nicholls and
Gladys, Lady Nicholls (reproduced with permission
from Mavis Thorpe Clark, *Pastor Doug: The Story
of Sir Douglas Nicholls, Aboriginal Leader*, first
published 1972).

73. Governor Sir Keith Seaman (at right) (courtesy *Advertiser*).

74. Right: Governor Lieutenant General Sir Donald Beaumont Dunstan (courtesy Virtual War Memorial).

75. Below: Major General Donald Beaumont Dunstan inspects a South Vietnamese Guard of Honour at Tan Sun Nhut airport, Saigon (now Ho Chi Minh City) (courtesy Australian War Memorial, 4098124).

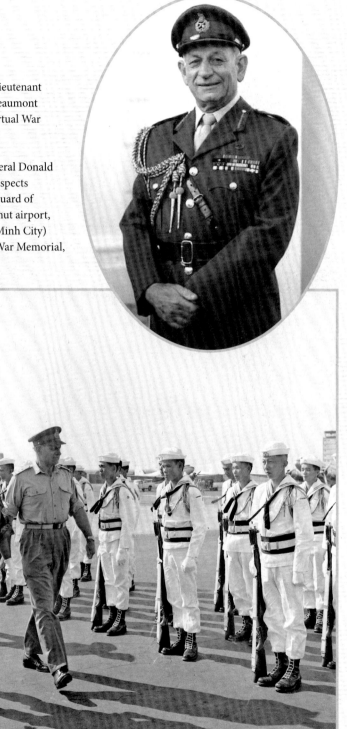

76. Above: Governor Dame Roma Flinders Mitchell, 1992 (courtesy *Advertiser*).

77. Left: Dame Roma Flinders Mitchell as Supreme Court Judge, 1965 (courtesy National Archives of Australia).

78. Governor the Honourable Sir Eric Neal, speaking in Adelaide (courtesy Wikipedia).

79. Governor the Honourable Marjorie Jackson-Nelson inspects the Guard at the opening of the State Parliament in 2006 (courtesy SLSA B70703).

80. Governor Marjorie Jackson-Nelson chats with two other women at the International Women's Day lunch at the Adelaide Convention Centre in March 2006 (courtesy SLSA B70666).

81. Governor Rear Admiral the Honourable Kevin Scarce speaking at the Adelaide Convention Centre in 2008 (courtesy SLSA B70753).

82. Mrs Elizabeth Scarce, wife of Governor Kevin Scarce, cutting a cake to celebrate the International Women's Day's 70th birthday on 7 March 2008 (courtesy SLSA B70766).

83. The Honourable Hieu Van Le, Governor of South Australia 1 September 2014 to 31 August 2021, and Mrs Le (courtesy Government House).

84. Governor Hieu Van Le, wearing Companion of Australia decoration (courtesy Government House).

Adelaide Club. One day, after a very liquid lunch, he returned to the Club feeling 'fuzzy'. The head porter explained that there was a message to ring a certain telephone number. Guard did so, and:

> To my surprise I found that I was speaking to Government House, and after a while I was put through to a Lady Muriel Barclay-Harvey, who was the wife of the Governor of South Australia. She asked me if I was able to go to lunch on the following day, and because of my state of mind I said yes. Then there was an awkward pause, and I found myself saying, greatly to my horror, 'What are you going to have?' She said, 'Oh, what would you like?' So I said, 'Roast beef and Yorkshire pudding', and she laughed quite loudly over the phone, and then said, 'Well! You shall have it'. On the next day in a rather shamed faced way I presented myself at Government House at the appointed time, where I had the most delightful meeting with Lady Muriel Barclay-Harvey and the Governor of South Australia. Also at the lunch were a bishop and an Australian naval captain, and it was a most enjoyable occasion. We had a good laugh about me ordering my lunch of roast beef.[64]

Lady Muriel thrived on all this, and threw herself with seemingly boundless energy into all that the vice-regal role demanded of her during the war years. Among her many duties, for example, was the launching of the corvette HMAS *Whyalla,* the first warship built at Whyalla, on 12 May 1941. Her husband, however, although equally committed, was not as robust. On a visit to Ceduna on the West Coast in October 1943, he was taken ill and rushed to hospital in Adelaide.[65] Suffering increasingly from ill health, Sir Malcolm Barclay-Harvey was advised to resign the governorship, which he did, retiring on medical grounds on 26 April 1944. He returned to his Scottish estate, not exactly for a quiet life, for he was appointed Deputy Lord-Lieutenant of Aberdeenshire in 1945, and served on Aberdeen County Council from 1945 until 1955. He died in London on 17 November 1969; Lady Muriel survived him. In 1971 she made a small donation towards the restoration of *Sir Malcolm Barclay-Harvey,* preserved by the Australian Railway Historical Society and today undergoing further refurbishment at the society's Steam Ranger Heritage Railway at Mount Barker.

Charles Willoughby Moke Norrie
(19 December 1944 – 19 June 1952)

Charles Willoughby Moke Norrie (usually known as 'Willoughby') arrived in Adelaide in time to take up office on 19 December 1944, having travelled across from Sydney by train with his wife Patricia, their two young children, an orphaned niece (Eleanor Kerans) for whom he had legal responsibility, and twelve staff. He had retired from the British Army in September 1944 in order to take up the governorship of South Australia, and had been knighted before leaving England. In contrast to the lavish receptions received by other recent vice-regal appointments, it was announced that Willoughby Norrie 'will not be greeted with the same ceremony normally accorded to the arrival of a Governor', there being a war on. As the Adelaide *News* explained, the 'war will mean that no salute of guns will be fired on the arrival of Sir Willoughby at Government House'.[66]

Nonetheless, the Melbourne *Age* thought the new Governor 'certain to win widespread popularity among the people'.[67] Sir Willoughby knew that Sir Malcolm Barclay-Harvey, the previous Governor, had had to retire prematurely, and that he was stepping into the breach at a difficult moment. The war in Europe against Nazi Germany was proceeding slowly but inexorably towards its victorious conclusion but the conflict in the Pacific – in Australia's backyard – against Japan remained far more uncertain, not least as to how it might be concluded. A no-frills arrival suited Willoughby Norrie, who immediately threw himself into the morale-building and war-effort activities pursued tirelessly by his predecessor.

In just two years as Governor, Norrie had visited every local government area in the State, including some 300 schools, making as many as ten speeches a day. He went out of his way to meet returned servicemen coming home from abroad, including repatriated prisoners of war. He likewise supported the RSL, which he considered would have an especially important role to play in creating social cohesion in the postwar years (as he told the Uraidla sub-branch), when returned servicemen and women would need to 'pull-together' and 'the RSL was certain to do its part. He liked the idea of a happy blending of youth and experience that was taking place in the sub-branches, which could not but result in good'.[68] Lady Norrie was similarly busy, supporting the usual range of voluntary and patriotic organisations, including the recently formed Food for Britain Appeal. As one correspondent to the *Advertiser* put it, echoing Lady Norrie's mantra: 'What old Britain did for the world deserves our all-in effort. Britain impoverished herself to save the world. In this land of ample foodstuffs anything we can do is not too much.'[69]

Willoughby Norrie's stoic and sometimes taciturn nature also lent itself to the difficult task in hand. The *Age* observed that he was 'a pleasant conversationalist' but by upbringing and life experience Norrie was cast in the old-school style of reserve, understatement and quiet fortitude.[70] For example, as his son George Norrie would explain much later, his relationship with his father 'would seem strange to many today'. In those years, George said, when his father Willoughby Norrie was overseas in the British Army: 'Public service and boarding school meant prolonged separation of parents from children and the difficulties of sea travel – this was long before routine transcontinental flights – made things worse.'[71] Indeed, according to George:

> It might seem shocking for many [today], for instance, that when in 1936 my sister tragically died young at school in England, neither my mother nor my father were able to travel home from India until many months afterwards. It was a different time, with different conditions and different expectations. As children we were expected to cope with the vagaries life cast up with that famous stiff upper lip and I had a nanny, a seminal figure, but nonetheless separation and tragedies took a toll that perhaps I was only to recognise much later in life.[72]

This was, of course, the austere tradition in which Willoughby Norrie himself had been raised. Charles Willoughby Moke-Norrie (as he was then), was born on 26 September 1893 at Brompton, London, the son of George Edward Moke-Norrie, barrister, and Beatrice Stephen. He was educated at Eton and the Royal Military College, Sandhurst, before joining the 11th Hussars in 1913. He landed in France in August 1914, as part of the 1st Cavalry Division in the British Expeditionary Force (BEF), and saw action during the retreat from Mons, participating in a cavalry charge which captured eight German guns at Nery in September 1914. He was at the Battle of Messines in October 1914, and the 2nd Battle of Ypres in 1915. Wounded four times, Norrie rose to the rank of Temporary Major, won the Military Cross in 1915 (with Bar, in 1916), and was awarded the Distinguished Service Order in 1919. He was twice mentioned in dispatches.[73]

After the Great War, Willoughby simplified his surname to Norrie, dropping the hyphen but retaining Moke as a middle name. In 1921 he married Jocelyn Helen Gosling, with whom he had three children: Diana (who died young), Rosemary, and George (mentioned above). Sadly, Jocelyn died in March 1938, and later in the year Norrie married Patricia Merryweather Bainbridge, with whom he also had three children: Guy, Sarah and Annabel (the latter born in Adelaide in 1944). Norrie had settled well into Army life. His pastimes, all appropriate to a cavalry officer, included polo, foxhunting and steeplechasing, as well as racehorse breeding. Having attended Staff College, Norrie was appointed Commanding Officer of the 10th Hussars in 1931, serving with his regiment in India. In 1936 he was promoted to command the 1st Cavalry Brigade, which was mechanised in 1938 (exchanging horses for armour) and renamed the 1st Light Armoured Brigade. By now, Norrie had required a reputation as a specialist in tank and armoured warfare, an assumed expertise which would profoundly influence the subsequent course of events.

Early in the Second World War, Willoughby Norrie became General Officer Commanding of the 1st Armoured Division, and was appointed Major General in June 1941. Five months later, the Division was deployed to Egypt, where Norrie found himself promoted to Lieutenant-General in command of 30 Corps, replacing his old friend Vyvyan Pope who had recently been killed in an air crash. Almost immediately, he was pitched into action against Italian forces in North Africa and Erwin Rommel's formidable German 'Afrika Korps'. Norrie fought gallantly against the Axis powers during Operation Crusader, but performed less well during the following Battle of Gazala from 26 May to 21 June 1942.

Gazala proved to be Rommel's most impressive victory in the North Africa campaign. He forced the British to abandon their prepared defences, allowing him to capture the strategic port of Tobruk as he pushed the British back to the Egyptian border. The overall British commander in the Middle East was Claud Auchinleck – 'the Auk' – but the commander on the ground of the British 8th Army in Libya was Neil Ritchie. In advance of Gazala, Ritchie had divided his force into two components: 30 Corps, commanded by Willoughby Norrie, which comprised the 1st and 7th Armoured Divisions with almost 600 tanks of various types, and 13 Corps (under William Gott), with nearly 300 tanks and most of the infantry. Ostensibly well prepared, with extensive minefields and dispersed defensive concentrations of brigade strength, the British were nonetheless out-manoeuvred by Rommel's bold assault, which mercilessly exploited British weak points, including an exposed southern flank. Ritchie quickly lost control of the battle, and was often hopelessly out of touch with events, while Norrie was subsequently criticised for his allegedly out-dated 'cavalry' tactics approach to armoured warfare.

Ritchie finally managed an orderly retreat, but the debacle at Gazala proved to be his undoing. He was replaced by Bernard Montgomery – 'Monty' – who would shortly reverse the 8th Army's fortunes. Auckinleck was likewise replaced (by Harold Alexander) but not before he had ordered the removal of Willoughby Norrie. Norrie was returned to Britain as Commander of the Royal Armoured Corps, and became an adviser to Bernard Paget, commander of the Anglo-Canadian 21st Army Group set up in July 1943 to begin preparations for the D-Day Allied invasion of Europe. However, there was consternation when the senior staff learned that Montgomery was to take command of 21st Army Group in early 1944. Monty had a reputation for bringing his own men with him, and dismissing those he did not like or trust. As Otway Herbert, one of Paget's staff, recalled:

> For example, Willoughby Norrie, who had been a Corps Commander in the desert – he and Monty didn't hit it off, so I remember him coming in to me, to my office: 'Well I'm off anyhow – that's absolutely certain', the moment he heard Monty was coming! And off he went!
>
> I don't think anyone expected to be kept on. 'Monkey' Morgan – he was already a lieutenant-general, Chief of Staff – I think he was a bit upset about being outed. But he expected it!

The BGS [Brigadier General Staff] Intelligence was no good at all – he should have been out before – so that he was a certainty to go . . . The major-general Administration – he was a bit of a dud too.[74]

Having anticipated Montgomery's cull and extricated himself before the axe fell, Norrie was in April 1944 appointed head of the Military Mission to the French Committee for National Liberation in Algiers, a post he held for only a few months before being recommended for the governorship of South Australia. This new position was exactly what he needed to restart his career afresh. The Australian press welcomed him 'as one of this war's Middle East heroes', noting that his 30 Corps had included the 9th Division Australian Imperial Force (AIF). Drawing a veil over the collapse at Gazala, journalists liked to imagine that Norrie had 'played a major part in the relief of Tobruk' and 'the now epic El Alamein push, which led to the ultimate defeat of Rommel'.[75]

Governor Norrie was also welcomed as an exponent of the 'Empire spirit'.[76] The *Advertiser* reported that Norrie was 'a zealous imperialist', adding its own helpful gloss to explain: 'Not so long ago among a few foolish people "imperialist" was a term of reproach, but the recent course of history has altogether disposed of the anti-imperial heresy. It has taught all concerned . . . that there is no folly quite to be compared with isolation'.[77] Australia's isolation, and its consequences in war, was indeed one of Norrie's concerns. But his perspective was more complex than the *Advertiser* allowed. He considered that in the pre-war years Britain should have invested far more (in industry as well as defence) in Australia, and far less in what he termed 'the East'.[78] He had served in India in the 1930s, observing the movement towards independence, and let it be known publicly that he opposed Churchill's rejection of Indian self-determination. Moreover, money spent in Malaya and (especially) Singapore, he thought, could have been more soundly invested in Australia. Similarly, he criticised Churchill's opposition to the postwar renewal of mass emigration from Britain to Australia, considering the flow vital to maintaining close links between the two countries as well as stimulating population growth and economic development.

Willoughby Norrie's belief in economic growth and industrial investment chimed exactly with that of his Premier, Tom Playford, as the two men discovered to their mutual satisfaction. As Governor, Norrie had close-quarters exposure to Government policy, expressed most intimately at State openings of Parliament when it fell to His Excellency to deliver the prepared speech detailing his Government's program for the forthcoming session. Thus, in June 1949, for example, Norrie found himself discussing superphosphate – his Government planned to import more from Tasmania to meet a current shortfall, while considering the construction of new plants at Port Pirie or Port Adelaide – and the continuing implementation of the soldier–settler scheme. There were proposals for the allotment of underdeveloped Crown land to large business organisations for the purpose of closer rural settlement. The provision of electricity to country towns was now a high priority, with the construction of waterworks also continuing apace in rural areas. Narrow-gauge railway lines in the south-east of the State were to be broadened, and afforestation efforts were to be redoubled.[79]

State intervention was critical to Playford's economic planning, and Norrie considered that, despite being labelled the Liberal and Country League, the conservative party in South Australia under Playford's leadership was really 'what in England would be termed sound Right Wing Labour'.[80] Interestingly, others tended to agree. The State's Labor Party had seemingly resigned itself to perpetual Opposition, and contented itself with the conceit that Playford was actually implementing its own program. R.S. Richards, Labor leader from 1938 to 1949, promised that as 'long as the Premier [Playford] continues to implement Labor's policy, I will give him 100% support'.[81] Lindsay Riches, another Labor MP, reckoned 'Playford was the best socialist who had ever occupied the treasury benches'.[82] Mick O'Halloran, who succeeded R.S. Richards as Labor leader in 1949, went further, insisting that Playford's policies were 'more socialistic than Labor could ever hope to implement even it is was in office'.[83]

But there were also those within his own party who reckoned that Playford was 'a socialist at heart'.[84] Such disquiet came to the fore with Playford's proposed nationalisation of the Adelaide Electricity Supply Company, which was to also to include State control of the coal supply used in generating electricity. The company strongly resisted the plan, condemning 'this socialism', but Playford pressed ahead, leading eventually to a Royal Commission into the company.[85] The Commissioners' report was tabled in October 1945, effectively giving Playford the 'green light' for his legislation. As ever, Playford could rely on Labor MPs for support but his own party was a different matter. In the vote on the nationalisation Bill, the Labor Party voted with the Government but in the House of Assembly seven Liberal County League (LCL) members voted against. In the Legislative Council, nine LCL members opposed the Bill, which was defeated on the casting vote of the President, Collier Cudmore.

Governor Norrie was not impressed with Cudmore's behaviour, and let his disapproval be known quietly behind the scenes. The result was that, when an amended version of the Bill was presented in 1946, Cudmore absented himself from the crucial votes. One LCL member in the Legislative Council, J.L.S. Bice, switched his support to Playford, and the vote was carried, leading to the creation of the Electricity Trust of South Australia. Bice was known thereafter as 'Wobbly Jack' and sent to 'Cudmore Coventry' by his conservative colleagues. Playford, meanwhile, attracted the long-term hostility of many of his former friends, in and out of parliament, and the atmosphere of malice and recrimination extended to his own family. Years later, Playford's daughter, Margaret Fereday, remembered the effect on her mother, Lorna:

My mother was repeatedly snubbed by Establishment ladies when she and my father went to Government House for dinner at this time. Backs were turned on them (not by the Governor) and they were left talking only to each other while pre-dinner drinks were being served. My mother's feelings of social inferiority, and anxiety about her style of dressing not being good enough, really came to the fore at this time. It was quite hard for her. The other guests' feelings about my father may have been understandable but their manners left a lot to be desired. My mother was a shy person, she had nothing to do with Government policy and to snub her was cruel.[86]

Governor Norrie had played a discreet but powerfully enabling role in nudging Playford's electricity Bill through Parliament. He also approved the 'sound judgement' and 'honesty of purpose' of Labor Prime Minister Ben Chifley.[87] But his support for progressive politics was always firmly pragmatic and he was inherently suspicious of what he considered wishful thinking or unrealistic aspirations. He criticised, for example, the 'misguided sentimentality' of Charles Duguid, the leading advocate for South Australia's Aboriginal communities.[88] However, Norrie had seriously underestimated Duguid's intent and his lasting impact on the State's Aboriginal affairs.

Charles Duguid was a prominent member of South Australia's seven-person Aborigines Protection Board, which reported annually to the Governor through the House of Assembly. Alongside routine accounts of the Board's activities, the annual submissions also included aspirational material and policy recommendations which, perhaps, to some did indeed appear 'sentimental'. Thus the report presented to 'His Excellency, Lieutenant-General, Sir Charles Willoughby Moke Norrie' for the year ended 30 June 1945 emphasised that an 'amendment to the Aborigines Act has been recommended to provide for the establishment of a Special Court presided over by a Magistrate with a knowledge of tribal law to hear charges that may be made against aborigines [sic] living in tribal conditions'. Likewise, it 'is intended to seek the powers necessary to enable the Board to control working conditions, wages etc., of aborigines employed on farms and stations in various parts of the State'. The Board also reported: 'Considerable dissatisfaction prevails amongst the aborigines that because many of them are not eligible to participate in the benefits available to members of the general community under Commonwealth social legislation.'[89]

Duguid, who had been instrumental in establishing Ernabella mission in the Far North of the State in 1936, became president of the Aborigines Advancement League of South Australia in October 1951. The League's aim, enthusiastically espoused by Duguid, was 'to secure for Aborigines and part-Aborigines an honourable status within the Australian nation by ensuring the economic security and development of the race'.[90] Aboriginal activist Lowitja O'Donoghue recalled the efforts of the League to press the 'case for the girls to get into the professions, like nursing and teaching and so on, and the fellas to get into apprenticeships'. As she put it, 'Dr Duguid was very much part of it, on side, he supported us . . . Really things started to happen from there'. What had appeared utopian only a few years before, now seemed possible and within grasp, leading in South Australia, as O'Donoghue put it, to broad 'acceptance of Aboriginal people'.[91] Such aspirations were no longer 'sentimental', in the way Governor Norrie had imagined, but serious, realistic and achievable.

In 1948, Governor Norrie's term was extended for another four years but he left South Australia early, in June 1952, to become Governor-General of New Zealand. He served in that post until July 1957, when he returned to Britain. In retirement, he became a director of the London branch of the Bank of New South Wales and president (in 1967) of the British Boys' Movement for Australia. Survived by his wife and their son and two daughters, and by the son and daughter of his first marriage, he died on 25 May 1977 at Wantage in Oxfordshire.

Robert Allingham George
(23 February 1953 – 7 March 1960)

Willoughby Norrie's successor was Robert ('Bobby' to his friends) Allingham George, an Air Vice-Marshall in the Royal Air Force, who was welcomed enthusiastically in South Australia 'as one of the most daring of the RAF's helldivers', a 'foundation member of the RAF [who] used his World War I experience in developing power diving'.[92]

Robert Allingham George was born at Cromarty in the Scottish county of Ross and Cromarty on 25 July 1896, twin child of William George, inspector of the poor, and Mary Allingham. Educated at Invergordon and Inverness, he enlisted in the Seaforth Highlanders in 1914 and was sent to France. He was commissioned in 1916 into the Gordon Highlanders. The following year he transferred to the infant Royal Flying Corps and quickly demonstrated his ability as a pilot, being awarded the Military Cross for his achievements in night bombing and strafing. He was appointed to a permanent commission in the Royal Air Force on its foundation in 1919, serving in India until 1924 and then at the RAF College at Cranwell, Lincolnshire. Every inch the dashing RAF officer, Robert George married eighteen-year-old Sybil Elizabeth Baldwin in May 1927.[93]

Graduating from the RAF Staff College in 1931, George took command of 33 Squadron, based at Bicester in Oxfordshire, where he won acclaim for his development of dive-bombing techniques, especially against naval and maritime targets.[94] He was senior Air Staff Officer in Singapore in 1934–1937, and then filled the all-important post of air attaché in Ankara (1939–1944) and Athens (1939–1941), developing extensive knowledge of the strategic and diplomatic complexities of the eastern Mediterranean and Middle East. His subsequent appointment as Air Officer Commanding Iraq and Persia (1944–1945) was a natural progression. From there he was air attaché in Paris from 1945, and was promoted substantive Air Vice-Marshall in 1952 prior to the award of a knighthood on his retirement from the RAF in 1952.

Sir Robert and Lady George arrived in Adelaide on 22 February 1953, and in his welcoming speech Premier Tom Playford observed that Governors were expected to be 'an inspiration in times of danger'.[95] These were prescient words indeed for in March 1954 – two weeks before the first visit to South Australia as Queen by Elizabeth II – Adelaide was hit by a severe earthquake, which damaged Government House and many other buildings in the city. The Governor oversaw the patching-up of the vice-regal residence in time for the Queen's visit. But worse was to come when, in January 1955, Marble Hill, the gubernatorial retreat in the Adelaide Hills, was destroyed in a bushfire (see p. 17). Sir Robert and Lady George had only recently moved their personal belongings to Marble Hill, to allow the full refurbishment of Government House, and all was lost. However, quick thinking and decisive action by Governor George ensured that his family and staff survived the conflagration with only minor injuries.

In among the many duties falling routinely to the Governor, the most high profile in this period was the royal visit to South Australia in 1954. The Queen and Prince Philip were accommodated at Government House and there was an array of official functions, including a grand parliamentary reception and banquet.[96] After the drabness and austerity of the war years, the accession to the throne of the young Queen Elizabeth was hailed across the Empire–Commonwealth as the dawn of a new Elizabethan Age. Indeed, the Queen's visit to Australia in 1954 has been described by historian Peter Spearitt as 'the most popular and elaborate ritual this country has ever seen'.[97] Labor politicians could on occasion be as enthusiastic as members of other parties. Clyde Cameron, Federal MP for the Adelaide seat of Hindmarsh, for example, hoped that arrangements would be made for the royal couple to visit the working-class suburbs of Hindmarsh, Brompton and West Adelaide. At a function at Wayville Oval, one hundred thousand voices singing 'God Save The Queen' farewelled Her Majesty into the night, Thomas Playford having presented her with a huge Andamooka opal on behalf of the people of South Australia. At Whyalla, Elizabeth II witnessed a corroboree performed by fifty members of the Pitjantjatjara people, who had travelled 300 miles to see their Queen.[98]

Much of this royalist enthusiasm rubbed off onto the office of Governor, the regal sheen surviving long after the Queen had departed these shores. Broadly, Robert George was a popular Governor, although he irritated Playford by his demands for a swimming pool and personal helicopter. His habit of carrying a fly whisk as well as a cane on parade was thought a pretentious affectation by some. Sybil, Lady George, performed the usual functions falling to Governors' wives, although she did not display the feisty proto-feminism of some of her predecessors. Opening laboratories and classrooms at a girls' school, she informed pupils that 'the most important thing for a girl is to learn how to run a home well'. Some eyebrows were raised but in those postwar years her comments perhaps reflected a general yearning for domesticity and order after the exigencies of conflict. After all, as Lady George added, if women 'had kept their menfolk better fed and more contented . . . many wars might have been prevented'.[99]

After the triumph of the royal visit, an unfortunate postscript was another domestic incident at Government House. Sir Robert and Lady George employed a cook named Mrs Badcock, who had been guaranteed the same salary and conditions as employees in licensed clubs. Not surprisingly, when the Arbitration Court increased these salaries, Mrs Badcock expected to be treated accordingly. But when she approached Lady George, she was told that she was already treated well, especially as she enjoyed free board and lodging. The cook then sought the advice of her trade union, and subsequently she was called to the Governor's study in Government House where she was confronted by Sir Robert and Lady George and dismissed for having failed to 'keep the Governor's secrets'.[100]

Mrs Badcock then consulted Don Dunstan, who as well as being an up-and-coming Labor MP in the House of Assembly, was still practising part-time as a solicitor. Dunstan examined her case and concluded that, as well being entitled to the Arbitration award, she was also due $14,000 in back pay as a result of her extensive hours of work. Arthur Pickering QC was retained and an action launched against the Georges in the Supreme Court. The forthcoming *Badcock v Air Vice Marshall Sir Robert Allingham George* did not auger well for vice-regal dignity. In Parliament, Playford had a quiet word with Dunstan, and subsequently the Premier funded an out-of-court settlement by inserting a line in the 1956–1957 Budget on condition that Dunstan and Labor members would not debate the item during the Budget's passage through Parliament. In the event, one MP, S.J. Lawn, attempted to raise the subject. Playford, duly incensed, reacted by extending the Governor's term of office.

Robert George eventually retired to Britain in 1959, where he became a director of the Bank of Adelaide and the Australian Estates Company. Survived by Lady George, his daughter and three sons, he died tragically outside Marylebone underground station in London on 13 September 1967, when he was knocked down by a car.[101]

Chapter 7

DUNSTAN'S DECADES

'Queen Elizabeth the Second had the mix of pageantry, dignity and humanity expected of a modern monarch; she also had youthfulness.'[1] Geoffrey Blainey's perceptive assessment helps to explain why three-quarters of the Australian population went out of its way to see the Queen and Prince Philip during the royal tour of 1954.[2] In South Australia, as elsewhere, there was an outpouring of affection for the royal couple but also for the institution of constitutional monarchy. The vice-regal role performed by Governors received new lustre, its constitutional dimension more readily apparent in the reflected glory of the royal visit, its status and relevance enhanced in the estimation of the general public.

Among those contemplating all this was Don Dunstan, Labor MP for Norwood in the State Parliament, first elected in March 1953. A lawyer by training, he was deeply interested in the gubernatorial role, appreciating its critical significance in the Westminster system of Government. But he was also a republican,[3] a paradox he had to resolve in his own mind so as to accommodate his equally strong commitment to the constitutional principles of the Westminster system. Moreover, in the Labor tradition, he was opposed to the Imperial practice of vice-regal appointment, criticising the predictable stream of London appointees, usually one senior British military officer after another. Dunstan wished to see Australians as Governors, especially those with strong South Australian connections. There was also Dunstan's telling brush with Government House, when he had championed the cause of Mrs Badcock, the cook summarily dismissed from the Governor's employ (see pp. 164–165). As Dunstan rose inexorably in the Labor hierarchy, from minister to party leader and Premier in the late 1960s and 1970s, so these experiences and opinions would impact on the manner in which South Australia's Governors would be chosen and appointed in the future.

Edric Montague Bastyan
(4 April 1961 – 1 June 1968)

Although it was not immediately obvious, least of all to Edric Bastyan himself, Bastyan's governorship of South Australia in the 1960s was to mark a turning point in the State's vice-regal history. Although Bastyan was seen by most observers as an exemplary and conscientious Governor, his was nonetheless the last 'Imperial' appointment. Yet there was little to suggest that this might be so when he was appointed in April 1961, although the *Canberra Times* did observe that a 'majority of Australians told a gallup poll recently that they preferred Australians to Englishmen as Governors and Governors-General'. But, as the *Canberra Times* also noted, 'Sir Edric Bastyan's appointment can be seen as evidence that the pro-British school are not going to surrender the tradition without a struggle'. Indeed: 'First indications are that as in the case of Field Marshal Slim [Governor-General, 1953–1959], it would be hard to find an Australian to match the quality of the latest Englishman nominated to SA.'[4]

Governor Bastyan's seemingly instant popularity in South Australia, 'a special ring of satisfaction', as the press had it, was due partly to the fact that for the very first time the initial vice-regal progress through the City of Adelaide was shown live on television, as were the official welcoming ceremonies. There was even a half-hour televised press conference, another gubernatorial innovation, when the Governor was seen 'by scores of thousands of people in their own homes' answering questions about himself. 'The overwhelming impression left by the new Governor', according to one report, 'was not merely of charm and grace – one expects that as a basic qualification for the job – but of a man with a clear mind of his own who can talk with good sense and handle extempore questions with quick skill'.[5]

The *Australian Women's Weekly*, sizing up the new 'SA Governor and his lady', announced confidently 'they will be popular', enthusing over 'Sir Edric Bastyan, with his military bearing, boyish stride, and the petite, charming Lady Bastyan'. Lady Bastyan explained that her main hobbies were languages (she spoke six fluently), music, and horseracing. 'I am rather naughty', she confessed, 'I love horseracing and a little dabble'. Surprisingly, perhaps, she also revealed that she and her husband often spoke German 'or some other language' together for fun, usually when they were alone at home or out motoring.[6] Both were excellent public speakers.

Edric Montague Bastyan was born on 5 April 1903 at Seaforth, Lancashire, in north-west England, eldest son of Lieutenant Samuel James Bastyan, Royal Field Artillery, and Maude Mary Dare.[7] He attended West Buckland School and was educated at the Royal Military College, Sandhurst, before being commissioned in 1923 and posted to India. Staff appointments in Malta and Palestine followed. In 1934, Edric Bastyan married Marjorie Dorothy Bowle; the marriage was dissolved in November 1943 on account of 'her misconduct'.[8] By then Bastyan was serving as a staff officer under Montgomery in the 8th Army in North Africa. Subsequently, he participated in the Allied invasion of Italy, his former North Africa colleague Oliver Leese having now assumed command of the 8th Army following Monty's return to Britain to prepare for D-Day. It was in Rome on 21 October 1944 that Bastyan married Victoria Eugenie Helen Bett, an Intelligence Officer who had served in Gibraltar, the Middle East and Italy, and had been mentioned in despatches. In 1945 Bastyan was appointed Major General in charge of administration under Oliver Leese, now Commander of Allied Ground Forces in South-East Asia.

Oliver Leese, who had taken over 30 Corps from Willoughby Norrie after the disastrous Battle of Gazala (see pp. 156–157), had served alongside Bastyan in the 8th Army in both North Africa and Italy. Like Montgomery, Leese had his favourites, and Bastyan was one of them. As William Slim later recalled, Leese's 'staff, which he brought with him ... had a good deal of desert sand in its shoes, and was rather inclined to thrust Eighth Army down our throats'.[9] Certainly, Leese singled out Edric Bastyan and G.P. Walsh (another ex-8th Army man) for special mention. 'I would like to place on record the splendid work done by my own staff officers', he wrote in his despatches. 'I consider that the success of my forces [in Burma and elsewhere] was to a great extent made possible by the work and ability of these two officers.' Bastyan, in particular, had 'carried heavy responsibilities'.[10] Slim, who had commanded the 14th Army in Burma and later succeeded Leese, was similarly effusive. He thought Bastyan 'outstanding', lynchpin of 'a first-class staff, in excellent running order'.[11]

After the war, Bastyan served in the British Army of the Rhine in 1946–1948, and was head of logistics during the Berlin Airlift. He then filled various staff appointments in Britain and, in 1957, he was knighted and promoted Lieutenant-General. Subsequently, he was posted as Commander British Forces, Hong Kong, where he also served as a member of the Executive and Legislative Councils until 1960. On retirement from the British Army, he was selected as Governor of South Australia, arriving in Adelaide in April 1961. One of his earliest public duties was taking the salute in Adelaide on Anzac Day.[12] Like many of his predecessors, Governor Bastyan took a close interest in the welfare of returned servicemen and women, and was keen to participate in veterans' activities. An enthusiastic golfer, he took part, for example, in the Diggers' Golf Cup competition at Victor Harbor in May 1964, an event that attracted some 200 contestants. As the *Victor Harbour Times* explained, 'His Excellency . . . has played at Victor Harbour [*sic*] on a number of occasions. He is very impressed with the links and is looking forward to his first competition on a country golf course'.[13]

Governor Bastyan's first major constitutional challenge arose in the State election of 1962, when Labor became the biggest party in the House of Assembly, with nineteen seats to the Liberal and Country League's eighteen, Labor also winning a convincing lead in the popular vote.[14] There were two Independents, who effectively held the balance of power in the House. Frank Walsh, Labor Opposition leader, waited on the Governor, arguing he had received a popular mandate to form a Government.[15] Governor Bastyan intimated that he might 'consult constitutional authorities' before announcing a ruling, later deciding that it should be left to the House of Assembly itself to resolve the crisis when next it met.[16] On that basis Thomas Playford's Government survived, the two Independents (who were both subsequently richly rewarded with appointments respectively as Speaker, and Minister of Lands, Repatriation and Irrigation) voting to support Playford. Playford himself reckoned Bastyan to be 'the most intelligent' Governor he had encountered in his career. Next year, the Playford Government purchased a vice-regal holiday home at Victor Harbor – which Bastyan called 'Anookanilla' (an Aboriginal word meaning 'thank you') – and granted the Governor a long overdue pay rise.[17]

In 1965, Labor at last won office, bringing the Playford era finally to an end, with Frank Walsh now Premier. Intriguingly, it emerged four months later that Governor Bastyan's term of office (still with almost twelve months left to run) had been extended for a further two years. Speculation was rife as to who had recommended the extension. The *Canberra Times* wondered whether the wily Playford, having anticipated electoral defeat, had 'acted to try to settle the vice-regal issue before it [the Playford Government] went out of office'.[18] But there was also suspicion that, despite Labor's traditional insistence that Governors should be Australian-born, Walsh had recognised Bastyan's popularity and acted accordingly. At any rate, according to the *Canberra Times*, the 'effect of the extension of Sir Edric's term will take the issue of a British-born Governor out of the field of controversy for the next State election in 1968'. Indeed, the newspaper ventured, 'it confirms the growing opinion that the new [Labor] Government is not going to let minor doctrinaire planks in the Labor platform impair its chances of re-election at that poll'.[19]

By now, Don Dunstan had emerged as a powerful player in the Labor Government. He was given the major portfolios of Attorney-General, Minister of Social Welfare, and Minister of Aboriginal Affairs. It was due largely to Dunstan's energy and initiative that the Walsh Government was able to achieve its early legislative pace. But by now the Liberal Country League had a new leader, the elderly Thomas Playford having been replaced by thirty-eight-year-old Steele Hall in July 1966. It was apparent to many in the Labor camp that ageing Frank Walsh would have to go too. Walsh duly stepped down, to be replaced as party leader and thus Premier by Don Dunstan.

However, despite Dunstan's undeniable popularity, Labor lost the State election of March 1968. The party's popular vote had held up well – 52% of the primary votes and an estimated 54% of the two-party preferred vote – but Labor had come to grief as a result of the so-called 'Playmander', the hugely inequitable constituency boundary system that had underscored Liberal County League hegemony for decades. The iniquity of the electoral system was now plain for all to see, and Dunstan made the most of it. He refused to resign as Premier until being formally defeated in the House of Assembly, which gave him six weeks to mobilise popular outrage and maximise Liberal Country League discomfort. Dunstan waited on the Governor and advised that he should do nothing, as in 1962, until the matter was resolved in the House.[20] As before, Bastyan hinted that he might take constitutional advice elsewhere but events played out much as Dunstan had envisaged. Dunstan was duly defeated in the House, and when Steele Hall finally became Liberal Country League Premier on 16 April 1968 he was already on the back foot. Governor Bastyan advised Hall to proceed with electoral reform, to restore the legitimacy of the system, and Hall recognised that change was inevitable.[21] Despite strong misgivings in his own party, especially in the Legislative Council, Hall was able to push through a reform Bill which, while perpetuating an element of rural over-representation, fundamentally shifted the balance towards a fairer apportionment.

Steele Hall had understood that it was simply not possible to defend the malapportionment of the Playford era but in achieving reform he had effectively signed his Government's own death warrant for the next State election. In fact, the election came sooner than expected. In April 1970 one of the Independents habitually supporting the Liberal Country League voted with Labor, and the Hall Government collapsed. In the ensuing election the outcome was very similar to that of 1968 in terms of votes cast, with Labor winning 51% of first preferences. But in numbers of seats gained in the House of Assembly, the result was radically different, Labor gaining twenty-seven to the Liberal Country League's twenty, a veritable landslide ushering in Dunstan's second period as Premier, which was to last until his resignation through ill-health on 15 February 1979.

In assessing Bastyan's conduct during the 1968 constitutional impasse, legal experts Castles and Harris considered that the Governor's apparent readiness to accept guidance from British Government sources 'followed a time honoured nineteenth century course . . . [where] relics of colonialism could still be treated as relevant in the conduct of South Australian affairs in the latter part of the twentieth century'.[22] Bastyan may have been within his legal rights to seek such advice, they argued, but 'what he did was not the act of a local constitutional sovereign. His was rather the action of an imperial representative . . . that of an imperial pro-consul'.[23] Paradoxically, Dunstan did not see it quite that way. Skating over the question of whether Bastyan had or had not sought the advice of the British Government, Dunstan insisted (not surprisingly) that the Governor had been right to let the issue resolve itself in the House of Assembly. 'I advised the Governor, properly, that the matter should be dealt with in the House of Assembly when it met', he explained. Dunstan added that, alternatively, he could have advised the Governor to delay calling a meeting of the House, thus enabling him to continue as Premier for as long as possible. But, he admitted, the 'Governor's proper course, had I done such a thing, would have been to reject such advice and threaten to withdraw my commission [as Premier] . . . His power to do this is a necessary public safeguard'.[24]

Once again, Dunstan was defending the tenets of the Westminster system. He had also developed more than a sneaking regard for Governor Bastyan, praising him in public and extending his term for a further year to 1 June 1968.[25] However, as we have seen (see p. 3), Dunstan and Bastyan clashed when the Premier had bypassed the Governor to ask the British Government directly about progress towards the next vice-regal appointment. Bastyan had phoned Dunstan 'in a fury and addressed me with all the courtesy of a British commander to an errant subaltern'.[26] For all his support for the Westminster system, Dunstan recognised that:

> Herein lies one of the problems of having British representatives of the Queen as State Governors. They inevitably see themselves as satraps of the British Government, and as the only means of authorised communication with it about matters concerning the government of the State. But the British Government is a foreign government, and it is unfortunate that the Queen continues to use its ministers and officials for advice and bureaucratic procedures concerning State and Provincial Governments

in other countries of which she is Queen. It can lead to real conflicts of interest.[27]

In February 1968, it was announced that Sir Edric Bastyan was to be appointed Governor of Tasmania. A measure of the goodwill that he and Lady Bastyan had accrued in South Australia, not least in its swelling multicultural immigrant communities, was the grand farewell ball held in their honour. Nearly a thousand people dressed in national costumes attended the function organised by the Good Neighbour Council of South Australia, of which Governor Bastyan was patron. Lady Bastyan, 'a fluent linguist, was able to speak to many of them in the languages of their former countries'. As the vice-regal couple made to leave, 'the guests broke into Wish Me Luck As You Wave Me Goodbye and They Are Jolly Good Fellows'. They were, it was reported, 'visibly affected'.[28]

Although the Bastyans enjoyed their time in Tasmania, it was South Australia that remained in their hearts. Sir Edric found the Tasmanians unpunctual, which offended his military sensibilities. He also developed emphysema while in Hobart. When he relinquished his post in Tasmania in November 1973, he and Lady Bastyan retired to North Adelaide. There he devoted much of his time to painting, selling many of his works for charity, and in 1974 held an exhibition in Hahndorf. Survived by his wife and son, he died in North Adelaide on 6 October 1980.[29]

James William Harrison
(4 December 1968 – 16 September 1971)

Don Dunstan as Premier had decided that he wished to have an Australian appointed as Bastyan's successor, preferably someone from outside the military tradition but with a record of distinguished service that would encourage an active and intelligent engagement with the vice-regal role. His thoughts turned to Mark Oliphant, the South Australian-born nuclear physicist of international repute. Dunstan approached Oliphant in February 1968, and Oliphant replied in the affirmative almost immediately. Before the month was out, Dunstan had sent a formal recommendation to Buckingham Palace.[30]

However, Dunstan had not reckoned with the possibility of losing the ensuing State election, but lose he did. By now news of the Queens's approval of Oliphant's appointment had reached Governor Bastyan, who briefed Dunstan accordingly, and, irritatingly, news of Oliphant's potential appointment had already been leaked to the press.[31] Dunstan agreed to approach Steele Hall, seeking bi-partisan support for Oliphant, and Bastyan decided that if such agreement could be made, there would be no obstacle to making an announcement once the Palace had been informed.[32]

But Steele Hall would not agree. Although he too believed it was time for an Australian appointment, Hall (according to Dunstan's account) considered that 'given the importance of the ex-service element in the community . . . the appointment should be of a distinguished soldier'.[33] Additionally, Hall saw the vice-regal role as largely ceremonial, and did not wish for a potentially proactive appointee such as Oliphant. Out of courtesy, Hall wrote to Oliphant to explain his position, emphasising his personal opinion that the Governor should be an individual 'who has had a distinguished career in one of the armed services'.[34] An embarrassed Dunstan amplified the point, noting that Hall 'considered the most important organisations in the community were Service Clubs', and that this should be reflected in gubernatorial appointments, adding that Hall 'regarded the [vice-regal] position as largely a ceremonial one'.[35] Oliphant, clearly disappointed, replied to Dunstan, saying that while it would have been a privilege to work with him for the benefit of South Australia, 'it would be intolerable to find myself in a situation where I was expected to serve in a purely ceremonial capacity, or to regard the Service Clubs as the most important organisations in the community . . . I count myself fortunate not to have been appointed [by Hall] as Governor'.[36]

In seeking his preferred mix of an Australian with an exemplary military career, Steele Hall as Premier alighted upon James William Harrison. Harrison was born at Camperdown, Victoria, the second child of James Samuel Harrison, a farmer, and Mary Eleanor Harlock, both Victorians. He was educated at Geelong College and the Royal Military College, Duntroon, where he graduated in 1932 as an artillery officer. He spent four years in Melbourne with the 2nd Heavy Brigade before training in India and Malaya in 1937–1938. He then returned to Australia, and in May 1940 was promoted Captain. In September of the same year, he married Patricia Helen MacLean Lennox.[37]

From 1940 until 1942, Harrison served in the Middle East theatre of operations, mainly in staff appointments, and was mentioned in despatches. When the Australian Army returned home from the Middle East, the New Guinea Force was formed in April 1942, a military command unit for Australian, United States and so-called 'native troops' in Papua New Guinea during the Second World War. By now a Lieutenant-Colonel, Harrison was attached to Headquarters New Guinea Force (established in Port Moresby in August 1942) from November 1942 to February 1943, where he 'displayed marked ability'.[38] During this period the Headquarters staff helped plan and direct successful operations at Milne Bay, Kokoda, Buna-Gona and Wau, denting the myth of Japanese invincibility and beginning the Allied fightback in the region. Subsequently, Harrison was attached to the Australian Army Staff, London, in 1943–1945, before being appointed to the Directorate of Military Operations, Melbourne, where he dealt with the major issues concerning the conclusion of the war in the Pacific and the occupation of Japan.

Thereafter, Harrison was attached briefly to the Long Range Weapons Board of Administration in Melbourne before attending the Joint Services Staff College in Britain in 1948. From there he became an instructor at the Australian Staff College at Queenscliff, Victoria, where in 1951 he was promoted Temporary Colonel and appointed as the first Commandant of the Officer Cadet School at Portsea. Promoted Temporary Brigadier in 1954, he was posted to London as Australian Army representative before completing the 1956 course at the Imperial Defence College. In August 1957, he assumed command of Western Command, Perth, as a Temporary Major General (the rank being made substantive in September 1959), and became chairman Joint Planning Committee in the Department of Defence, Canberra, 1960–1962. Further appointments culminated in his becoming General Officer Commanding Eastern Command, Sydney, from 1966.

In 1968 James Harrison was invited to become Governor of South Australia. He was knighted in the October, and was seconded from military duties to allow him to take up the vice-regal position, which he assumed on 4 December. He was Steele Hall's ideal appointment. The Premier recognised that the salary was unattractive, so his Government relieved the Governor of paying his domestic staff salaries once he had reached the prescribed Army retirement age on 25 May 1968. Harrison was widely welcomed as 'the first Australian to become Governor of the State',[39] but those who expected much from this novelty were to be disappointed. From the first his governorship was low-key, typically routine events such as the formal opening of The Levels campus of the South Australian Institute of Technology on 22 October 1970.[40] Renovations in Government House in 1969–1970 limited the number of social events, and the hospitalisation, first of Lady Harrison and then the Governor himself, were further constraints. By early 1970, Harrison had developed angina, and was clearly in considerable pain during the opening of the State Parliament in April. In his discomfort, he may not have noticed that the text prepared for him by Hall had omitted the traditional words 'my ministers advise me' at a key point, promoting a storm of (largely disingenuous) protest that this had 'politicised' the Governor's speech, making it appear that it reflected his own opinions rather than those of his Government.[41]

Governor Harrison struggled on but it was clear by now that he was a sick man. On 9 May 1970 he suffered a coronary occlusion and was out of action for two months. He was advised to rest, and in the following year he and Lady Harrison set out for a round-the-world holiday. Sadly, he was taken ill on a QANTAS flight to Honolulu on 16 September, and was pronounced dead by a doctor on the aeroplane when it was about an hour away from Hawaii. His body was cremated in Honolulu before the remains were returned to Sydney. As the *Canberra Times* mused, 'Sir James had a history of heart trouble'.[42] He was only fifty-nine.

Dunstan was once again the Premier, having won the 1970 election. He recalled the shock of receiving the news that the Governor had died en route to Hawaii: 'It was a very sad occasion – he had served the State as he had been asked to do and had been kind courteous and conscientious in his office. It was a tragic loss for his wife, a universally liked and likeable woman'.[43] But, characteristically, Dunstan also had the last word:

He [Harrison] was a very pleasant man, but Hall intended that his office be ceremonial, and that's what it was. Sir James filled his role as Governor quietly and in the traditional way, and left very little mark on the State. It is ironic that later it was I, who had a different view of the Governor's role, and promoted it, who should be attacked by the Establishment and their lackeys for 'endeavouring to downgrade and neutralise' the office of Governor.[44]

Likewise, Dunstan had the last act. He lost no time in contacting Oliphant once more, asking him again to accept the office of Governor. He explained that the Governor's salary would now be $15,000 tax free, with a tax-free expense allowance of $17,000. The Government would also pay the salary of Government House staff, as well as covering the costs of providing cars (including petrol), holding receptions, utility bills, and the upkeep of a vice-regal holiday home at Victor Harbor.[45] In this Dunstan had gone further than Hall's sympathetic treatment of James Harrison, finally putting to rest the erstwhile Imperial assumption that candidates for gubernatorial posts were men of private means, or should be.

Oliphant accepted at once, and the nomination was dealt with swiftly by the Palace. Sir Mark was sworn-in at an open-air ceremony at Government House in December 1971. The press recognised the historic nature of the occasion, observing that it 'broke an Australian precedent' in that Sir Mark Oliphant was neither an ex-military man nor British born.[46] Dunstan had now achieved his aim, and all three vice-regal appointments during his term as Premier would meet the same criteria. But, as Peter John Boyce would later remark, with almost wry amusement, Dunstan's 'choices were bold and imaginative, though not in each case entirely successful'.[47]

Marcus Laurence Oliphant
(1 December 1971 – 30 November 1976)

Dunstan, for his part, soon discovered that Oliphant 'was a strange mixture of idealism, naivete, kindliness, cantankerousness, restlessness, concern with status, and fervour for causes, some great, some petty'.[48] But he was in no doubt that Oliphant was a great man, and hoped that his appointment as

Governor would stimulate interest in the development of high-technology science-based industries in South Australia.

Marcus (generally known as 'Mark') Laurence Oliphant was born on 8 November 1901 in Kent Town, Adelaide, son of Harold George 'Baron' Olifent [*sic*], a public servant and part-time lecturer with the Workers' Educational Association, and Beatrice Edith Fanny Tucker, an artist.[49] He was the eldest boy, and had four younger brothers. He attended Unley High School and, in his final year, Adelaide High School. In 1919 Oliphant began studying at the University of Adelaide, where Professor Kerr Grant, the distinguished physicist, arranged a cadetship worth ten shillings a week. He graduated in 1921, followed by an Honours year, his thesis supervised by Grant. When Grant went overseas on sabbatical, Roy Burden, the acting head of department, took Oliphant under his wing, co-authoring with him two scientific papers on mercury and surface tension. Oliphant's academic career was about to take off, his intellectual abilities and theoretical insights complemented by his practical skills, where he soon gained a reputation for his facility in manufacturing and erecting laboratory apparatus. When Oliphant married Rosa Louise Wilbraham, his childhood sweetheart, in Adelaide, on 23 May 1925, he fashioned her wedding ring from a gold nugget (from the Coolgardie goldfields in Western Australia) that his father had given him.

Oliphant's burgeoning interest in physics was further encouraged by the visit to Adelaide of Ernest Rutherford and his wife Mary, Lady Rutherford. As Oliphant recalled, in 'September 1925, the Rutherfords visited Adelaide, where I was working as an assistant to the Professor of Physics, Kerr Grant. Rutherford gave a talk in the Department of Physics on the work going on in the Cavendish Laboratory [at the University of Cambridge]'.[50] That Rutherford was a New Zealander lent Oliphant a sense of Antipodean affinity with the famous nuclear physicist, 'and I was determined that I would work under him, if this was at all possible'. As Oliphant added, in those days 'members of the University as humble as I were not introduced to such illustrious visitors' but nonetheless he applied for – and got – an overseas scholarship in the hope of travelling to Cambridge. Kerr Grant, on sabbatical leave, had just visited the Cavendish and apparently had put in a good word for Oliphant. 'I had already telegraphed to Rutherford', explained Oliphant, 'and had received a reply saying that he would reserve a place for me'.[51]

Years later, Mark Oliphant could still vividly recall his first encounter with Rutherford at the Cavendish:

> I arrived in the Cavendish in October 1927, as a raw research student from the antipodes, who Rutherford had kindly admitted to what was then, by far, the greatest physical laboratory in the world. I was told to wait outside by a formidable little man, Mr Hayles, who while primarily the lecture assistant, acted as his secretary. [I waited] in the passage, with uncarpeted board floor, dingy varnished pine doors and stained plastered walls, indifferently lit by a skylight with dirty glass.[52]

As he queued, Oliphant soon found himself in the company of another Australian, Cecil Eddy, and a young physicist from Trinity College, Dublin, E.T.S. Walton:

> Each of us expressed agreement at the unprepossessing appearance of the Laboratory tucked away obscurely in the narrow Free School Lane, behind Corpus Christi College, and we speculated about the Cavendish Professor [Rutherford] who would interview us shortly. When my turn came, I entered a small office littered with books and papers, the desk cluttered in a manner which I had been taught in school indicated an untidy and inefficient mind. It was raining, and drops of water ran reluctantly down the grime covered glass of the uncurtained window.[53]

Unprepossessing or not, the Cavendish Laboratory was to be Oliphant's academic home for the next decade, while Rutherford's relations with Oliphant became, in the estimation of James Chadwick, a senior colleague, 'akin to those between father and son'.[54] In 1972, while Governor of South Australia, Oliphant published his *Rutherford – Recollections of the Cambridge Days* (the title page proudly boasts, 'Government House, Adelaide'), part biography and part autobiography, a pen picture of Rutherford during those times but also a memoir of Oliphant's own experiences.

Ernest Rutherford had been knighted in 1914, was awarded the Order of Merit in 1925, and later elevated to the peerage in 1931. Early in his career, with the help of Frederick Soddy, a junior demonstrator, Rutherford had proposed the then revolutionary theory that radioactivity was the spontaneous disintegration of an atom, with the simultaneous emission of energy in the form of radiation. It was a discovery that opened up the whole vista of nuclear physics, leading ultimately to the generation of nuclear energy and, of course, the atom bomb. But when Oliphant joined the Cavendish in 1927, these developments were a long way off, the laboratory a hive of experimental buzz and excitement. Oliphant found Rutherford's lectures somewhat chaotic. He spluttered and 'hummed and hahed too much, repeating himself when he lost his place, but he was so enthusiastic, so imbued with the excitement of physics, that he was inspiring. He was convinced that nature was inherently simple, and that apparent complexity reflected lack of knowledge'.[55] As Rutherford himself put it: 'I believe these things to be simple, being a simple man myself'.[56]

By observing Rutherford and the other academics at the Cavendish, Oliphant added the art of good lecturing and public speaking to his repertoire of skills. He abhorred those who merely read their papers, considering it lazy and boring, and thought that one particular academic's 'lectures on isotopes and mass-spectroscopy were dull because he read them directly from his book on the subject'. Another lecturer failed to attract many attendees to his classes, 'not because the subject lacked interest, but because the lecturer himself was so clearly embarrassed by his inability to express himself'.[57] When Rutherford, scribbling mathematical formulae on the blackboard, lost his way or made a mistake, he would turn upon the students and exclaim, 'You sit there like a lot of numbskulls and, and not one of you can tell me where I've gone wrong'.[58] But, despite the occasional outburst of irritability, Rutherford was gently supportive of his students, as he was of his research staff, and went out of his way, for example, to put PhD students at their ease during the nerve-wracking experience of the viva.[59] Here was another lesson that Oliphant never forgot.

Oliphant and his wife Rosa soon became part of the Rutherford's social circle, with a privileged place within the Rutherford home. They holidayed with them at their Welsh retreat Celyn, near Snowdonia, and were frequent guests at Newnham Cottage, their house in Cambridge. Here were opportunities to observe the Rutherfords at close quarters. 'Rutherford was a large man', recorded Oliphant, 'and since he was talkative and did not pay much attention to what he was doing, he was apt to spill tea or food, which settled upon his waistcoat. When this happened, Lady Rutherford would say loudly: "Ern, you're dribbling."'[60] Oliphant also noted that the 'Rutherfords occupied separate bedrooms ... There were no overt acts of affection between them. Yet they were devoted to one another'.[61] However, for several years until about 1936, the Rutherfords had living with them Miss Eileen de Renzi (apparently a relation of Lady Rutherford). She was then in her mid-thirties, 'a mercurial mixture of Irish and Latin ancestry', according to Oliphant, and while Lady Rutherford was 'cool, competent and never demonstrative, Miss de Renzi's great affection for Rutherford was shown in countless ways, and he obviously enjoyed being fussed over at times'.[62] In difficult moments, Rutherford 'accepted many acts of care and affection from Miss de Renzi'.[63] In this somewhat eccentric household, Eileen de Renzi was Rutherford's inspiration and muse, as Oliphant appeared to recognise, for him another telling insight into his mentor's intriguing make-up.

Mark Oliphant thrived in this environment, exalting in both the intimacy and social milieu of the Rutherfords and the intellectual stimulus of the Cavendish Laboratory. He gained his PhD in 1930, became a Fellow of St John's College, Cambridge, in 1934, and in 1937 was elected Fellow of the Royal Society. He was also Assistant Director of Research at the Cavendish. Deploying his practical skills, he built a particle accelerator, demonstrating the artificial disintegration of an atom's nucleus, and became the first to show nuclear fusion experimentally. As Oliphant explained later, referring to his early work in nuclear physics, 'we had no idea that this would one day be applied to make hydrogen bombs. Our curiosity was just curiosity about the structure of the nucleus of the atom, and the discovery of these reactions was purely, as the Americans would put it, coincidental'.[64]

But despite all this exhilaration, there were sad times too. Oliphant and Rosa's son, Geoffrey, born in 1930, died from meningitis just before his third birthday. The Oliphants found that they could not have further children but were delighted when they were able to adopt, first a son, Michael, in 1936, and then a daughter, Vivian, in 1938. In October 1937, unexpectedly, Rutherford died after what was supposed to be a routine operation. Oliphant, like all Rutherford's close associates, was devastated. He thought Rutherford 'the greatest experimental physicist since Faraday', and reckoned that in 'some ways Rutherford's work was more significant than that of Faraday or Einstein'.[65] Writing in 1972, by now Governor of South Australia, Oliphant still found himself asking so very often: 'what would the professor have done under those circumstances, and what would he have thought of this idea? So long as we live he will live in our hearts, and if we can do a little to hand on the flaming torch, we shall be content.'[66]

In fact, shortly before Rutherford's death, Oliphant had moved to the University of Birmingham to take up the Poynting Chair of Physics. It was a change of direction that had caused heartache for both Oliphant and Rutherford yet they agreed it was a necessary next step for Oliphant's career. Oliphant assumed his new post in September 1937, a month before Rutherford died. He had laid down exacting and ambitious terms for accepting the chair, and initiated a funding campaign to construct a cyclotron, a new type of particle accelerator in which charged particles were propelled by an alternating electric field between two electrodes in a constant magnetic field created by two large magnets. Oliphant travelled to Berkeley, California, to consult with Ernest Lawrence, the inventor of the cyclotron, and hoped to have his version operational by the end of 1939. In the event, the Second World War intervened, and it was not completed until after the war.

However, Oliphant had now become embroiled in secret war work. By 1938 he was already engaged in the development of radar, struggling with the task of designing a device small enough to fit into an aircraft. Along with his Birmingham team, he came up with the short wave-length 'magnetron', small yet powerful, which was operational by 1941, playing a significant part in detecting U-boats, intercepting enemy aircraft, and directing Allied bombers.[67] The Birmingham physicists had also studied the theoretical possibilities of developing atomic bombs, discovering that it might require as little as one kilogram of uranium-235 to trigger a chain reaction equivalent to the explosion of hundreds of tons of TNT. Oliphant presented the team's findings to the British Government, which studied the data and concluded that such a bomb might be ready by 1943. Oliphant also pushed for American involvement, travelling to the United States in August 1941, meeting officials and also convincing his friend Ernest Lawrence to join the research effort. In November 1943, the British project, coyly known as Tube Alloys, was merged with the emergent American Manhattan Project, with Oliphant playing a key role at Lawrence's laboratory at Berkeley. But he soon detected that the Americans intended to monopolise the nuclear weapon program, sidelining the British contribution, which Oliphant duly reported back in timely fashion, insisting the United Kingdom should pursue its own independent nuclear strategy.[68]

Oliphant had returned to Britain in March 1945, resuming his post at Birmingham, and was on holiday in Wales when news of the atomic bombing of Hiroshima and Nagasaki came through. Any slight satisfaction that the bombs had worked in practice was immediately overtaken by the sheer horror of what had happened, his vivid imagination picturing the immense destruction and the appalling levels of death and human suffering. For the rest of his life, Oliphant kept a cutting from the *New Yorker*, annotated in the margins, a report from the American war correspondent, John Hersey. Hersey had watched a small man reach 'down to help a woman into his boat but when he took her by the hands her skin slipped off in huge glove-like pieces . . . Then he got out into the water and, though a small man, lifted several of the men and women, who were naked, into his boat'. This small man recalled that their 'backs and breasts were clammy, and he remembered uneasily what the great burns he had seen during the day had been like: yellow at first, then red and swollen, with the skin sloughed off, and finally, in the evening, suppurated and smelly'. As he lifted these hideous slimy living bodies out of the water, 'he had to keep consciously repeating to himself: "These are human beings."'[69]

Oliphant maintained a glimmer of hope that the peaceful use of atomic technology might outweigh the continuing dread of nuclear war, but as time went on he became less optimistic.[70] In the 1970s, even as Governor of South Australia, he was an outspoken critic of French nuclear testing in the Pacific.

In 1972, his thoughts returned to his late mentor, Ernest Rutherford. He remembered how, in the 1930s, Rutherford had called for an international treaty to limit the use of aerial warfare, fearing the wholesale destruction of cities by waves of bombers. As Oliphant reflected: 'How much more strongly would Rutherford have spoken now, when chemical, biological and nuclear weapons can be delivered anywhere on earth with great accuracy by unmanned rockets?'[71]

In April 1946, Prime Minister Ben Chifley asked Oliphant to join an Australian delegation (which included H.V. 'Doc' Evatt, the Minister for Internal Affairs, and Paul Hasluck, Australia's representative at the UN) to the new United Nations Atomic Energy Commission, which was seeking ways of securing the international control of nuclear weapons. Their deliberations came to little but Chifley and H.C. 'Nugget' Coombs, the Minister for Post-war Reconstruction, shared with Oliphant their ideas for a new research institute in Australia, one which would be a focus nationally and internationally and raise Australia's academic profile. This would lead eventually to the foundation of the Australian National University in Canberra, and Oliphant was committed from the first. It was an uphill battle, however, with Robert Menzies' victory in the 1949 Federal election threatening to derail the process, many Liberals considering the proposed university an extravagance. But Menzies turned out to be supportive, although Oliphant became frustrated by the slow progress of construction. Nonetheless, he soon established the new university as a worldwide centre for research in the physical sciences. In 1954 he founded the Australian Academy of Science, based in Canberra on the Australian National University campus, and was knighted in 1959. He continued to serve the university at professorial level until his retirement in 1967, when he was appointed Emeritus Professor.

Oliphant was restless in retirement. In November 1970, his son Michael, then thirty-five, was found to have inoperable cancer, dying shortly after.[72] Oliphant was devastated. Not surprisingly perhaps, he jumped at the invitation to become Governor of South Australia, embracing a new direction in his life and hoping for a fresh start after the loss of his son. Oliphant remained popular with the South Australian public throughout his appointment, and initially it appeared that he and Dunstan got on well together. Both were radical visionaries, democrats though with elitist tendencies, and strong-willed. Perhaps they were too similar. Oliphant had told Dunstan that, as Governor, he wished to retain the right to speak out on great issues and 'that he should not be limited in speaking out against nuclear warfare or French atomic tests'.[73] Dunstan readily agreed, although pointing out that the Governor should avoid 'entry into matters of party political difference and particularly within the State – on these the Governor must of course remain neutral and above the fray'.[74] But Dunstan also hoped that Oliphant would comment on things he felt to be of importance in the community. Indeed, Oliphant had marched through the streets of Adelaide in 1970 in an anti-Vietnam War demonstration, and Dunstan was quietly impressed.[75]

One issue that the new Governor felt strongly about was the despoliation, as he saw it, of the Adelaide Hills environment, especially by the continuing quarrying for dolomite stone. He said so in a public dinner in Norwood (Dunstan's own constituency), creating a flurry of press interest.[76] Dunstan was embarrassed, and visited Government House to explain that the Government had already stopped the spread of quarrying on the Hills' face, and now required all quarries to produce environmental rehabilitation plans to be implemented once their extractive work was complete.[77] During 1972 there was another difference of opinion between Governor and Premier, when Dunstan announced that he would not recommend to the Queen any further honours under the Imperial system, hinting perhaps that he would introduce his own South Australian system. Oliphant scoffed at the latter suggestion, telling the Premier that no one would take such 'honours' seriously, and he also upheld his belief in the Imperial system. Dunstan quietly abandoned his plan, which was soon overtaken by Gough Whitlam's introduction of a new Australian Honours system.[78]

There was another spat in 1972, when Governor Oliphant visited Mount Gambier in the south-east of the State. Local dignitaries asked Sir Mark to say something about the possibility of the city becoming a government-supported centre for regional development. Oliphant did as he was asked, unwittingly unleashing a storm of protest. 'The Premier was very angry',

Oliphant later recalled: 'He reminded me that his government had a policy of developing a new city at Monarto . . . He said I had no right as Governor to advance Mount Gambier's claims . . . It was the first sign to me that all was not well between us.'[79] As Dunstan pointed out, the Liberals had campaigned in Mount Gambier on the basis that Monarto was a waste of money, and Oliphant had allowed himself to become embroiled in this party-political dispute.[80]

Matters seemed to go downhill thereafter. Oliphant resented what he saw as attempts to water down the ceremonial role of the Governor. He protested that he had not been consulted over plans to alter the State's vice-regal flag, and objected strongly when Dunstan suggested that the Governor's aides-de-camp need not dress in full military uniform when presenting themselves at the Bar of Parliament to deliver vice-regal messages. He felt that his role was being undermined, and decided he would resign.[81] His mood was not helped by the arrival at Government House of a formal visitation from the Legislative Council, for which occasion he had donned morning dress. The councillors, however, were informally attired, in the Governor's opinion 'a bunch of scruffy-looking Australian politicians' and an affront to the dignity of his office.[82] This redoubled his intention to draft a letter of resignation. Only quick thinking by an aide-de-camp, who contacted Dunstan and arranged for him to visit Government House to mollify Oliphant, prevented the situation from getting out of hand. The Governor decided he would not be resigning after all.

Oliphant, perhaps, had not fully recovered from his traumatic experience at Flinders University a day or two before. Earlier, he had been appointed Visitor to the University and, priding himself on his ability to relate to young people, had enjoyed himself immensely when attending the annual freshers' camp. Now, however, a group of radical students had staged a 'sit-in' at the university's Registry, and Oliphant offered his services as a mediator. It was a mistake. He was made to feel unwelcome and out of touch by the students, and amid the shouting and jeering decided it was time to leave. It also reinforced his prejudices about the nature of contemporary higher education. As he explained to Revd Paul Barnett, Rector of Holy Trinity Church in Adelaide, in the sit-in students 'of medicine, engineering and science were totally absent . . . The rebels were students of history and of the social sciences, with a few arts students'. These subjects had no future, he thought, and in terms of 'employment only school teaching was an obvious avenue. Even that is beginning to dry up'. That left 'only the pursuit of personal satisfaction, in motor cars, alcohol, drugs, eating, uninhibited sex, and the rejection of all authority'.[83]

Revd Paul Barnett, Rector of Holy Trinity, was to play an important role in another disagreement between Oliphant and Dunstan. The Premier had relaxed the State's censorship code, and Barnett complained of a resultant upsurge of pornography, pleading with the Governor to use his influence to rectify the situation. Oliphant obtained examples of such pornography from his friend, Harold Salisbury, Commissioner of Police, and invited Dunstan to visit Government House to view this explicit material. He also asked Walter Crocker, his Lieutenant-Governor, to the meeting. As Crocker recalled:

> When Sir Mark Oliphant, after being shown by Police Commissioner Salisbury a hundred or so examples of the pornography available in delicatessen shops and around schools, and after bringing myself as Lieutenant-Governor into the matter, had a conference with Dunstan, the latter took the line that censorship would not be tolerated by the Government: people could see or hear whatever they wanted.[84]

According to Oliphant, Dunstan added that personally he found pornography boring and disliked children being exploited in the ways depicted in some of the material he was shown.[85] Dunstan's recollection was more nuanced. He indeed told Oliphant that his was a libertarian Government. But he also confirmed that the production of child pornography within the State was a crime, and that those importing such material from elsewhere would henceforth be liable to prosecution.[86] Oliphant had had greater influence as Governor than perhaps he had realised.

Oliphant's close friendship with Harold Salisbury would lead to further friction with Dunstan, when in 1978 the Premier dismissed the Police Commissioner for calculatedly misleading him about the activities of the

South Australian Special Branch, which had for years kept secret files on 'subversive' individuals (including Labor MPs, Dunstan among them) and those with suspected homosexual tendencies.[87] A Royal Commission later vindicated Dunstan, but there was widespread public concern about the turn of events. Fortuitously, no doubt, Oliphant's term of office had been completed before the Salisbury affair blew up, for he was forthright in his defence of the erstwhile Commissioner. 'Harold Salisbury', he told the press, 'is one of the few people of absolute integrity whom I have known in my lifetime. His concern for his State and for Australia generally was absolute.'[88] Oliphant might no longer be Governor but his comments caused a sensation.

Earlier, in 1975, while still in post, Oliphant had made Dunstan 'almost uncontrollably angry' when he decided, following Sir John Kerr's dismissal of Whitlam and his Government, that he should issue a statement supporting the Governor-General and insisting that he had acted correctly and constitutionally.[89] Dunstan gave very firm advice that this would be beyond a Governor's competency, and that should he issue such a statement, Dunstan would have to consider Oliphant's position and advise the Queen accordingly. Oliphant retreated but twelve months later, in a farewell press conference, returned to the subject when he asserted that Kerr had indeed been right to sack Whitlam. As Boyce remarked, looking back over Oliphant's time as Governor, 'he knew little about the conventions of the constitution.'[90]

For most South Australians, however, unconcerned with legal niceties, 'Sir Mark Oliphant had exercised his Vice-Regal role with extraordinary success.'[91] He and Rosa, Lady Oliphant, retired to Canberra. Oliphant survived into a sprightly old age, living to be ninety-eight before dying on 14 July 2000. Unfortunately, however, he had witnessed Rosa's suffering in a long illness which led to her death in 1987, making him a late convert to the cause of voluntary euthanasia. He was survived by his daughter Vivian.

Douglas Ralph Nicholls
(1 December 1976 – 30 April 1977)

As Oliphant's term of office drew to a close, Dunstan considered a suitable successor. Various names had crossed his desk but he was drawn overwhelmingly to Douglas ('Pastor Doug') Nicholls, a Church of Christ minister and in 1972 the very first Aboriginal Australian to be knighted by the Queen. An Aboriginal rights activist, Nicholls was also a noted athlete and Australian Rules footballer. But when news of this impending appointment leaked out, there were those, expressing incredulity, who reckoned that Nicholls had not even learned to read and write until he was a young man. Some wondered, indeed, whether he would be able to cope with all the papers he would be expected to peruse as Governor, or whether he would be able to read the Governor's speech at the State opening of Parliament.[92]

Oliphant had similar concerns, and, while still in office, wrote to Dunstan. He warned that 'there are grave dangers in your proposal':

> there is something inherent in the personality of the aborigine [*sic*] which makes it difficult for him to adapt fully to the ways of the white man . . . The first problem likely to be faced by an aborigine as Governor, would be the natural assumption by all other aborigines that what is his is theirs. The house [Government House] may well be filled to overflowing by his relatives and tribesmen to whom, by custom and duty, he cannot say no. The results could be chaos, inability to find or keep domestic staff, and even loss of valuables because of the 'sharing' habits of his people.[93]

This outburst, which historian Angela Woollacott has described as 'shocking racism',[94] stood in stark contrast to the sentiments expressed only a few years before in the foreword 'by Sir Mark Oliphant, Governor of South Australia' to Charles Duguid's autobiography *Doctor and the Aborigines*. Here, in more measured tones, Oliphant had welcomed the recent 'awakening interest of government, institutions and people generally in the welfare of the Australian Aborigines'.[95] Dunstan, perhaps, thought Oliphant's irrational claims strangely uncharacteristic of an otherwise humane man committed to scientific reason, and his response was calm, even friendly. He regretted, he told Oliphant, that 'there is still racial feeling in the community', and counselled that 'it is necessary constantly to war against it'.[96] The appointment of Sir Douglas Nicholls as the Queen's representative in South Australia would be a significant step in the right direction, he said.

News of Oliphant's concerns leaked out, prompting the *Canberra Times* to warn that the 'next Governor may test community's racial tolerance'. The newspaper conceded that the appointment of Douglas Nicholls would be seen by many as 'an inspired act of both symbolism and atonement' but it also noted that the ABC's television program *This Day Tonight* had reported 70% opposition among its anonymous viewing audience.[97] Nicholls' personal embarrassment was compounded when he and Lady Nicholls were interviewed in their own home for the television station GTV9. The journalist asked Lady Nicholls how she thought she would be received by 'the garden-party set in Adelaide', at which point Sir Douglas exploded, declaring 'you are a racist' and ordering the offending interviewer to leave his house immediately.[98] Nicholls requested that the interview not be shown but it was broadcast anyway on the station's *A Current Affair*, GTV9 not issuing an apology until after the event.[99]

On 1 December 1976, the great day of swearing-in, Governor Nicholls welcomed his appointment as an 'historic' occasion for the Aboriginal people of Australia. But he also recognised his wider responsibilities to all South Australians. 'I am an Aborigine', he proclaimed, 'and I'm aware that in holding this high office I have equal duties to every citizen of this State, irrespective of creed, colour, standing or age'.[100] It was a sentiment echoed by Premier Don Dunstan. In his speech, Dunstan acknowledged that 'South Australia is proud that it is the first State in which a member of the original race of Australians has attained the highest office'. However, 'We also know that you have come not as aboriginal [sic] governor of South Australia, but as the Governor of the whole people'. Dunstan dwelt too on the constitutional aspect of the Governor's role. Remembering, perhaps, Oliphant's sometimes cavalier approach, he emphasised that a Governor must act 'in accordance with constitutional precedent and convention', and that he or she has 'the duty of staying above dissension and uniting the people of the State'. But more than this, Dunstan stressed that the office of Governor 'is of vital importance in any system of Government which follows the Westminster precedent', because, he argued, it 'ensure[s] that the Executive of the State acts in accordance with the authority given to the Executive by the legislature and generally by law'.[101] In welcoming Australia's first Indigenous Governor, Dunstan had also laid down the constraints and duties of vice-regal office, as he understood them.

'I know that you will be a much loved Governor of this State', Dunstan exclaimed: 'We believe that your stay in South Australia will be a great one.'[102] Alas, Sir Douglas Nicholls remained in post for only 150 days, until 30 April 1977, when he was forced to retire through ill-health, following a stroke. But in his short time as Governor, 'Pastor Doug' hosted the Queen in March 1977 during her royal tour, although the task fell principally to Lady Nicholls and his Lieutenant-Governor as he was already ill. More profoundly, perhaps, as the first Aboriginal Governor, he was an honoured guest at Proclamation Day at Glenelg. As Robert Foster and Amanda Nettelbeck have observed: 'One can only wonder what Governor Nicholls thought when he attended the Proclamation Day ceremony in 1976 and heard the 1836 promises of justice to Aboriginal people read out loud.'[103]

Douglas 'Doug' Ralph Nicholls was born on 9 December 1906 at Cummeragunja Aboriginal Mission on the Murray River in New South Wales, the fifth child of Herbert Nicholls and Florence Atkinson.[104] He grew up at Cummeragunja in what Richard Broome has described as the settlement's 'golden years of Aboriginal autonomy'.[105] Yet this veneer of independence was steadily chipped away, the Aborigines Protection Board in New South Wales in 1909 acquiring new powers which, among other things, allowed it to disperse Indigenous communities. Aboriginal workers were now expected to find employment in the wider world, taking their chances where they could. In 1915, Doug Nicholls' sister Hilda was forcibly removed from the Mission and sent to Cootamundra Girls' Home, some 185 miles away, to train as a domestic servant. For Nicholls this was a traumatic but formative experience, the police's rough handling of his mother as she fought to prevent her daughter's removal, seared into his consciousness for all time.[106] Four years later, in 1919, when the Aborigines Protection Board decided to cease all farming activities in the vicinity, Nicholls himself was forced to leave the security of the Mission and his family to seek employment elsewhere. Aged fourteen, he found work initially with the dredging teams constructing levees on the Murray.

Nicholls' introduction to the world beyond Cummeragunja led him inexorably to the bright lights of Melbourne. He had already demonstrated exceptional ability (and acquired something of a reputation) in Australian Rules circles, and, after trying out unsuccessfully for Carlton in 1927, signed with Northcote Victorian Football Association team. Although short he was extremely fast, earning him the nickname 'the Flying Abo', a term devoid of the pejorative connotations one would detect today and instead a mark of affection and esteem.[107] In 1931, Nicholls decided to try his hand as a professional boxer, joining a travelling boxing show. But he proved a better footballer than boxer, and a year later he had signed on with the Fitzroy Victorian Football League team, playing fifty-four games for Fitzroy over six seasons before knee trouble led him to reluctantly give up the game.

By then another chapter had opened in Nicholls' life. Following his mother's death, he revisited the Northcote Church of Christ chapel they had briefly attended together, and on 17 July 1932 he experienced a religious conversion. He 'confessed Christ', as he put it.[108] A fortnight later he was baptised, the beginning of a journey that would lead to his being ordained as a Churches of Christ pastor in 1945. But his Christian faith also led him into Aboriginal activism, encouraged by William Cooper, a fellow Christian and founder of the Australian Aborigines' League (AAL), who recognised Nicholls' leadership abilities. Together, they lobbied the Commonwealth Government, pressing for Federal control of Aboriginal affairs, aiming to place Aboriginal aspirations centre stage and to achieve nation-wide policies and standards instead of the widely different treatment afforded by individual States. Nicholls was at the seminal Aboriginal 'Day of Mourning' protest in Sydney on 26 January 1938. As 'footy' star and devout Christian, he attracted respectful attention in the wider community, enhanced by his demure manner. As John Ramsland and Christopher Mooney have observed:

> The juxtaposition of Doug's conservative image and his provocative stance made his contribution that more important ... Doug's conservative persona (broad smile, greying hair, smartly dressed genteelness now with broad-rimmed black glasses) provided the AAL with a non-threatening spokesman who was known and liked by many in the white community.

The familiarity, comfort and security that Doug engendered made it easier for the AAL to communicate its radical message. With Doug as spokesman, the white community was more willing to listen, to be challenged and perhaps to accept the possibility of change.[109]

This was to be Nicholls' public strategy for the rest of his career, to project an almost 'Establishment' image but to use this effectively to promote his radical agenda in support of Aboriginal rights. In June 1941 he enlisted in the Citizen Military Forces, and after training was posted to the 29th Battalion. However, his military service was short-lived, and he was discharged on compassionate grounds in January 1942, allegedly to act as mediator in attempts to diffuse the growing tensions between servicemen and Aboriginal residents in Fitzroy, Melbourne. Less than three months later, Nicholls' beloved brother Dowie died as a result of a road accident, and on Boxing Day that year Doug Nicholls married Dowie's widow, Gladys. Initially a compassionate gesture, designed to care for Gladys and her three children, the marriage soon developed into a loving partnership. Together, they had another three children.

Nicholls had begun religious services and pastoral care activities in an Aboriginal home in Fitzroy in 1942, and in January 1943 he inaugurated 'Aboriginal Sunday', with memorable performances by a gum leaf orchestra and choir. By 1955, Aboriginal Sunday had shifted to July and had laid the foundations for what would become later the National Aborigines and Islanders Day Observance Committee (NAIDOC) week.[110] Following his ordination, Nicholls established an energetic ministry at Gore Street chapel, Fitzroy, where he and Gladys proved adept fundraisers, among other things founding an Aboriginal Girls' Hostel in 1956 and purchasing holiday units for Indigenous people. He protested against the Woomera rocket range and its impact on the Aboriginal population of the Warburton Ranges, and in 1957 joined the reconstituted Aborigines Welfare Board in Victoria as one of its two Indigenous representatives. In May of the same year he help set up the Victorian Aborigines Advancement League, one of his collaborators being the prominent Federal Labor MP Gordon Bryant, Nicholls working as the League's paid field officer and spokesman. In 1958, with his gift for organisation, he helped found the Federal Council for Aboriginal Advancement, serving as field officer in 1961 and Victorian secretary (1962–1963).

By now Nicholls was a prominent figure of national stature. In September 1963, for example, he was a member of an Aboriginal deputation that met Prime Minister Robert Menzies to discuss Indigenous participation in the new 'developing the North' program. Nicholls had met Menzies on a number of occasions, so it was natural he should lead the discussion. The banter between Nicholls and Menzies is revealing, indicating not only friendly intimacy but also Nicholls' assured self-confidence and innate sense of equality. As Mavis Thorpe Clark tells it:

> As an old campaigner, Doug softened up the approach. He knew that Sir Robert followed Carlton football team and held the club's No. 1 ticket, so he asked, 'What are you going to do to liven up Carlton next season Sir Robert?'
>
> Sir Robert replied, 'The same as you're going to do at Fitzroy.'
>
> While the Aborigines had been waiting at the airport for a car to pick them up to take them to Parliament House, they had seen a group of Indian diplomats arriving. The Indians had been greeted with great ceremony – they received 'the red carpet treatment', according to Doug. He now asked the Prime Minister, 'Why doesn't Australia have an Aboriginal diplomat, Sir Robert?'
>
> Sir Robert looked sideways at Gordon Bryant, who is the Labor Member for Wills.
>
> 'You stand for the Liberals in Wills, Doug,' he said, 'and I'll make you a diplomat.'[111]

Nicholls many achievements did not go unnoticed. He was appointed MBE in 1957 (his son Ralph insisted that the initials stood for 'More Black than Ever'), OBE in 1958, and knighted in 1972, the first Aboriginal person to receive the honour. Typically, he remarked, 'I hope being called "sir" will make officialdom listen more closely to me. Officialdom gave it to me – maybe now they'll take notice of me.'[112] However, as Nicholls was aware, he was facing criticism from younger, yet more radical Aboriginal activists who saw him as staid and too ready to be happily accommodated within the 'white man's world'. He had opposed the introduction of American 'black power' ideology into the AAL, resigning in 1969, although later re-joining once the League had moderated its position. Nonetheless, the 'black power' controversy had affected his physical and mental health, and when in low spirits he admitted to himself:

> I have failed ... Some of the younger Aborigines don't regard me as progressive. But in public life I am dealing with men of my age. Young people can't get through to these people . . . I have bellowed from Parliament House and from the ashes of the camp-fire. I have represented the State [Victoria] six times at football, dined with the Queen, walked with the highest in the land, yet what have we accomplished? What more can be done? What more can I do? Eventide has come. We have finished our course. We have kept faith.[113]

Douglas Nicholls had once dreamed of becoming the first Aboriginal Member of the Federal Parliament. That honour fell to Neville Bonner, who was elected to the Senate in 1971. However, Nicholls did become the first Indigenous State Governor in Australia, arguably a far higher honour. It was a pity that his appointment prompted such prejudice and controversy, and more so that he was forced by ill health to resign after only 150 days. Poor health continued to dog his retirement. He died on 4 June 1988, and was buried in the Aboriginal cemetery at Cummeragunja. Gladys, Lady Nicholls had predeceased him in 1981.

Keith Seaman
(1 September 1977 – 28 March 1982)

The sudden departure of Douglas Nicholls from Government House presented Premier Don Dunstan with a major problem. As he explained, when 'Sir Douglas Nicholls did not recover from his stroke he was obliged to resign, and we looked for a new nominee to the office. It was difficult to find someone who was above political commitment to party, and who was also prominent and of proven public service'.[114] Dunstan alighted upon Revd Keith Seaman, 'the minister of the Central Methodist Mission, who had an outstanding record of care for the poor and underprivileged'.[115] Indeed, in 1976 Seaman had been appointed OBE for his services to aged care, social welfare and the Uniting Church (of which the Methodist Church had become an integral part). When the invitation arrived, Seaman found it 'a complete shock', totally unexpected and not something he had ever considered.[116] Nonetheless, he accepted with alacrity, becoming Governor of South Australia on 1 September 1977.

Less than six months later a scandal of sorts broke. The Adelaide journalist Stewart Cockburn came to see Dunstan 'in some excitement and asked was the Governor going to resign. I told him no, nor did I know of any reason why he should. I was mystified'.[117] On 23 February 1978, Dunstan was approached by Robin Millhouse, the Australian Democrat MP in the State Parliament. He too asked whether the Governor was about to resign, and warned that he was going to raise the matter in the House. Again, Dunstan expressed bewilderment, until Millhouse explained 'that the Governor, prior to his appointment, had signed the register at a motel to spend time there on an assignation, and that this had been his habit up till not long before his appointment'.[118] As Angela Woollacott put it bluntly, Seaman had been having an 'extramarital affair'.[119] The news soon leaked to the press, with an embarrassed Seaman having to admit publicly his 'grave impropriety'.[120]

As Millhouse explained in letters to inquiring constituents and others, he was shocked by Seaman's erstwhile behaviour: 'I regarded it, and still do, as quite wrong in one who is now Governor of South Australia.' He added that he had spoken personally to Governor Seaman: 'I expressed my opinion and told him that I saw no alternative to his resigning his office.' More generally, Millhouse insisted, the 'holder of the office of Governor as the Queen's representative should be above reproach and seen to be above reproach. If he is not, then the high office itself may be damaged. The Governor will not be accepted with the respect and confidence accorded to his predecessors'.[121]

Dunstan, however, took a more relaxed view – as well he might, for he was hardly in a position to cast the first stone, given his own complex personal life. He pointed out that the indiscretion had been committed before Seaman was appointed as Governor, and had not continued thereafter. Moreover, Dunstan observed, Seaman 'had appeared before the disciplinary tribunal of his Church, which counselled him and found him to be a minister of good standing. That being so', Dunstan continued, 'it was a matter between his Church, his family, and himself, and nobody else's business'.[122] The South Australian public appeared to see it this way too, and the media frenzy soon abated as vice-regal life returned to normal. When the Queen and Prince Philip visited in October 1981, they stayed at Government House for several days. Her Majesty invested Governor Seaman as a Knight Commander of the Victorian Order – a very public royal seal of approval, and a high point of her visit.

Quite why Robin Millhouse had made such a fuss is open to debate. Known for his libertarian views on a range of topics – abortion, nudism, sex workers – his uncompromising stance on this issue seemed out of character, perhaps. But, as Robert Martin has noted, Millhouse often claimed to be the 'real opposition' in Parliament, effective where the Liberals were not, and in particular had since 'the 1950s . . . enjoyed sparring and feuding with Mr Dunstan'.[123] The Seaman affair, it seems, was another stick with which to beat Dunstan, not least as his two earlier vice-regal appointments – Oliphant and Nicholls – had in their separate ways not been entirely successful. Paradoxically, after this initial glitch, Seaman proved an adept and popular Governor, as Dunstan had hoped. He performed his routine duties quietly and efficiently, and there were no constitutional crises. When Dunstan resigned, the premiership moved smoothly to his deputy, Des Corcoran, and when Labor lost the State election in September 1979 the baton was passed without incident to David Tonkin, the Liberal leader.

Keith Douglas Seaman was born at McLaren Vale, South Australia, on 11 June 1920. He attended Unley High School and the University of Adelaide, where he gained BA and law degrees. During the Second World War he enlisted in the Australian Army but soon transferred to the Royal Australian Air Force, where he served as a Flight Lieutenant. One of his major tasks was assisting in the location and release of 300 Australian and New Zealand prisoners of war in Germany on the cessation of hostilities. In August 1946, shortly after his return from duty overseas, Seaman married Joan Birbeck. They had two children, a son John and daughter Chris. Seaman joined the

Methodist ministry and was ordained in 1954, his first appointment being to Renmark Methodist Church in the Riverland.

Four years later, Keith Seaman became Associate Minister at the Adelaide Central Mission, elevated to Superintendent in 1970. As Arnold Hunt has explained, the Mission was 'essentially a social service agency' whose 'dynamic was the Christian message', at its height employing hundreds of staff and volunteers.[124] Its activities ranged from alcohol rehabilitation to relief of the poor, and in the postwar era in which Seaman was involved there was great expansion in aged care, both the provision of care homes and day-care facilities for those who remained in their own properties. Funding came from individual donations and legacies, with increasing subsidies from government agencies to support the homes for the aged program.[125] As governments became ever more aware of the importance of such Mission work, so they were keen to enhance their levels of co-operation. On this basis, Keith Seaman was in 1973 appointed to the National Commission on Social Welfare set up by Gough Whitlam. And all this, as we have seen, caught the attention of Don Dunstan, leading to Seaman's appointment as Governor of South Australia in September 1977.

Sir Keith Seaman served as Governor for four years and 208 days, retiring on 28 March 1982. He and Joan, Lady Seaman, moved to Victor Harbor where they became deeply involved in local life. Sir Keith lectured to the local University of the Third Age, and led historical walking tours around Victor Harbor.[126] His growing interest in serious historical research led to his completion of a Master's thesis, 'The History and Influence of the Press in South Australia, 1836–1856', at Flinders University in 1987, and he was the author of several important articles. In 1986 he contributed a chapter on 'The South Australian Constitution Act of 1856' to the *Flinders History of South Australia*, a fitting subject for a former Governor versed in the law.[127] Likewise, he wrote on 'The Press and the Aborigines: South Australia's First Thirty Years' for the *Journal of the Historical Society of South Australia* in 1990. His summary was trenchant and discomforting:

Not surprisingly, the newspapers of the Colony's first thirty years reveal significant changes in the attitude of the white settlers to the native

Aboriginal population. From the original benevolent paternalism, it became irritation and then hostility. From the hostility there developed confrontation and killing. And through it all there was manipulation to satisfy the desire for more land occupation with less interference.[128]

In his retirement, Keith Seaman had become an historian of note, a specialist on his home State's early European settlement and its consequences. His wife Joan had predeceased him, and two years before his death aged ninety-three on 30 June 2013, he moved to Hobart to live with his daughter. A memorial service was held at Port Elliot Uniting Church on 16 July 2013.

Looking back over Don Dunstan's vice-regal appointments, Walter Crocker thought that Mark Oliphant could do no wrong. But he poured scorn on the two later Governors, perfunctorily dismissing Keith Seaman as 'a Methodist social-worker clergyman' and characterising the appointment of Douglas Nicholls as something of a gimmick, part of Dunstan's 'predilections' for Aboriginal affairs 'on a level that now seems more emotive than constructive'.[129] Dunstan's plans had certainly not always gone as intended but that is the nature of human affairs. What Dunstan had achieved, building on Steele Hall's earlier appointment of James Harrison, was the full 'Australianisation' of the vice-regal role in South Australia.

Chapter 8

ANOTHER DUNSTAN, A NEW MILLENNIUM

'Oh no! Haven't we had enough of that man!'[1]

Thus exclaimed an exasperated old lady in 1982 on learning that Donald Dunstan had been appointed Governor of South Australia. The horrified outburst was overheard by Robert Martin, author of the second volume of the prestigious *Responsible Government in South Australia*, who observed that this woman's angst was just one example among many of 'some sad temporary confusion' caused by the 'coincidence of his name with that of the recent Premier', Don Dunstan.[2] In fact, it was not entirely coincidental, as the new Governor and erstwhile Premier were distantly related, the former hailing from Murray Bridge and the latter having numerous relatives in the same area. 'Dunstan', after all, was a common Cornish surname in South Australia.[3] However, a shared name and heritage was about all the two men had in common.

Donald Beaumont Dunstan
(23 April 1982 – 5 February 1991)

David Tonkin, as Premier, was committed to the appointment of an Australian as Governor of South Australia. However, taking his cue from fellow Liberal and former Premier Steele Hall, whose recommendation had led to the appointment of Major General Sir James Harrison in 1968, Tonkin decided the State needed another senior military figure. Such individuals were invariably discreet and a safe pair of hands, with personal and leadership qualities honed over many years' service.

But there was, perhaps, another reason. Although Australia had withdrawn the last of its combat troops from Vietnam in March 1972, the divisive legacy of the war lived on.[4] Initially, public opinion had supported the war, and troops returning from Vietnam in the amphibious transport HMAS *Sydney* had been feted, according to Clem Lloyd and Jacqui Rees in their history of repatriation, 'with a patriotic fervour reminiscent of 1918–19 and 1945–46'.[5] However, later returnees came home by air, often arriving in the dead of night and dispersing in civilian clothes, this lack of visibility coinciding with an increasing hostility to Australia's participation in the war and to those who fought it. The Moratorium Movement emerged to organise large-scale anti-war demonstrations across Australia, attracting more than 200,000 participants. As the Department of Veterans' Affairs admitted: 'For Australia, the Vietnam War was the cause of the greatest social and political dissent since the conscription referendum in the First World War.'[6]

Many veterans felt they had returned home to an uncertain welcome, one alleging, for example, that 'the men and women who fought in Vietnam were, on their return, largely ignored by a society and abandoned by a government which ordered them to conduct its war'.[7] Another Vietnam veteran recalled that on his return to Australia in 1972, 'I was advised not to wear uniform as the public hated the sight of us! We were "rapists, murderers and war mongers"'.[8] In South Australia, Premier Don Dunstan echoed the growing opposition to the war. But he also joined in public criticism of Australian combatants: 'It is my belief that the war in Vietnam is totally immoral, and it is equally immoral to remain silent as Australian troops participate in its terror and slaughter.'[9]

Although the Vietnam legacy would rumble on into the third decade of the twenty-first century, by the early 1980s those troubled by the continuing divisions began to look for healing mechanisms. A more sympathetic assessment of those who had fought in Vietnam recognised that many had been traumatised by their experiences. Post-traumatic stress disorder (PTSD) had been clinically recognised in 1980, and in 1982 the Vietnam Veterans' Counselling Service was set up, initially in Adelaide, to help those who were suffering.[10]

It is against this background that the appointment of Lieutenant-General Sir Donald Beaumont Dunstan as Governor of South Australia in April 1982 is perhaps best understood. Dunstan was revered by the veteran community, especially those who had served in Vietnam, but also proved immensely popular with the general public. He was Governor for all of eight years and 288 days, at that time a record, and was credited with bringing the vice-regal role closer to the people. As a Vietnam veteran himself, he brought the war's legacy out of the shadows, and by his personal example showed the contributions that veterans could make to society. He later unveiled the Vietnam War Memorial in Torrens Parade Ground, Adelaide, former Premier Mike Rann commenting that 'I know Sir Donald's presence at the memorial unveiling meant a great deal to those who served in Vietnam'.[11]

Donald Beaumont Dunstan was born at Murray Bridge, South Australia, on 18 February 1923. In February 1940 he entered the Royal Military College Duntroon, graduating from what was a shortened wartime officer training course in June 1942.[12] He was posted to 27th Battalion as a platoon commander, seeing action against the Japanese during the Bougainville campaign in 1945, for which he was mentioned in despatches. After the war, Dunstan served as a staff officer in the British Commonwealth Occupation Force in Japan and was part of the cadre that formed the newly established Australian Regular Army in 1947. He married Beryl Dunningham in 1948, and that year relocated to Keswick Barracks in Adelaide, where he filled a number of staff appointments. In 1953, Dunstan was posted to 1st Battalion the Royal Australian Regiment (1RAR) and was appointed second-in-command before the unit's deployment to Korea in 1954–1955.

Between May 1964 and February 1965, Dunstan commanded 1RAR. He was then appointed to 1st Recruit Training Battalion, and thus commenced his long entwinement with Vietnam. Newly conscripted national servicemen, bound for Vietnam, were instructed to report to him directly. One such conscript, Rick Bentley, received his call-up notice in the post on 15 June 1965. 'You are hereby called up for national service', the letter read: 'You are required to present yourself to Colonel Dunstan at Army Training Depot, Docker Street, Wagga . . . You will catch the train leaving Albury at 8.47 am.'[13] The steely words were harbingers of strict military discipline and the harrowing operational deployments that would follow. But Dunstan himself had a reputation in the Army as a kindly and thoughtful man. One of the 'nashos' – national servicemen – eventually became Dunstan's batman. 'He and I got on very well, and I had a lot of respect for him', recalled the batman: 'He called me "Killer". He became a great man.'[14]

In January 1968, Dunstan arrived in Vietnam on the eve of the North Vietnamese TET offensive, becoming Deputy Commander of the Australian Task Force. A few months later, he took command of the Australians at Fire Support Base Coral and established a similar redoubt at Balmoral, strong points guarding the approaches to Saigon, the South Vietnamese capital. Dunstan swiftly endeared himself to the troops under his command. He was reckoned a 'leader of uncommon gifts', a man 'of few words and a winning smile'.[15] He was also a great delegator, one colleague commenting that he 'knew how to be lazy when it was sensible to be lazy'.[16] Ever concerned with improving morale, Dunstan overturned the 'dry' routine at Coral, ordering crates of beer. The bemused Americans responded by delivering sarsaparilla by helicopter, then Reschs Diet Lager.

Before Dunstan's arrival, Coral had already repulsed a determined enemy assault. The Australians had taken casualties but had consolidated their position. Having put his own stamp on Coral, Dunstan then decided to move one Australian battalion 4.5 kilometres to the north, to a new Fire Support Base he designated Balmoral, effectively taking the fight to the enemy. He also arranged the deployment of Centurion tanks of the 1st Armoured Regiment, whose immense firepower would soon prove their worth. Dunstan had witnessed the 'bunker busting' capacity of tanks in Bougainville during the Second World War and knew such capability would be important in Vietnam. As anticipated, the North Vietnamese attacked Balmoral in the small hours of 26 May 1968. Overall, the action around Fire Support Bases Coral and Balmoral lasted for almost four weeks. It was the first time an Australian all-arms brigade-size operation of some 3000 men had taken place since the Second World War. Twenty-six Australians were killed and ninety-nine wounded.[17] A conservative estimate put the number of North Vietnamese dead as more than 300.

From his pivotal role in the early days of Vietnam, first at Wagga Wagga and then at Coral and Balmoral, Donald Dunstan was also there at the end. In the rank of Major General, he was the last commander of the Australian Task Force in Vietnam, and in July 1971 was tasked with planning a phased withdrawal of Australian troops, to be completed by May 1972 in what became known as Operation Interfuse. His complex task was made more difficult by Prime Minister Billy McMahon's surprise announcement that all Australians would be home 'by Christmas', and that the National Service commitment would be reduced from two years to eighteen months with immediate effect. When it was pointed out that this would enable half of the 'nashos' to return to Australia at once, leaving other troops dangerously exposed, McMahon was forced to backtrack and adopt an alternative phased plan.[18] The withdrawal, masterminded by Dunstan, began in October 1971, with Australian commitments progressively handed over to the South Vietnamese, and indeed most were home by Christmas, the last of the combat troops leaving in March 1972.[19]

On his own return from Vietnam in early 1972, Donald Dunstan served in a number of staff and command jobs until January 1977 when he was promoted Lieutenant-General and appointed Chief of the General Staff. It was the highpoint of his military career, yet it was another daunting task. As the *Australian Army Journal* observed:

> After the turbulent 1960s, the acrimonious debate over conscription, and the end of the Vietnam War, the Army risked losing its way. It had lost much of the public regard that had been its birthright since the landing at Gallipoli. It was reduced in size and starved of resources. The challenges that faced the Army leadership of the late 1970s were quite simply daunting. But their response was both inspired and inspiring. They preserved the ethos and morale of our Army. Sir Donald Dunstan's finest contribution was made during this critical period.[20]

Dunstan's reorganisation of the Army in the early 1980s was crucial. The military's ability to respond so effectively to the East Timor crisis in 1999 was routinely attributed to Dunstan's reforms, his rapid response model also informing later deployments and operations. Likewise, he worked to rebuild self-esteem in the face of public criticism in the post-Vietnam era. As one Vietnam veteran recalled, soldiers were often reluctant to wear their uniform outside barracks 'but Don[ald] Dunstan changed that, and said you're in the Australian Army and you should be proud to wear your uniform.'[21]

At the height of his powers in the early 1980s (he was knighted in 1980), Dunstan on retirement from the Army would have been an attractive recruit for any senior position. It was to Premier David Tonkin's credit that he recognised the qualities Dunstan could bring to his home State, and he acted accordingly. As Beryl, Lady Dunstan, told the *Canberra Times* on the eve of her husband's appointment, 'I think it will be a challenge and I think it will also be just like another [Army] posting for us, only it will be a bit different. But I've got no doubt my husband will cope with it very well'. The newspaper decided that Lady Dunstan's experience of Army life – 'or, as she describes it, her marriage to the Army'– would also stand her in good stead for her role as 'South Australia's first lady'. She and her husband, she explained, had learned by long experience that you 'keep your opinions to yourself. That's the way it's got to be and that's the way it will be'. Indeed, she added: 'You're not political, you're not allowed to be political.' As in the Army, so in vice-regal office: 'Whatever Government's in is just fine and that's how it's got to be.'[22]

Contemplating Dunstan's forthcoming appointment as a presumed 'peaceful overseer', the conservative *Canberra Times* could not resist a less than thinly veiled jibe: 'Sir Donald will take up the reins after three controversial governors – Sir Mark Oliphant, Sir Douglas Nicholls, and Sir Keith Seaman – all appointed by the former [State] Labor Government.'[23] In the event, Governor Dunstan served happily with both Liberal and Labor Governments, David Tonkin being replaced by Labor's John Bannon, the latter enthusiastically extending Sir Donald's term of office. As Dunstan completed almost nine years in the post, the Adelaide *Advertiser* reflected on his achievements:

> Although publicly adopting a low-key profile, he has subtly brought Government House closer to the people ... Early in his term he noted that among the 3000 people invited to Government House each year, very few were young people. So he invited students from secondary schools to

vice-regal receptions. He also opened Government House and its gardens to regular public tours. Sir Donald and Lady Dunstan have travelled across the State in the vice-regal Rolls-Royce visiting major rural centres and remote Outback outposts.[24]

Not quite everyone agreed with this positive assessment, however, as the caustic and sometimes jaundiced pen of Walter Crocker revealed. According to Crocker, Dunstan was 'a bully, unbalanced about personal loyalty to him, unfair, unjust, violent temper'.[25] Moreover, the Dunstans could not keep staff, Crocker alleged, some twenty-six employees at Government House supposedly having been dismissed during the Governor's term of office. Yet Governor Dunstan's conciliatory public persona seemed entirely benign. He had brought people together and was a unifying influence in the State, especially after the trauma of Vietnam, his lengthy term of office conferring a sense of stability and continuity. In his retirement, Dunstan continued to cultivate his low-profile style, enjoying his fly-fishing hobby and pursuing cross-country skiing whenever he got the chance. In the military way, having relinquished his post, he wished to give his successors a free hand and to be seen not to interfere. Unfortunately, when subsequently he declined invitations to Government House, this was interpreted as a snub.[26] Sir Donald Dunstan lived quietly in Adelaide until his death on 15 October 2011, aged 88.

Roma Flinders Mitchell
(6 February 1991 – 21 July 1996)

When it was announced that Dame Roma Mitchell was to be appointed Governor of South Australia in succession to Sir Donald Dunstan, she was invited to visit Government House to be shown the ropes.[27] She felt, rightly or wrongly, that Sir Donald and Lady Dunstan gave her a frosty reception. She was a woman. She was not married. She was also somewhat advanced in years, being 78 years old when she took office. Yet none of these attributes, considered 'unusual' at the time by some, proved in any way an impediment. Quite the contrary – throughout her career Roma Mitchell had achieved a number of outstanding 'firsts', and the governorship of South Australia was to be no exception.

Roma Flinders Mitchell was born in Adelaide on 2 October 1913, the second and youngest daughter of Harold Mitchell and Maude Wickham. Her father was killed in the battle of Dernancourt on the Western Front in April 1918, leaving her mother to struggle on a widows' military pension and by taking in lodgers. But Maude was determined that her daughter should have a good education, and Roma, a Catholic, attended St Aloysius College in Adelaide run by the Sisters of Mercy. She finished dux of the school and won a bursary to study law at the University of Adelaide. There she became involved in student politics, displaying the keen sense of social justice that would motivate her throughout her life, and when prevented from joining the all-male Law Students' Society formed the Women's Law Students' Society instead. Completing her studies, she won the award for the most outstanding law student of her year.[28]

Roma Mitchell was admitted to the Bar in 1934, practising as a barrister. She also taught Family Law at the University of Adelaide. Over the next twenty-eight years she developed what Sir William Dean, himself a senior judge and later Governor-General of Australia, would call 'a formidable professional reputation, particularly as a noted advocate'.[29] In 1962 she became the first woman in Australia to be made Queen's Counsel, and in 1965 was appointed judge of the Supreme Court of South Australia, the first woman ever to serve in an Australian superior court. Her singular ambition, penetrating powers of analysis and forensic skills led some to imagine that Roma Mitchell QC must be an unsmiling and somewhat intimidating practitioner of the Law, dedicated to her career and possibly little else. But those who knew her well were aware that the exact opposite was true. Rex Jory, writing in the *Advertiser*, thought her 'courteous, lively, amusing, frank, with an enchanting lateral view on most subjects'. People, he said, 'were enthralled not only by her logic but by her freedom and originality of her argument'.[30]

Close friends were always delighted by Mitchell's impish sense of humour, and sometimes the stories told by and about her reached wider currency. In the estimation of Susan Magarey and Kerrie Round in their splendid biography, such anecdotes 'have become legend'.[31] For example, not long after having been appointed to the Supreme Court, an insensitive (presumably male) journalist asked cheekily: 'You are not married?' 'I am not,' she replied brusquely. 'And you do not drive a car?' 'I do not,' responded Mitchell. The journalist continued, pushing his luck: 'The Chief Justice, Dr Bray, is also unmarried. Is there any chance that the two of you might get together?' 'No,' shot back Roma Mitchell, 'that would be no good at all. He doesn't drive a car either.'[32] (That Bray was reputedly gay was neither here nor there.)

The Honourable Justice Mitchell, as a Supreme Court judge, had a small secretarial staff, complemented by tipstaves and associates. Tipstaves were general assistants, while associates had a formal legal background and spent a term each as interns, assisting in court matters and other legal business. In all, Roma Mitchell had thirteen associates over her eighteen years as Supreme Court judge, and not surprisingly most had a story to tell. In one colourful tale, Mitchell had gone out for lunch on a Thursday, as was her usual routine, but on this occasion had decided to return early to chambers. She surprised her associate and a companion in an intimate embrace, 'locked together in a tangle of half-discarded clothes on the table'. 'Oh really,' she exclaimed: 'That's where I eat my lunch!'[33] A further story was recounted by another associate:

> When we were in Sydney, we were going out, and while Dame Roma changed, she asked me if I would pop into the laundry and pick up her washing that she'd . . . stuck in the dryer. When I picked it up, I discovered it was leopard-print underwear. So I dashed back to the room. 'Roma, you're wearing leopard-print underwear!' She said, 'Yes, I know. Isn't it gorgeous?'[34]

As Magarey and Round admit, Roma Mitchell 'looked fierce enough, facing the court in her long black robe and horsehair wig with fashionably heavy black-rimmed glasses'. But, they explained, 'her fierceness was most often reserved for counsel not doing their job properly'.[35] The pompous would be taken down a peg or two and those who had not prepared their cases sufficiently would be subject to her devastating wit. According to the *National Times* newspaper, on one occasion a private investigator had appeared before her, giving evidence in a divorce hearing. The investigator told Justice Mitchell that, pursuing the case, he had lingered outside a bedroom, 'and had heard the unmistakeable sounds of sexual intercourse'. 'And what,' retorted Justice Mitchell, 'are the unmistakeable sounds of sexual intercourse?'[36]

Such stories, told and retold, and enjoyed by Roma Mitchell herself, reflected her status as a woman in what had been considered hitherto a man's world. But it would be wrong to imagine that she was in any way complicit in what might look like attempts to trivialise or belittle. Again, quite the contrary – alongside her sometimes self-deprecating humour was a profound commitment to the feminist cause. In her early days as Queen's Counsel, she had supported efforts to allow women to sit on juries, and was credited with changing Premier Thomas Playford's mind on the issue.[37] Likewise, as a QC, she had persistently advocated equal pay for equal work in an era when women generally were remunerated poorly compared to their male counterparts. At a time when the Women's Liberation movement was often viewed with alarm, Roma Mitchell became the 'acceptable "face" of the new feminism', and as such was invited by the Australian Broadcasting Commission to present the prestigious Boyer Lectures during 1975, International Women's Year.[38] Her stand sometimes brought her into conflict with Chief Justice John Bray, not least when he warned juries to treat warily uncorroborated testimony of sexual assault. Bray even refused to use the increasingly popular prefix 'Ms', an obstinacy Mitchell criticised publicly on several occasions, her comments serving as both condemnation of his misogyny and 'a fond tease' – for they were actually firm friends.[39]

From 1970 to 1981, Roma Mitchell chaired the South Australian Criminal Law and Penal Methods Reform Committee, which under her vigorous leadership led to major reforms in areas as disparate as rape, suicide, the bail system, protection of the rights of the accused, and compensation for victims of crime.[40] More generally, Roma Mitchell was a vocal advocate of human rights, and in 1981 became the first chair of the Australian Human Rights Commission, a position she held until 1986. In this role she was especially concerned for the human rights and needs of Indigenous Australians. Likewise, she lent her support to a wide range of charitable organisations, notably the Ryder-Cheshire Foundation of which she became

Australian national president. Her engagement with public life was reflected in her appointment in 1983 as Chancellor of the University of Adelaide, the first woman to hold the position, serving until 1990. In the previous year she had been appointed DBE.

As a judge of the Supreme Court, Roma Mitchell was often in the public eye, notably in February 1978 when she was appointed to lead a Royal Commission to inquire into and report upon the dismissal of Police Commissioner Harold Salisbury (see p. 188). She found the sacking was justified. Moreover, she observed that Salisbury's expressed belief that his responsibility was to the Law and to the Crown, and not to any popularly elected representative government, 'suggests an absence of understanding of the constitutional system of South Australia or, for that matter, of the United Kingdom'.[41] During the Vietnam War, Mitchell was sometimes a dissenting voice on the Full Court, unwilling to consent without careful analysis to the conviction of (usually young) people charged with public order offences. On another occasion, when an elderly woman appeared before her on abortion charges, Justice Mitchell noted that the woman had been charged with similar offences six times between 1932 and 1968, and had served four prison sentences. Drawing attention to the woman's age and ill health, Justice Mitchell observed that on this occasion the woman had not been entirely responsible for her actions. She had been pressured into performing an abortion, and Mitchell told her that 'you are coming towards the end of your life and you don't want to be doing these things now'.[42] The woman was released on a bond of $500, with a requirement to be of good behaviour for three years. This included a proviso that she should move from the house where she had lived for forty-six years, so as to be less readily approached by those seeking abortions.

Roma Mitchell retired from the Bench in 1983, aged seventy, devoting subsequent years to a variety of good works (including personally delivering Meals on Wheels), until approached by Premier John Bannon with the suggestion that she become the next Governor of South Australia. Having duly accepted, she took up her post in February 1991, in the process becoming the first woman to hold any vice-regal position in Australia. She brushed aside comments from the press about being single – would she play at being both Governor and Governor's wife? – and created the position of comptroller, a live-in official who would oversee all domestic arrangements in Government House. Having settled in, Governor Mitchell swiftly established her daily routine. She rose at 7 am, partaking of a light breakfast in her upstairs rooms. By 9 am she was at her desk, a schedule to hand detailing her forthcoming commitments, including preparations for Executive Council meetings when Parliament was sitting. She wrote all her own speeches.

No sooner had Governor Mitchell commenced her duties, than Premier John Bannon briefed her about the unfolding crisis in the State Bank. Bannon took full responsibility for the Bank's failure, averting the possibility of a constitutional crisis in which the Governor might possibly have to intervene. Bannon resigned his commission in September 1992, and Lynn Arnold smoothly replaced him as Premier. As Governor Mitchell observed: 'This is South Australia. We do not have constitutional crises.' There was never, she said, the likelihood of any situation 'which would call for any intervention'.[43] Her role, she emphasised, was to watch, and if necessary to warn.

Like Governor Dunstan before her, Roma Mitchell had set out to promote cohesion and optimism across the State, although her style was very different. She was warm, down-to-earth, approachable and amusing, as well as genuinely keen to meet people from all walks of life. She particularly relished the opportunity to visit far-flung parts of the State, including the Anangu Pitjantjatjara Yankunytjatjara (AYP) Aboriginal lands in the remote north-west of South Australia. A staunch monarchist – at least while Elizabeth II remained on the throne – Governor Mitchell welcomed a succession of royal visitors to the State: the Queen herself and Prince Philip in February 1992, the Duke of Gloucester in March 1993, Prince Edward in March and November 1994 and Princess Michael of Kent in April 1995. She went on to visit the Queen in Windsor Castle, and made official trips to New Zealand and to China. She remained actively supportive of the Women's Movement, albeit discreetly in non-political ways. On 11 February 1994, for example, she attended an ecumenical service in St Peter's Cathedral in Adelaide to commemorate the Women's Suffrage Centenary.[44]

Governor Mitchell became a much-loved figure throughout the State. She was also loved by Government House staff. She remembered their birthdays and gave them gifts at Christmas. When it was time for her to relinquish her post, the staff found it difficult to say goodbye: 'They wept when she walked out of that front door and away.'[45] Sir William Deane, himself a very popular Governor-General, mused: 'For my part, I venture to suggest that there has been no better loved vice regal representative in the whole history of this land.'[46]

In her retirement, Roma Mitchell remained characteristically active in numerous organisations and events, until being diagnosed with terminal bone cancer in February 2000. She died less than a month later, on 5 March. She was accorded a State funeral. John Bannon, the former Premier, summed up Roma Mitchell's life with telling accuracy: 'She epitomised Australia in the 20th Century. She was in the van of social legislation changes throughout the second half of the century. She wouldn't shirk from being a standard bearer.'[47]

Eric James Neal
(22 July 1996 – 3 November 2001)

Among the tributes to Dame Roma Mitchell after her death, was that paid by the then Governor, Sir Eric Neal. 'She was a lady for whom I had the utmost respect, admiration and affection', he said. 'Her advice was always freely given, pragmatic and helpful, she had wisdom, a commonsense approach to issues, a ready sense of humour . . . She believed in service.'[48]

Governor Neal had succeeded Roma Mitchell in July 1996. He was the first Governor of the State from an Australian business background but alongside his commercial success he too had long experience of service in promotion of the public good. Born in London, England, on 24 June 1924, Eric Neal immigrated to South Australia with his parents when he was two-and-a-half years old, the family settling in Adelaide. In 1950, he married Thelma Joan Bowden at St Peter's Church, Glenelg. They had two sons, the first born in Broken Hill in 1951, the second at Ballarat in 1963.

Eric Neal's childhood was described as 'Happy but financially constrained'.[49] Unfortunately, family circumstances 'foreshortened his early education', but this disability only 'redoubled his passion for learning over the years that followed'.[50] He was required to leave school at the age of sixteen as his parents could not afford for him to stay on but, undaunted, he was soon training to be an engineer at the South Australian School of Mines (later part of the South Australian Institute of Technology, now the University of South Australia). Alongside his undoubted technical abilities, Neal quickly demonstrated entrepreneurial skills and a commercial acumen which would propel him shortly into the forefront of Australian economic life, in the process earning him a reputation as a 'tough, frequently autocratic businessman'.[51] His fourteen years as Chief Executive Officer (CEO) of Boral are routinely cited as the pinnacle of his career but his commercial activities extended in numerous directions, including as director of Broken Hill Proprietary, John Fairfax Holdings, Cocoa-Cola Amatil, and AMP Limited, as well as chair of Westpac and Atlas Copco Australia Pty Ltd.

Yet it was Boral that made Neal's reputation. When he took over as CEO in 1973, the Australian economy was in the doldrums, reflected in weakening business confidence. Neal was looking for opportunities to expand Boral's activities, including overseas acquisitions, but bided his time until conditions improved. His big chance came in 1978 when Neal learned that Amalco, a Hawaiian-based company manufacturing concrete products, was in difficulties. Amalco had entered the Australian market in the early 1970s, acquiring concrete plants in Sydney, Melbourne and Adelaide. The Adelaide factory had recently purchased a concrete roof tile machine, a considerable advance in its manufacturing capability, and it was part of the package acquired by Neal in his negotiations with Amalco. Following some modifications, the machine was soon working efficiently, allowing Boral to corner a sizeable part of the South Australian roof tile market. Subsequently, Amalco approached Neal with a 50–50 share plan to shore up an ailing tile plant in California. The deal was clinched, with Boral acquiring 55% in 1979. This proved to be the lynchpin of Boral's expansion in North America. Six months later they bought the California plant outright, to which was added a new tile-making factory in Texas and another in California.[52]

Historically, California had used timber shingles or 'shakes' for roofing but bushfires had made these vulnerable. Soon after the Boral acquisitions, shakes were outlawed, opening the way for concrete tiles. In 1980, concrete tiles had only a 5% share of the Californian roofing market – by 2020 it stood at 75%. Indeed, by the late 1970s, under Eric Neal's leadership, Boral had established itself as a major player in the building and construction industries, both in Australia and the United States. A brick company had been purchased in Augusta, Georgia, in 1980, for example, as Boral sought further diversification. Closer to home, Boral acquired a controlling share of Quarry Industries, 'the jewel in South Australia's quarrying crown', including the historic Stonyfell Quarry in the Adelaide Hills, which had been worked since the State's early days.[53] The variety of acquisitions was not as ad hoc as sometimes appeared, as Neal oversaw the introduction of a computer modelling program that assessed the numerous variables involved to indicate whether a proposed purchase was viable or not. This was reckoned to be 'Eric Neal's secret weapon', as the *Australian Business Magazine* put it in October 1991: 'If the computer says "go", Boral moves.'[54]

Such modelling gave Boral the confidence to acquire BMI in 1982, a company which operated quarries in New South Wales and had interests in quarries elsewhere in Australia. In doing so, Boral also gained BMI bases in the United Kingdom and Indonesia, further strengthening its international profile. Despite the complexity of acquisitions, Neal maintained a simple, small management team. There were only fifty employees in Boral's head office in the early 1980s, and strategic planning was confined to an elite group. As the *Business Review Weekly* reported, Neal's team operated in a manner 'straight out of the management textbooks'.[55] In the eight years since taking over, Neal had added some $400 million worth of new businesses to the Boral Group. He retired as Boral's CEO in June 1987, but remained on the board until April 1992. In the year Eric Neal retired, Boral's operating profit was $178.1 million, compared with $12.6 million in 1973 when he took over – an increase of 141.3%. It had been an impressive performance.

Eric Neal was knighted in 1982. Alongside his business career was a distinguished role in public life. He chaired various government advisory bodies, and served as National Chairman of the Duke of Edinburgh's Award (1984–1992), President of the Order of Australia Association (1989–1992), and chair of the Opera Foundation (1990–1996). Neal was also Chief Commissioner of the City of Sydney (1987–1988). His interest in the armed forces led to his appointment in 1981 to the committee charged with reshaping Australia's defence organisation, and in 1992 he was awarded the United States Department of Defense Medal for Distinguished Public Service in recognition of his contribution to managing Australian events commemorating the 50th anniversary of the Battle of the Coral Sea.

Sir Eric Neal's appointment as Governor of South Australia in July 1996 reflected his wide experience in commercial and public life. He and Lady Neal settled swiftly into Government House routine, with the usual round of events and receptions. As ever, guests invited to garden parties and the like were selected from a broad spectrum of South Australian life. Even for the most worldly wise, such occasions could be daunting, as Adelaide journalist Des Ryan revealed. 'When the invitation arrived to attend a drinks party at Government House to celebrate the Queen's Birthday, I must admit I left the gold embossed card on my desk for a good while', he recalled. Eventually the evening in question arrived, and he and 'The Escort' set off for Government House. As they walked along North Terrace, having parked the car, Ryan suddenly remembered that he had not received an entrée card:

I casually mentioned to The Escort that for some reason no entrée card for the occasion had arrived, as should have been the case once you've RSVPeed.

Never mind, I added lightly, the original invitation in my pocket would no doubt suffice. In fact, without the entrée card, I seriously doubted we would get past the front gate but there was no point in putting The Escort in more of nervous tizz than she was already in.

You can imagine my surprise, then, when the security guards simply waved us through. As we crunched our way up the gravel driveway, however, an even more horrible thought struck me – I could not actually recall RSVPeeing.

Here we were, me in a tux and black tie and her dressed to kill, about to gatecrash Government House.

By now we were at the front door and I expected to be turned away, embarrassingly, at any moment. I felt obliged at this stage to whisper to The Escort that there may have been just the teeniest oversight concerning the RSVP. She stiffened and I had to pull her along by the wrist, whimpering.[56]

Much to his surprise (and relief), Des Ryan and The Escort were ushered straight through, their coats taken, and they found themselves in the queue, waiting to be welcomed by the Governor, Sir Eric Neal, and Lady Neal:

> I began to relax – then noticed the liveried man around the corner who was taking people's entrée cards and calling out their names as they were being greeted by Sir Eric. The Escort groaned and wobbled.
>
> Here, finally, crunch time had come and it was too late, with the Governor in arm's reach, to quietly slip away. Oh St Jude, I thought, we're done for here.
>
> I handed over the invitation card, to the man in livery, with a whispered, 'Ahem, this is rather embarrassing but . . . ' and the dear chap did not bat an eyelid but announced us loudly as if we were to the manor born.
>
> 'So nice to meet you again,' said Sir Eric, shaking hands. Again? Er, I could not say for certain that I had never met him, not one-to-one anyway, but who was I to argue in the circumstances?[57]

This story, although no doubt tongue-in-cheek, says much about the anxieties and self-doubts experienced by many hesitant Government House guests over the years. Likewise, Sir Eric's calm familiarity, designed to put the guest at his or her ease, was a technique that successive Governors had honed with consummate skill. This was a polished but routine courtesy. Diplomacy of a higher order was required when Governor Neal attended the Proclamation Day ceremony at Glenelg on 28 December 1999. Although Proclamation Day remained an important event in South Australia's diary, the contrast between the noble aspirations in Governor Hindmarsh's original address and the reality of the subsequent treatment of Indigenous Australians was for many now an acute discomfort. Just a month earlier, the Ngarrindjeri people had issued their own proclamation at the construction site of the controversial Hindmarsh Island bridge and, now, at Glenelg on 28 December, Sir Eric Neal formally accepted a declaration from representatives of South Australia's Aboriginal community, the statement echoing the Ngarrindjeri proclamation, 'denouncing the unlawful nature and genocidal impact of colonisation, and . . . asserting ongoing Aboriginal sovereignty in South Australia'.[58]

85. East Entrance, Government House, Adelaide

86. Federation Window, Government House

87. The Library, Government House

88. The Small Dining Room, Government House

89. The Small Drawing Room, Government House

90. The State Dining Room, Government House

91. The Adelaide Room, Government House

92. Government House today

93. The State Entrance, Government House

Eric Neal's diplomatic skills had also been developed during his Boral years, especially when dealing with senior executives in America during acquisition negotiations. Now, as Governor, this international experience was put to good use, as he led trade missions to Malaysia, Sweden, Shan Dong province in China, and the United States.[59] Following his retirement as Governor in November 2001, Eric Neal was no less active. He chaired the South Australian Government Road Safety Advisory Council between 2003 and 2011, and supported the Australian Institute of Company Directors, of which he was a life member.[60] Listing the qualities required of a company director in the twenty-first century, Sir Eric stressed the importance of a 'listen-and-learn approach', of asking probing questions of management, getting 'out of the boardroom at every opportunity', and, above all, undertaking 'continuing education'.[61]

Neal reiterated the latter point in his role as Chancellor of Flinders University from early 2002 to 2010. As he explained, when he became CEO at Boral in 1973 he recognised the value of forging closer links between universities and business. 'When we started working together', he said, 'the academics realised that industry could use their services and would pay them for their work, while industry realised they had access to a whole range of people with skills and knowledge that they could never assemble themselves in an in-house research department'. Moreover, he continued: 'Education is even more important today than when I was young. People take on roles today with the chance that in 20 or 30 years that role will have changed, or even disappeared.'[62]

Alongside his educational work, Eric Neal also pursued his interest in military and defence matters. He was Honorary Colonel of the Royal South Australia Regiment, and led the fundraising appeal to erect a war memorial in the Torrens Parade Ground in Adelaide for all Aboriginal and Torres Strait Islander people who had served in the armed forces. He was the inaugural chair of the Veterans' Advisory Council, formed in April 2008 to promote the wellbeing of South Australian veterans and to advise the State Government on veterans' affairs. Sir Eric was commended by the Minister for Veterans' Affairs 'for his capable leadership and splendid example', and he also acted as a 'community pulse' to help gauge public perceptions of the then forthcoming ANZAC Centenary preparations.[63] By now, of course, Eric Neal was also enjoying his retirement pursuits, which included sailing and watching horseracing and football.

Marjorie Jackson-Nelson
(3 November 2001 – 8 August 2007)

Eric Neal, like Roma Mitchell before him, had been an important 'first' in the gubernatorial history of South Australia. Now it was the turn of Marjorie Jackson-Nelson to add to the list of vice-regal 'firsts'. She was the second woman to be appointed Governor of South Australia but was the first (and to date, only) Olympian athlete to hold the position. As Flinders University observed at the award of her honorary doctorate, Marjorie Jackson-Nelson was 'a breaker of barriers. She was the first Australian female runner to break a world record. She was the first Australian woman to win an Olympic athletics medal; indeed the first of either gender to win gold on the track since Edwin Flack (1896)'. Moreover, 'she was the first female manager of an entire national team – the 500 strong Australian contingent at the 1994 Commonwealth Games in Victoria, Canada'.[64]

Marjorie Jackson (as she was then) was born at Coffs Harbour, New South Wales, on 13 September 1931, and moved to Lithgow as a young child with her parents, William Jackson and Mary Robinson.[65] Her prowess as a runner was apparent at an early age. Her father bought her a second-hand pair of spiked shoes, made her a set of starting blocks, and arranged a part-time coach. Aged fifteen, Marjorie Jackson won the 100-yards sprint at the New South Wales Combined Girls' High Schools' carnival, breaking a record of eighteen-year's standing in the seventy-five yards on the same occasion. Just after turning sixteen, she was invited to compete in the State trials for the possibility of selection for the 1948 London Olympics. But Marjorie Jackson did not really catch the public eye until 5 February 1949 at the Sydney Sportsground, when a large crowd had gathered to watch Fanny Blankers-Koen, the 'Flying Dutchwoman', hailed as the world's greatest female athlete, taking on local sprinters. To the spectators' astonishment, Blankers-Koen was pipped to the post by Jackson, the 'Lithgow Flash' as she was soon dubbed by the press. Demonstrating that this was no fluke, a few days later

Jackson beat Blankers-Koen again in the 100 yards, setting a new Australian record, one-tenth of a second faster than Blankers-Koen's previous winning Olympic time.

Thereafter, there was no looking back. Between 1950 and 1954, Marjorie Jackson won every State and Australian title for the 100 yards, 100 metres, 220 yards and 200 metres. At the 1950 Empire Games in Auckland she won four gold medals. In 1952 she flew to Helsinki to participate in the Olympic Games. On the plane she met and fell in love with Peter Nelson, a cyclist from Adelaide who was on his way to compete in his first Olympics. He had never seen Marjorie run and years later she recalled that at Helsinki she 'wanted to show off a bit to Peter'.[66] The result was that Jackson set a new world record of 23.4 seconds for the semi-final of the 200 metres and went on to win gold in the final by an impressive five metres. She had hoped to gain another gold medal in the 4 x 100 metres relay, her team having set a new world record in the heats. Alas, the baton was dropped in the final handover, and the Australians were disqualified. Ironically, a week after the Olympics, the Australian team defeated the Americans who had snatched victory in the relay. Meanwhile, Peter Nelson had not performed as well as he had hoped in the cycling events.[67] But meeting Marjorie Jackson had changed his life – they were married on 7 November 1953.

In 1952 Marjorie Jackson's achievements were recognised when she became ABC's Australian 'Sportsman [sic] of the Year'. In the same year the prestigious Helms Foundation in the United States named her 'Outstanding Athlete 1952'. She went on to win a further three gold medals at the 1954 Empire Games in Vancouver. But by then, she and Peter Nelson had made their joint decision to retire from competitive sport, and together they opened a sports shop in the Adelaide suburb of Unley. They were both active in the local community. Peter Nelson was involved with the Unley Rotary Club, and in the mid-1960s was a key player in establishing the Unley Memorial Swimming Pool, where he taught swimming.[68]

Tragically, Peter Nelson died of leukaemia on 2 February 1977. Subsequently, Marjorie Jackson-Nelson launched the Peter Nelson Leukaemia Research Fellowship, raising funds across Australia to sponsor research into combating the disease. 'I'm a possibility thinker', she explained in the early 1980s. 'I believe the solution to every problem is there if you look for it. I'd rather attempt something great and fail than succeed at less.'[69] By 2019, she had raised $7 million and funded ten research projects, a great success story by any standard.[70] Among these projects were the sponsorship of a leukaemia laboratory in Adelaide, the appointment of a leukaemia researcher at the Flinders Medical Centre, and the establishment of a research fellowship in the Department of Microbiology and Immunology at the University of Adelaide.

Alongside her commitment to leukaemia research, Marjorie Jackson-Nelson's dedication to Australian sport remained undiminished. She was a president of the South Australian Division of the Australian Olympic Federation, and served as Women's Section Manager of the Australian Commonwealth Games teams in 1982, 1986 and 1990, as well as leading the Australian national team in Vancouver in 1994. She was appointed a board member of the Sydney Organising Committee for the 2000 Olympic Games, and carried the Olympic Flag into Stadium Australia at the opening ceremony. In the following year, she became Governor of South Australia.

As Governor, Marjorie Jackson-Nelson proved adept at fulfilling the myriad public roles associated with the office. Her duties took her to regional South Australia, for example, such as northern Yorke Peninsula when she officially opened the biennial Kernewek Lowender Cornish festival in the former mining towns of Moonta, Wallaroo and Kadina. She hosted a visit by the Queen in February 2002, during which time she was appointed Commander of the Royal Victorian Order by Her Majesty. One of her more unusual tasks during her period as Governor was being one of the four runners who carried the Queen's Baton around the MCG stadium during the 2006 Commonwealth Games opening ceremony in Melbourne. She remained outspoken on sporting issues generally, and, as well as continuing to encourage young women in their endeavours, was scathing about the 'excesses and disappointments of contemporary sport'.[71] On completion of her term as Governor, Marjorie Jackson-Nelson was awarded the Olympic Order, the highest order bestowed by the International Olympic Committee. The Committee explained that the award was for her 'having illustrated the

Olympic ideal through her actions, having achieved remarkable merit in the sporting world and having rendered outstanding service to the Olympic movement through her community work and as Governor of South Australia.[72]

Kevin John Scarce
(8 August 2007 – 1 September 2014)

After the innovative appointments of Roma Mitchell, Eric Neal and Marjorie Jackson-Nelson, the selection of Rear Admiral Kevin Scarce as Governor of South Australia in 2007 looked like a return to the tried-and-tested formula of a having a senior military officer in post. Yet here were other 'firsts' too. Kevin Scarce was the first Naval officer to hold the position since Admiral Sir Day Bosanquet was appointed in 1909. Moreover, he was the very first (and currently, only) former member of the Royal Australian Navy (RAN) to become Governor of the State.

Kevin John Scarce was born at Toorak Gardens, Adelaide, on 4 May 1952. He spent his early years at Woomera in outback South Australia and was educated at Elizabeth East Primary School and Elizabeth High School in Adelaide. He joined the Royal Australian Navy College (HMAS *Creswell*) in 1968 as a Junior Entry Cadet Midshipman. He undertook his sea training in 1971 during the Vietnam War, serving in HMAS *Sydney*, the former aircraft carrier turned amphibious troop transport with the unflattering nickname the 'Vung Tau Ferry' on account of its role in transporting servicemen and women to the South Vietnamese port where Australia had established a logistical base.[73] Returning to HMAS *Creswell*, Kevin Scarce graduated in 1972 with full colours for basketball and cricket, as well as winning the Farncomb Cup as best all-rounder in cricket and the Morgan Trophy for best batsman. He also played in the College's first XVIII for Australian Rules football, and perhaps not surprisingly was awarded the Governor-General's Cup for the best individual performance in all sports.[74]

Armed with these glowing accolades, Sub-Lieutenant Scarce proceeded to the United Kingdom in 1973 for further training with the Royal Navy. Returning on completion to Australia, he attended professional supply (logistics) training courses, pursuing his chosen area of Naval specialisation, and was then appointed in turn to HMA Ships *Vendetta, Yarra* and *Duchess*. In 1975 he was promoted Lieutenant and posted to HMAS *Watson*, the Sydney shore base. In the same year, he married Elizabeth Anne Taylor, an officer in the Women's Royal Australian Naval Service (they later had two children, Kasha and Kingsley). Subsequently, Kevin Scarce joined the aircraft carrier HMAS *Melbourne* in 1977, participating on 28 June in the Review of the Fleet at Spithead, near Portsmouth in England, as part of the Queen's Silver Jubilee celebrations. Back in Australia once more, he was posted to the RAN Staff College Project, which led to the establishment and inauguration of first Naval Staff Course in 1979.[75]

A prestigious appointment to the Naval staff of the Australian Embassy in Washington followed in 1979, from where he was promoted Lieutenant Commander. Scarce then joined the destroyer HMAS *Perth* as Supply Officer and, following promotion to Commander in June 1985, was appointed to the Directorate of Service Requirements – Navy in the Navy Office in Canberra. In 1987 he became Base Supply Officer at the Naval Air Station HMAS *Albatross*. Thereafter, his rise was meteoric. In 1990 he completed a one-year Masters of Economic Management course at the University of New South Wales (Australian Defence Force Academy campus in Canberra), and in the December was promoted to Captain. In that rank, he became Fleet Supply Officer, and in 1994 completed a further Masters degree, this time in National Security Strategy at the United States War College in Washington DC. In 1995, Captain Scarce assumed command of HMS *Cerberus*, the Royal Australian Navy's principal shore training establishment, before being promoted Commodore in early 1997 and serving as Flag Officer Naval Training Command during 1997–1998. In 1999 he was appointed Commodore Logistics Support – Navy, based in Sydney, and following promotion to Rear Admiral in December 1999 moved to Melbourne to become Support Commander Australia – Navy. From 2000 to 2003, Rear Admiral Scarce was Head of Maritime Systems Division in the Defence Material Organisation (DMO), the culmination of his career as a Naval Supply (logistics) officer.[76]

Kevin Scarce retired from the Royal Australian Navy in 2003, and was briefly the Acting Under Secretary of the DMO in 2004. Shortly after, he was appointed Chief Executive Officer of the South Australian Government Defence Unit, with responsibility for expanding the State's defence industry, serving until 2005. During this period, he played a leading role in securing South Australia's winning bid for a $6 billion contract to build three air-warfare destroyers for the Navy.[77] He was also chairman of the Defence Industry Advisory Board, and in 2006 became a board member of the Port Adelaide Maritime Co-operation Board.

The development of South Australia's maritime defence industry was an important strategic objective for successive State Governments, and it was clear that Kevin Scarce was a fine ambassador for the State's maritime capacity as well as a key influencer within the industry. His appointment as Governor in August 2007 was welcomed widely. In 2010, he told *Defence Business SA* magazine: 'My major role as Governor is helping to sell the opportunities of investing in South Australia. I welcome visiting delegations and travel overseas helping to promote the state's capabilities and aspirations.'[78] However, those who imagined that Governor Scarce would slip seamlessly into 'the Establishment' role of his military predecessors were surprised when, deviating from normal vice-regal apolitical protocol, he announced that he was a confirmed supporter of the Australian republican movement – an interesting position for Her Majesty's appointed representative in South Australia.[79]

Among the Governor's annual responsibilities was attendance at the Proclamation Ceremony at Glenelg on 28 December. In December 2008, with Governor Scarce present, the ceremony struck a distinctly different note compared to its predecessors. In the previous twelve months, the Kaurna Heritage Committee and Holdfast Bay City Council had worked together to devise a more inclusive format for the event. The 2008 ceremony was watched eagerly by Robert Foster and Amanda Nettelbeck, distinguished historians of Aboriginal South Australia. As they observed, an Aboriginal 'welcome to country' performance introduced the formalities:

> When the Governor arrived, the official Aboriginal delegation presented him with a bunch of seven emu feathers, representing the seven 'Rs'

of reconciliation: Recognition, Respect, Rights, Reform, Reciprocity, Responsibility and Reparations. Much of the ceremony that followed accorded with past formalities, but the atmosphere had changed from the previous year. Where the reading of the Proclamation promising justice to the Aboriginal people had been redolent with irony, there was now a different air in its sentiments.[80]

As a gesture of reconciliation, Governor Scarce also offered to hold a special event at Government House, which took place on 19 February 2009. Here he recalled the unfulfilled 'good intentions' of the original founding documents, and emphasised that 'it is necessary for us now to renew the spirit of these good intentions, and define our resolve.'[81] A year later, it fell to Governor Scarce to present the title deed of the Maralinga Tjarutja Section 400 at a special 'handback ceremony' at Maralinga village, marking the return of the land to its traditional Aboriginal owners. Hitherto they had been denied access to Section 400 due to continuing radioactive contamination, following British nuclear weapons testing in the 1950s and early 60s. Now, eventually made safe, the land was restored at last to its rightful custodians.[82]

Governor Scarce was Chief Scout for Scouts South Australia from 2007 to 2014, the term of his vice-regal appointment, and was likewise involved in any number of charitable and voluntary organisations across the State.[83] As Premier Jay Weatherill put it: 'I know many South Australians appreciate the contribution His Excellency has made as patron of more than 200 charities and organisations across the state. He has been tireless in his efforts to support the economic and social wellbeing of South Australians.'[84] On his retirement as Governor, Kevin Scarce continued many of his not-for-profit activities, including an appointment as National President of the Scouts. He became chairman of the Cancer Council of South Australia in November 2014, in the same month also becoming president of Novita Children's Services, which provided assistance to disabled children, their families and carers. He was Chancellor of the University of Adelaide from 2014 to 2020. Along with his wife Elizabeth, he was also joint Patron of Anglicare SA.

More controversially, freed from the constraints of vice-regal convention, Kevin Scarce spoke out in favour of nuclear energy, suggesting that South Australia should develop nuclear industries to compensate for the decline in manufacturing.[85] Subsequently, Premier Jay Weatherill appointed Scarce to lead a Nuclear Fuel Cycle Royal Commission to enquire into the possible expansion of nuclear industries in the State, covering areas as diverse as uranium mining, enrichment, power generation and radioactive waste storage. In May 2016, Scarce presented his report, which argued that the greatest economic opportunity for the nuclear industry in South Australia was the creation of deep underground repositories for imported spent nuclear fuel. Many found the report persuasive but, in the light of perceived majority public opinion, the State Government decided not to proceed with the recommendation. Nonetheless, undeterred, Kevin Scarce continued to strongly advocate the development of nuclear industries in Australia.[86]

Further controversy surrounded Scarce's claim that Australia's political and defence establishment had failed to admit the extent of the nation's precarious position in the Indo–Pacific region. He argued in 2019 that Australia had not responded sufficiently to changing geo-political circumstances, including the rise of China and India and the assertiveness of other regional powers such as Indonesia and Pakistan. Although he did not believe that China posed an imminent territorial threat to Australia, he warned that it 'will simply not be sufficient to assume that US diplomatic and military strength will always come to our aid'.[87] Sooner or later, he said, the growing influence, ambitions and increasing assertiveness of China would need to inform public debate and policy calculations.

Kevin Scarce's wideranging portfolio of interests and activities expanded still further in April 2018, when, at a time of the Oval's critical diversification and expansion, he was appointed chair of the Adelaide Oval Management Authority for three years. Despite his lengthy term as State Governor (extended by two years in 2012), Scarce's post-gubernatorial career had been energetic and ambitious in a way that only a relative few of his predecessors had achieved.

Hieu Van Le
(1 September 2014 – 31 August 2021)

'G'day mate. Welcome to Australia!'[88]

Such was the greeting extended to Hieu Van Le, along with his wife Lan and some forty other Vietnamese 'boatpeople' refugees, who in 1977 had braved treacherous seas, monsoon storms and even a volcanic eruption before finding themselves drifting off the coast near Darwin. The cheery welcome and friendly wave from two men fishing from a nearby aluminium 'tinny' was somehow reassuring and deeply Australian: Hieu Van Le later recalled fondly that each fisherman had 'some zinc on their nose and a can of beer in their hands'.[89] The tinny sped off and Hieu Van Le and the other refugees approached a larger vessel. 'Excuse me, sir,' he called out in impeccable English, 'where is the nearest police station?'[90] They had to wait a day or two before permission to land was given. But Hieu Van Le had made it to Australia, 'with nothing but an invisible suitcase filled with dreams, [and] a dream to live in a peaceful, safe and free country and to live a meaningful and fulfilling life'.[91]

Hieu Van Le was born on 1 January 1954, the year Vietnam was partitioned, at Quang Tri in what became South Vietnam. His father had been killed in the first phase of the Indochina conflict just before his birth, leaving him to be brought up by his mother.[92] He was educated in the city of Da Nang, and studied Economics and Business Management at Dalat University. Yet these were the terrible years of the Vietnam War. As he recalled:

> Never a day in my childhood went by when I did not hear gunshots or feel the terrible loss of friends and family . . . War was part of my life and it has left me with a painful soundtrack of my childhood – rockets firing, roaring helicopters hovering overhead, endless firing of weapons . . . and the haunting sound of people suffering.[93]

These were the years when the South, assisted by America and Australia among others, fought to resist the onslaught from Communist North

Vietnam. By the time Saigon (now Ho Chi Minh City), the southern capital, fell on 30 April 1975, South Vietnam had been comprehensively overrun, with imminent reunification with the North under Communist rule. By now, the Americans and Australians had gone. Educated southerners were met with suspicion and sometimes hostility by the new regime, with many singled out for 're-education' or worse. It was in this climate that Hieu Van Le and his wife Lan and a great number of other South Vietnamese decided it was time to leave, many heading for the enticing shores of Australia, their erstwhile ally.

Early on the morning of 24 November 1977, Hieu Van Le, his wife and a number of other Vietnamese refugees, arrived in Adelaide, having spent a short period in the old quarantine centre in Darwin. Years later, he remembered that they 'were a group of exhausted, ragged-looking people', at a low ebb after their arduous journey, 'but excited at the prospect of a new life'.[94] Housed in Nissan huts at the Pennington Migrant Hostel, Hieu Van Le explained that 'while finding our feet in our new home' the refugees were able to brush-up their English, find their way around the city, and discover how administrative systems such as healthcare worked.[95] Meals at Pennington were the standard meat-and-two-veg, and Hieu Van Le, tiring of this basic fare, visited a fruit and vegetable store in Port Adelaide in search of his favourite lemongrass. 'Mate, we don't eat grass in Australia' was the bemused response of the greengrocer.[96] Cultural misunderstanding could lead sometimes to anti-migrant feeling, such as fears that boatpeople would bring strange diseases to these shores or otherwise threaten the cohesion and wellbeing of Australian society.[97]

Yet, like the smiling Aussies in their tinny off Darwin, the vast majority of Australians felt empathy for the plight of the Vietnamese refugees. Many of those who had fought in Vietnam, as well as those who had opposed Australia's participation in the war, felt a responsibility towards the boatpeople, especially when the refugees quickly became self-sufficient and adapted swiftly to their new home, as many did.[98] Years later, when he was Governor of South Australia, Hieu Van Le paid an official visit to the outback town of Coober Pedy. After he had laid a wreath at the war memorial, he was approached by a man. 'He shook my hand and held on for a long time,' the Governor said: 'He told me he had been conscripted and served in Vietnam and, upon returning to Australia, he and his fellow soldiers were confronted with a very negative response from some of the community.'[99] As the Governor went on to explain, the former national serviceman:

> felt disappointed with this treatment he received. And so he decided to 'hide himself away' in Coober Pedy, digging opals for a living and pursuing a solitary life. He told me that, when he heard my story and my appointment to the Vice Regal office, he felt a profound relief and said to himself that his service and sacrifice in Vietnam had not been in vain. There were tears falling from his eyes . . . and from mine. It was a moment I will never forget.[100]

Hieu Van Le also remembered the 'kindness and generosity' of Australian troops he had encountered in Vietnam all those years before.[101] And, indeed, there had been many 'South Australian Vietnam Veterans [who] were overjoyed when a loyal and long serving friend was elevated to the high honour of State Governor'.[102] But all that lay in the future. For now, Hieu Van Le was still a new migrant, striving to find his way in strange and sometimes bewildering country.

A few weeks after arriving at Pennington in November 1977, Hieu and Lan Van Le heard that an Australian couple in the Riverland, Ken and Daphne Schwarz, wished to invite some refugees to join them for the festive season, and so they set off for Loxton on the River Murray for their first Christmas in Australia. As Hieu Van Le recalled:

> Ken and Daphne were extremely warm and welcoming hosts . . . I'd come from a country that was so crowded, and always surrounded by so much chaos and unrest. To find myself in a place of such spaciousness and quiet beauty – surrounded by apricot trees, as far as the eye could see – was a profound experience. For the first time in my life, I felt what it was like to experience an environment of true peace. There was an overwhelming sense of awe for the mesmerising landscape, with its vast blue skies, gentle beauty and pristine environment.[103]

On Christmas Eve 1977, they joined the Schwarzs at an evening service at the Lutheran church in Bookpurnong, where Hieu Van Le read a passage from the Bible. As he put it:

> The church community greeted us with such friendship and warmth, and a real sense of family. We were strangers in a foreign land; we had no family, no friends, and yet the people welcomed us into their community with open arms. The expression of such genuine friendship and warmth by the people in Bookpurnong instilled in us a profound sense of belonging and confidence. It made us feel we could move mountains. The community showed empathy and understanding of our circumstances and made us feel like members of their own families.[104]

Spurred on by such uplifting experiences, Le went on to attend the University of Adelaide, where he gained a degree in Economics and Accounting. This was followed by a Master of Business Administration from the same university in 2001. He had already acquired a Certified Practising Accountant accreditation, and from 1991 was employed at the Australian Securities and Investments Commission, working at a high level and reaching a senior position in the organisation before his retirement in March 2009. At the same time, he had become involved in a wide range of community affairs, in 1995 being appointed a member of the South Australian Multicultural and Ethnic Affairs Commission, of which he became chair in 2007 – the first person of Asian heritage to hold the position. In 2007 Hieu Van Le was sworn in as Lieutenant-Governor of South Australia, supporting the then Governor, Rear Admiral Scarce, retaining the appointment until 2014 when he himself became Governor – the first Asian migrant to achieve the position, and the first Vietnamese-born individual ever to have been elevated to a vice-regal role anywhere in the world. He was also the first Lieutenant-Governor to have been appointed to the role of Governor in South Australia.

Although he had served as Lieutenant-Governor for all of seven years, Hon. Hieu Van Le professed himself humbled as well as honoured by his appointment as Governor. 'It is the stuff of fairy tales to be honest,' he said when he heard the news, 'and I'm still trying to come to terms with it right now . . . to be bestowed with the greatest honour and the privilege of holding vice-regal office is absolutely beyond my wildest dream.' But, he was quick to add, the appointment 'says much more about our society than about me. It sends a powerful message affirming our inclusive and egalitarian society'.[105]

In office, Governor Hieu Van Le remembered those formative early days in the Riverland, and made a conscious effort to visit rural and regional communities across the State whenever he could. As he explained, on 'each visit we always meet with the local Mayor and Councillors, community organisations like the CFS, RSL, Aboriginal organisations and communities, Men's Sheds, charitable organisations, schools, hospitals and many arts, cultural and historical places'.[106] Of especial significance, he said, was 'experiencing local Aboriginal culture . . . I was truly moved standing at the Breakaways Conservation Park in Coober Pedy, an Aboriginal sacred land. To me it was a magic place with a powerful sense of spirituality'. Likewise, 'I was in awe in many sacred places of the local Aboriginal people in the Flinders Ranges. And I was impressed by the Aboriginal Art Gallery in Ceduna, which displayed many extraordinary works of local Aboriginal artists'.[107]

The Governor's passion and commitment to Australia was shared by his wife Lan Le (they even named their sons Don and Kim after cricketing legends Sir Donald Bradman and Kim Hughes), and she too has played an important role in the life of the State. She attended the South Australian Institute of Technology (now University of South Australia) and in 1985 graduated with a Bachelor of Social Work degree, subsequently working as a social worker/rehabilitation consultant in various Commonwealth Government departments, and acting as a senior rehabilitation consultant with CRS Australia for twenty-eight years. Mrs Le also developed a strong interest in the resettlement of newly arrived migrants, running cross-cultural awareness training workshops for those staff working in complex cultural settings.

The Governor and Mrs Le found themselves working hand-in-glove on many occasions, official and otherwise, but perhaps never as closely as during the early days of the COVID-19 lockdown in South Australia when they were confined to Government House with only a minimal staff. As Hieu Van Le told Adelaide journalist David Penberthy in April 2020, he usually attended around 900 community events each year, shaking hands with 200 to 300 people every day. 'Now I can't even shake my own sons' hands,' he exclaimed: 'It is extraordinarily bizarre. I love people, so this is a big adjustment. I miss meeting people. I miss hearing their wonderful stories, but we all have to put our heads down so we can get through this.'[108] As he explained, he had spent lockdown liaising through telephone calls or video meetings with community groups he would normally meet face-to-face, assessing their needs, learning about their pressures and concerns, and relating these to the Premier at their weekly meetings. 'At a time when people feel vulnerable and scared, when people are sick, anxious about their jobs', continued the Governor, 'there is a vice-regal role to help societal cohesion'.[109] It was an initiative applauded by the Premier, who described the Governor as 'an inspiration and a role model for all South Australians . . . I am particularly grateful for his calm and considered leadership through the COVID pandemic'.[110]

It was a role that the Governor had also played during the bushfires that had swept through parts of South Australia during the summer of 2019–2020. In their aftermath, he had visited Kangaroo Island and the Adelaide Hills to view the devastation and meet those who had lost so much.[111] Later, in January 2021, he displayed a similar concern for the recent bushfire in Lucindale, near Naracoorte, telephoning the local mayor to discuss the extent of its impact.[112] In the COVID pandemic, as in the bushfires, Governor Hieu Van Le had observed time and again the 'resilience, determination and unwavering community spirit' of South Australia.[113] It was, he said, exactly the same spirit that he and his wife Lan had experienced more than forty years before, when 'we were welcomed with open arms and received generous support from South Australians to help us find our feet in our new home'.[114] It was for him an enduring impression of the State, and, perhaps, the defining feature of his profoundly humane governorship.

AFTERWORD

From the final months of William IV's reign to the third decade of the twentieth century, the office of Governor has played a major role in the constitutional life of South Australia. But, as we have seen, this role has changed markedly over time. In the early years, the Governor exercised executive power, determining matters of policy and law, as well as being directly responsible to the United Kingdom for the management and good governance of the colony. The achievement of responsible government in 1856 effectively redefined the vice-regal position, now mirroring that of the Queen – a constitutional monarch – in the United Kingdom, acting on the advice of the Premier but retaining various reserve powers. However, the Governor remained the eyes and ears of the United Kingdom Government, a function that survived Federation in 1901, so that South Australia – like other Australian States – continued strictly speaking as a self-governing dependency of the British Crown.

This essentially 'Imperial' status was increasingly anomalous and under pressure by the 1960s, not least in South Australia where a deliberate policy of 'Australianisation' by successive State Governments ensured that henceforth all Governors would be Australian citizens. Moreover, the *Australia Act(s)* of 1986 and attendant Letters Patent issued by the Queen on 14 February 1986 set the powers, responsibilities and duties of the modern governorship. In effect, this reinforced the Governor's status as local 'head of state' in South

Australia, lynchpin of the Westminster system of government as practised in the State.

Alongside his or her constitutional duties, the Governor plays – and always has played – a significant role in the community life of South Australia. As well as entertaining in Government House and attending functions in Adelaide, successive Governors have been anxious to visit rural and regional South Australia, often travelling to far-flung parts of the State to meet people from a wide variety of different backgrounds. In times of stress, such as war and the Depression years, such visits have been vital in maintaining morale as well as affording Governors opportunities to gauge the popular mood and detect current concerns. In the digital age, new forms of communication became important when physical contact was not always possible, not least during the COVID-19 lockdown.

This community role has also evolved over time, and the traditional vice-regal task of maintaining stability and cohesion has widened considerably in modern times. The divisive legacy of the Vietnam War has been addressed in different ways by recent Governors, assisting in the healing process that rehabilitated those veterans who had felt alienated from society. Governors have also celebrated the spirit and practice of multiculturalism, embracing enthusiastically the new diversity apparent after the Second World War as immigrants arrived in South Australia from an increasingly wide range of overseas countries.

Recognition of Aboriginal rights and the centrality of Indigenous culture has likewise been emphasised by successive Governors, for whom reconciliation and the acknowledgement of past wrongs has become a significant imperative. Tellingly, Governors (and their spouses) have often acted as South Australia's collective conscience, a trend observable as early as the late nineteenth century, when Governors were apt to contrast the original good intentions of European settlers with the subsequent reality of dispossession, death and destruction.

Governors' wives (all but two of South Australia's Governors have been men) have usually complemented their husband's activities. An unspoken but universally acknowledged rule was that Governor's wives should act as supportive 'first ladies' (as they have occasionally been addressed) on social occasions but also on rural visits where, for example, they might meet local women's groups or (typically) view hospital facilities. In wartime, Governor's wives played impressive leading roles in patriotic fundraising activities and organisations such as the Red Cross. As well as frequent commentators on the plight of Indigenous Australians, vice-regal wives were often keen observers of social conditions, on which they were prepared to comment, even to the extent of buttonholing Premiers. Some were highly literate as well as observant, and their shrewd commentaries have survived as important windows into South Australian life over the decades. Perhaps more than their husbands, they were in a position to tell us what they really thought. Certainly, gubernatorial reputations, good and bad, could sometimes depend partly on the activities of Governors' wives.

As we have seen, against the background of the evolving vice-regal office, some Governors have been more successful than others, some popular and some not. A number left a lasting mark on the State, still recalled in popular memory; others disappeared quickly and quietly from general view. Yet despite this variation in impact, what is most noticeable is a remarkable sense of continuity, from early times to the present day, together with an unswerving devotion to duty demonstrated by the overwhelming majority of Governors. On balance, South Australia has been extremely well served by its first thirty-five Governors.

NOTES AND REFERENCES

Chapter 1

1 P.A. Howell, 'Varieties of Vice-Regal Life with Special Reference to the Constitutional Role of the Governors of South Australia, 1890–1927', *Journal of the Historical Society of South Australia*, No. 3, 1977, p. 26.

2 Bradley Selway, *The Constitution of South Australia*, Federation Press, Sydney, 1997, p. 33; P.A. Howell, *The Office of Governor of South Australia*, South Australian Constitutional Advisory Centre, Adelaide, 1995, p. 8.

3 Peter John Boyce, *The Queen's Other Realms: The Crown and its Legacy in Australia, Canada and New Zealand*, Federation Press, Sydney, 2008, p. 25.

4 *ibid.*, p. 25.

5 Howell, 1977, p. 19.

6 Max. C. Castles and Michael C. Harris, *Lawmakers and Wayward Whigs: Government and Law in South Australia 1836–1986*, Wakefield Press, Adelaide, 1987, p. 249.

7 *ibid.*, p. 250.

8 *ibid.*, p. 251.

9 Boyce, 2008, p. 149.

10 Don Dunstan, *Felicia: The Political Memoirs of Don Dunstan*, Macmillan, Melbourne, 1981, p. 152.

11 Boyce, 2008, p. 157.

12 Philip Payton, *Australia in the Great War*, Robert Hale, London, 2015, p. 208.

13 Castles & Harris, 1987, p. 250.

14 Roma D. Hodgkinson, 'Tennyson, Hallam (1852–1928), in *Australian Dictionary of Biography*, National Centre of Biography, Australian National University, http://adb.anu.edu.au/biography/tennyson-hallam-8773/text15379, published first in hardcopy 1990, accessed online 11 May 2020.

15 Howell, 1977, p. 15.

16 Boyce, 2008, p. 29; P.A. Howell, 'Weigall, Sir William Ernest George Archibald (1974–1952)', in *Australian Dictionary of Biography*, National Centre of Biography, Australian National University, http:/adb.anu.edu.au/biography/weigall-sir-william-ernest-george-archibald-9037/text15917, published first in hardcopy 1990, accessed 11 May 2020.

17 *(South Australian) Register* (Adelaide), 2 January 1924.

18 Howell, 1995, p. 10.

19 Don Dunstan, 'The State, the Governors and the Crown', in Geoffrey Dutton (ed.), *Republican Australia*, Sun Books, Melbourne, 1977, pp. 202–204. It should be noted that Dunstan was himself a republican but also a champion of the Westminster

system of government which, he argued, would require appointed 'heads of state' at State and Commonwealth levels in any republican arrangement.

20   Howell, 1995, p. 8.

21   *ibid.*

22   *ibid.*, p. 9.

23   *ibid.*, p. 14, citing *South Australian Statutes, 1837–1975,* Vol. 11, p. 756.

24   Howell, 1995, p. 16; see also Castles & Harris, 1987, p. 258.

25   For example, there was considerable discussion of the role and powers of the Governor-General in John Arnold, Peter Spearritt and David Walker (eds.), *Out of Empire: The British Dominion of Australia,* Mandarin, Melbourne, 1993, a volume which examined arguments for and against a republic, but there was no mention whatsoever of State Governors. Likewise, Malcom Turnbull, *A Bigger Picture*, Hardie Grant, Melbourne, 2020, pp. 94–104, in describing the referendum campaign, concentrates on the role of Governor-General but ignores that of State Governors.

26   Anne Twomey, *The States, the Commonwealth and the Crown – the Battle for Sovereignty*, Papers on Parliament No. 48, Parliament House, Canberra, 2008, p. 12.; see also Anne Twomey, *The Chameleon Crown: The Queen and her Australian Governors*, Federation Press, Sydney, 2006.

27   Howell, 1995, p. 17.

28   *ibid.*, p. 18.

29   *South Australian Government Gazette,* http://www.governmentgazette.sa.gov.au/2014/june2014_043.pdf, accessed 30 June 2020.

30   *Register*, 2 January 1924.

31   *Advertiser*, 28 July 1934.

32   Howell, 1995, pp. 18–19; the issue of the potential re-use of Government House appeared again (albeit somewhat tongue-in-cheek) as recently as 2017; see *Advertiser*, 9 January 2017.

33   K.T. Borrow, *Government House, Adelaide (1837–1901)*, The Pioneers Association of South Australia, Adelaide, 1982, p. 6.

34   *ibid.*, p. 17.

35   John Blackett, *History of South Australia,* Hussey and Gillingham, Adelaide, 1911, p. 142.

36   *Register*, 22 June 1887.

37   *Register*, 15 January 1878.

38   *South Australian Gazette*, 9 March 1839.

39   Borrow, 1982, p. 23.

40   Governor.sa.gov.au/node/21, accessed 30 June 2020.

41   *ibid.*

42   *Register*, 15 January 1878.

43   *Register*, 16 January 1841.

44 John Stephens, *The Royal South Australian Almanack for 1846*, Stephens, Adelaide, 1846, available as CD ROM, Archive CD Books Australia, Modbury (Adelaide), c. 2008.

45 governor.sa.gov.au/node21, accessed 30 June 2020.

46 *ibid.*

47 Alexandra Hasluck (ed.), *Audrey Tennyson's vice-regal Days: The Australian Letters of Audrey Lady Tennyson to her mother Zacyntha Boyle, 1899–1903*, National Library of Australia, Canberra, 1978, p. 27.

48 *ibid.*, p. 28.

49 *ibid.*, p. 29.

50 *ibid.*, p. 28.

51 Governor.sa.gov.au/node21, accessed 30 June 2020.

52 Hasluck (ed.), 1978, pp. 126–127.

53 Pam Tamblyn, *Haven on the Hill: Old Government House, Belair*, Friends of Old Government House, Adelaide, 2007.

54 *Advertiser*, 25 April 1942.

55 *South Australian Chronicle*, 15 February 1879.

56 *Register*, 21 March 1922.

57 *Advertiser*, 9 February 1911; *Mail* (Adelaide), 8 March 1913.

58 *Advertiser*, 19 September 1944.

59 Cas Middlemiss, 'View from the Verandah: Marble Hill', *Australian Garden History*, 26 (4), April/May/June 2015, pp. 11–12.

60 National Trust of South Australia, *Marble Hill: South Australian Vice-Regal Summer Residence 1879–1955*, National trust of South Australia, Adelaide, 1973.

61 Hasluck (ed.), 1978, p. 85.

62 *ibid.*, p. 139.

63 *Register*, 22 February 1910.

64 Howell, 1977, p. 34.

65 *ibid.*, p. 45. Eric Richards in his then recent essay 'History from Below', *Journal of the Historical Society of South Australia*, No. 1, 1975, p. 7, noted the history of colonial elites in the Pacific region and observed: 'A colleague of mine at Flinders calls this kind of history – "history from the verandah".'

Chapter 2

1 Cited in K.T. Borrow, *Government House (1837–1901)*, The Pioneers Association of South Australia, Adelaide, 1982, p. 6.

2 Reprinted in the *Register*, 23 August 1920.

3 Paul Sendziuk and Robert Foster, *A History of South Australia*, Cambridge University Press, Cambridge, 2018, pp. 10–12; see also J.M. Main, 'The Foundation of South Australia', in Dean Jaensch (ed.), *The Flinders History of South Australia: Political*

History, Wakefield Press, Adelaide, 1986, pp. 1–25.

4   Douglas Pike, *Paradise of Dissent: South Australia 1829–1857*, Melbourne University Press, Melbourne, 1957, pp. 75–76; P.A. Howell, 'Cleaning the Cobwebs: A Reconsideration of the Beginnings of the Province of South Australia', *History Forum*, Vol. 13, No. 1, 1991, pp. 7–10.

5   Eric Richards, 'Wakefield Revisited Again', in Carolyn Collins and Paul Sendziuk (eds.), *Foundational Fictions in South Australian History*, Wakefield Press, Adelaide, 2018, pp. 40–42.

6   See Heidi Ing, 'South Australia's First Expedition: Three Generations of Settler-colonial Mobility', unpub. PhD, Flinders University, 2020, especially chapter 2.

7   Pike, 1957.

8   Sendziuk and Foster, 2018, pp. 13–14.

9   C.J. Napier, *Colonisation, Particularly in Southern Australia*, London, 1935, p. xviii.

10   *ibid.*, p. 213. I am grateful to Heidi Ing for drawing my attention to this statement.

11   Brian Dickey and Peter Howell (eds.), *South Australia's Foundation: Select Documents*, Wakefield Press, Adelaide, 1986, p. 31.

12   Robert Foster and Amanda Nettelbeck, *Out of the Silence: The History and Memory of South Australia's Frontier Wars*, Wakefield Press, Adelaide, 2012, p. 1.

13   House of Commons, Sessional Papers, 1837, 7, No. 425. Report of the Select Committee on Aborigines (British Settlements), p. 77. See also Foster and Nettelbeck, 2012, p. 1.

14   Sendziuk and Foster, 2018, pp. 15–17.

15   Cited in Pike, 1957, p. 103.

16   For biographical details of Hindmarsh's career, see: 'Hindmarsh, Sir John (1785–1860)', *Australian Dictionary of Biography*, Australian National University, http//:adb.anu.edu/biograph/hindmarsh-sir-john-1315/text2809, accessed 11 May 2020; F. Stewart Hindmarsh, *From Powder Monkey to Governor: The Life of Rear Admiral Sir John Hindmarsh*, Access Press, Geraldton, 1995.

17   'Stevenson's Journal', *South Australiana*, Vol. 1, No. 2, September 1962, p. 50; see also R.M. Gibbs, *Under the Burning Sun: A History of Colonial South Australia, 1836–1900*, Southern Heritage, Adelaide, 2014, p. 54.

18   Historical Publications Sub-Committee, *A Pioneer History of South Australia: In the Wake of Flinders and Baudin*, The Pioneers Association of South Australia, Adelaide, 2001, p. 52.

19   Gibbs, 2014, pp. 52–53.

20   Dickey and Howell (eds), 1986, p. 77.

21   Gibbs, 2014, p. 56.

22   Dickey and Howell (eds), 1986, p. 31.

23   Robert Foster, Rick Hosking and Amanda Nettelbeck, *Fatal Collisions: The South Australian Frontier and the Violence of Memory*, Wakefield Press, Adelaide, 2001, p. 3; see also Robert Foster, 'True Lies: South Australia's Foundation, the Idea of

"Difference", and the Rights of Aboriginal People', in Collins and Sendziuk, 2018, pp. 64–78; and Chapter 1 'The Aborigines and Their Law', in Alex C. Castles and Michael C. Harris, *Lawmakers and Wayward Whigs: Government and Law in South Australia 1836–1986*, Wakefield Press, Adelaide, 1987, pp. 1–28.

24   Castles and Harris, 1987, p. 13; Alan Pope, *One Law for All? Aboriginal People and Criminal Law in Early South Australia*, Aboriginal Studies Press, Canberra, 2011, p. 13; see also G. Jenkin, *The Conquest of the Ngarrinderi*, Rigby, Adelaide, 1979, pp. 52–53, and R. Clyne, *Colonial Blue,* Wakefield Press, Adelaide, 1987, p. 8.

25   SRSA GRG 2/5, Hindmarsh to Lord Glenelg, 20 May and 1 June 1837; see also Sendzuik and Foster (eds.), 2018, p. 23.

26   G.L. Fisher (ed.), 'Captain Hindmarsh's Letters to George Fife Angas: Part 1, 1835–1837', *South Australiana*, Vol. 1, No. 1, March 1962, pp. 5–31, and 'Part 2, 1837–1839', Vol. 1, No. 2, September 1962, pp. 49–83.

27   Sendzuik and Foster, 2018, p. 24.

28   Gibbs, 2014, p. 63.

29   Robert Foster and Amanda Nettelbeck, 'Proclamation Day and the Rise and Fall of South Australian Nationalism', in Robert Foster and Paul Sendziuk (eds.), *Turning Points: Chapters in South Australian History*, Wakefield Press, Adelaide, 2012, pp. 48–62.

30   For biographical details of Gawler's career, see R. Hetherington, 'Gawler, George 1797–1869', *Australian Dictionary of Biography*, Australian National University, http://adb.edu.autobiography/gawler-george-2085/text2615, accessed 11 May 2020.

31   Pike, 1957, p. 499 and p. 511.

32   *Gazette and Colonial Register*, 20 October 1838.

33   *South Australian*, 3 November 1838.

34   Foster, Hosking and Nettelbeck, 2001, pp. 13–28.

35   *Register*, 19 September 1840.

36   *ibid.*

37   James Penn Boucaut, *Letters to My Boys*, Gay and Bird, London, 1906, p. 118.

38   H.Y.L. Brown, *Record of the Mines of South Australia*, South Australian Government Department of Mines, Adelaide, 1908, p. 173.

39   Seymour Tremenheere, 'Notice respecting the Lead and Copper ores of Glen Osmond Mines. Three miles from Adelaide, South Australia', *Transactions of The Royal Geological Society of Cornwall*, Vol. VI, 1841–46, pp. 348–349.

40   Hetherington, accessed 11 May 2020.

41   'Grey, Sir George (1812–1898)', *Australian Dictionary of Biography*, National Centre of Biography, Australian National University, https://adb.anu.edu/biography/grey--sir-george-2125/text2691, accessed 11 May 2020; see also James Rutherford, *Sir George Grey*, Cassells, London, 1961.

42   Pike, 1957, pp. 187–188.

43   Gibbs, 2013, p. 101.

44   *ibid.*, p. 102.

45   Pike, 1957, p. 511.

46   Sendziuk and Foster, 2018, pp. 30–32; see also Foster and Nettelbeck, 2012, pp. 35–39.

47   Sendziuk and Foster, 2018, p. 32; see also Foster and Nettelbeck, 2012, pp. 42–54.

48   G. E. Drew, *Captain Bagot's Mine: Kapunda Mine 1844–1916*, Drew, Adelaide, 2017; Ian Auhl, *The Story of the 'Monster Mine': The Burra Burra Mine and its Townships 1845–1877*, Investigator Press, Adelaide, 1986.

49   Francis Dutton, *South Australia and its Mines, with An Historical Sketch of the Colony*, Boone, London, 1846, p. 244.

50   Philip Payton, *The Cornish Overseas: A History of Cornwall's 'Great Emigration'*, University of Exeter Press, Exeter, 2020, pp. 173–174.

51   *ibid.*, pp. 174–181.

52   Dutton, 1846, p. 41.

53   *ibid.*, pp. 75–76.

54   *ibid.*, p. 76.

55   Philippa Mein Smith, *A Concise History of New Zealand*, Cambridge University Press, Cambridge, 2005, p. 65.

56   *ibid.*, pp. 66–67.

57   *ibid.*, pp. 70–71.

58   'Grey, Sir George', accessed 20 May 2020.

Chapter 3

1   Paul Sendziuk and Robert Foster, *A History of South Australia*, Cambridge University Press, Cambridge, 2018, pp. 10–11;

2   Douglas Pike, *Paradise of Dissent: South Australia 1829–1857*, Longmans, London, 1957, p. 517.

3   Keith Seaman, 'The South Australian Constitution Act of 1856', in Dean Jaensch (ed.), *The Flinders History of South Australia – Political History*, Wakefield Press, Adelaide, 1986, pp. 76–77.

4   *South Australian*, 19 April 1844.

5   R.M. Gibbs, *Under the Burning Son: A History of Colonial South Australia, 1836–1900*, Southern Heritage, Adelaide, 2013, pp. 102–103.

6   Cited in Seaman, 1986, p. 78.

7   P.A. Howell, 'Constitutional and Political Development, 1857–1890', in Dean Jaensch (ed.), *The Flinders History of South Australia – Political History*, Wakefield Press, Adelaide, 1986, p. 96; E.J.R. Morgan, 'Robe, Frederick Holt (1802–1871), *Australian Dictionary of Biography*, National Centre of Biography, Australian National University, http://adb.edu.au/biography/robe-frederick-holt-2594/text3561, accessed 11 May 2020.

8   Alex C. Castles and Michael C. Harris, *Lawmakers and Wayward Whigs: Government*

Notes and References

and Law in South Australia 1836–1986, Wakefield Press, Adelaide, 1986, p. 35.

9   Gibbs, 2013, pp. 122–123.

10   Pike, 1957, pp. 358–359.

11   Gibbs, 2013, pp. 123–126.

12   He was named after his godfather General Henry Edward Fox, brother of the noted Whig politician, Charles James Fox.

13   H.J. Gibbney, 'Young, Sir Henry Edward Fox (1803–1870)', *Australian Dictionary of Biography*, National Centre of Biography, Australian National University, https://adb.edu.au/biography/young-sir-henry-edward-fox-4902/text8207, accessed 11 May 2020.

14   Caroline Quarrier Spence, 'Ameliorating Empire: Slavery and Protection in British Colonies, 1783–1865', unpub. PhD, Harvard University, 2014, pp. 233–235.

15   ucl.ac.uk/lbs/person/view/42069, Legacies of British Slave-ownership, Charles Marryat, accessed 29 July 2020.

16   ucl.ac.uk/lbs/person/view/2146630485, Legacies of British Slave-ownership, Joseph Marryat senior, accessed 30 July 2020.

17   Gibbs, 2013, p. 128.

18   *South Australian*, 19 September 1848.

19   See Philip Payton, *One and All: Labor and the Radical Tradition in South Australia*, Wakefield, Adelaide, 2016, pp. 62–74.

20   State Records of South Australia (SRSA), GRG 24, series 6, Colonial Office Correspondence, A (1848) 1432, 15/9/1848.

21   *South Australian*, 19 September 1848.

22   *Register*, 20 September 1848.

23   *Register*, 20 September 1848.

24   Payton, 2016, pp.33-9.

25   Ibid., pp.66-9.

26   *Register*, 13 October 1851.

27   Gibbs, 2013, p.142.

28   Cheryl Williss, *Miss Maryatt's Circle: A Not so Distant Past,* Wakefield Press, Adelaide, 2018, pp. 32–33.

29   Sendzuik and Foster, 2018, p. 49.

30   *ibid.*, p. 50.

31   Williss, 2018, p. 23 and p. 32.

32   C.C. Manhood, 'MacDonnell, Sir Richard Graves (1814–1881)', *Australian Dictionary of Biography*, National Centre for Biography, Australian National University, https://biography/macdonnell-sir-richard-graves-4084/text6523, accessed 11 May 2020.

33   *Register*, 7 December 1855.

34   *Register*, 19 May 1856.

35   Despatch, Governor MacDonnell to Lord Russell, 22 August 1855, cited in Gordon
      D. Combe, *Responsible Government in South Australia: Volume One – From
      Foundations to Playford*, 1957, repub. Wakefield Press, Adelaide, 2009, p. 46.

36   *ibid.*, p. 47.

37   Cited in Anna Munyard, 'Making a Polity: 1836–1857', in Jaensch (ed.), 1986, p. 71;
      see also Anna Munyard, 'Governor MacDonnell and the Transition to Responsible
      Government in South Australia, *Journal of the Historical Society of South Australia*,
      No. 5, 1978, pp. 41–65; Anna Munyard, 'Governor MacDonnell and the Transition
      to Responsible Government in South Australia', unpub. BA (Hons) thesis, Flinders
      University, 1979.

38   *Register*, 27 October 1856.

39   *Register*, 27 October 1856.

40   Combe, 2009, p. 88.

41   P.A. Howell, 'More Varieties of Vice-Regal Life', *Journal of the Historical Society of
      South Australia*, No. 9, 1981, p. 1.

42   Eric Richards, 'British Emigrants and the Making of the Anglosphere: Some
      Observations and a Case Study', in Philip Payton and Andrekos Varnava (eds.),
      Australia, Migration and Empire: Immigrants in a Globalised World, Palgrave
      Macmillan, Basingstoke, 2019, p. 37.

43   *South Australian Advertiser*, 2 March 1868.

44   Marjorie Findlay, 'Daly, Sir Dominick (1798–1868)', *Australian Dictionary of
      Biography*, National Centre of Biography, Australian National University, https://adb.
      anu.edu/biography/day-sir-dominick-3359/text5065, accessed 11 May 2020.

45   *Register*, 2 March 1868.

46   Howell, 1981, p. 1.

47   *Register*, 20–28 February inclusive; *Age* (Melbourne), 3 March 1868.

48   Combe, 2009, pp. 100–101.

49   *ibid.*, pp. 102–104.

50   *Register*, 7 December 1872.

51   Gibbs, 2013, p. 238.

52   *Register*, 25 January 1877.

53   *Australasian*, 15 June 1889.

54   Cited in H.J. Gibbney, 'Musgrave, Sir Anthony (1828–1888)', *Australian Dictionary of
      Biography*, National Centre for Biography, Australian National University, http://adb.
      anu.edu.autobiography/musgrave-sir-anthony-4283/text6929, accessed 11 May 2020.

55   *ibid.*

56   *ibid.*

57   Anthony Musgrave, *Studies in Political Economy*, Henry S. King, London, 1875, p. vii.

58   Gibbs, 2013, p. 404.

59   *Register*, 7 November 1874.

60   Gibbney, accessed 11 May 2020.

61   Robin W. Winks, 'Jervois, Sir William Francis Drummond (1821–1897)', *Australian Dictionary of Biography*, National Centre of Biography, Australian National University, http://adb.anu.edu/biography/jervois-sir-william-francis-drummond-3856/text6133, accessed 11 May 2020.

62   Philip Payton, *Tregantle and Scraesdon: Their Forts and Railway*, Dyllansow Truran, Redruth, 1988, pp. 4–6.

63   Gibbs, 2013, p. 236.

64   Combe, 2009, p. 111.

65   *ibid.*, pp. 231–232.

66   William Jervois, *Defences of Great Britain and Her Dependencies*, E. Spiller, Adelaide, 1880, p. 13.

67   *ibid.*, p. 23.

68   *ibid.*, p. 25.

69   *ibid.*

70   Gibbs, 2013, p. 277.

71   *Register* reports 6, 8, 9, 10 January 1883 detail Jervois' farewell.

72   *Bulletin*, 16 December 1882.

73   F.K. Crowley, 'Robinson, Sir William Cleaver Francis (1834–1897)', *Australian Dictionary Biography*, National Centre of Biography, Australian National University, https://adb.anu.edu/biography/robinson-sir-william-cleaver-francis-4494/text7329, accessed 20 May 2020.

74   'Unfurl the Flag', Words by Francis Hart, Composition by William Robinson, W.H. Glen, Melbourne, n.d.

75   Gibbs, 2013, pp. 298–299.

76   *Our Commonwealth*, 4 September 1886.

77   *Register*, 26 September 1884.

78   Richard Refshauge, 'Kintore, ninth Earl of (1852–1930)', *Australian Dictionary of Biography*, National Centre of Biography, Australian National University, https://adb.anu.edu/biography/kintore-ninth-earl-of-3963/text 6251, accessed 11 May 2020.

79   Payton, 2016, p. 23 and p. 147.

80   Howell, 1977, pp. 19–20.

81   Gibbs, 2013, p. 498.

82   *ibid.*

Chapter 4

1   P.A. Howell, 'Varieties of Vice-Regal Life, with Special Reference to the Constitutional Role of the Governors of South Australia, 1890–1927', *Journal of the Historical Society of South Australia*, No. 3, 1977, pp. 20–21.

2   *ibid.*, p. 21.

3   Cited in Howell, 1977, p. 21.

4   Paul Sendzuik and Robert Foster, *A History of South Australia*, Cambridge University Press, Cambridge, 2018, p. 95.

5   John Bannon, *The Crucial Colony: South Australia's Role in Reviving Federation, 1891 to 1897*, Federalism Research Centre, Australian National University, Canberra, 1994, p. 3.

6   Howell, 1977, p. 24.

7   George W.E. Russell, *Lady Victoria Buxton: A Memoir with Some Account of Her Husband*, Longmans, Green & Co., London, 1919, p. 164.

8   *ibid.*, p. 165.

9   Howell, 1977, pp. 25–26.

10   Russell, 1919, p. 40.

11   P.A. Howell, 'Buxton, Sir Thomas Fowell (1837–1915), *Australian Dictionary of Biography*, National Centre of Biography, Australian National University, http://adb.edu.au/biography/buxton-sir-thomas-fowell-5455/text9265, accessed 11 May 2020.

12   Russell, 1919, p. 110.

13   Howell, 1977, p. 29.

14   Russell, 1919, p. 128.

15   *ibid.*, p. 136.

16   *ibid.*, p. 137.

17   *ibid.*, p. 115.

18   *ibid.*

19   Howell, 1977, p. 30.

20   *Register*, 21 December 1898.

21   Russell, 1919, p. 171.

22   *ibid.*, pp. 177–178.

23   *Quiz and the Lantern*, 21 November 1895.

24   *Register*, 22 December 1923.

25   Russell, 1919, p. 145.

26   *South Australian Parliamentary Debates (Hansard) (SAPD)*, 1893, p. 1514; Stephanie McCarthy, *Tom Price: From Stonecutter to Premier*, Wakefield Press, Adelaide, 2015, p. 70 and pp.76–81.

27   Russell, 1919, p. 145.

28   *ibid.*, pp.145–146.

29   *Advertiser*, 11 April 1899.

30   *Register*, 29 September 1898.

31   Howell, 1977, p. 35.

32   Russell, 1919, p. 178.

33   Alexandra Hasluck (ed.), *Audrey Tennyson's Vice-Regal Days: The Australian Letters of Audrey Lady Tennyson 1899–1903*, National Library of Australia, Canberra, 1978, p. 324.

34   *ibid.*, p. 211

35   *ibid.*, p. 4.

36   Roma D. Hodgkinson, 'The Role of State Governors at the Time of Federation', unpub. BA (Hons) thesis, Flinders University, 1985.

37   *ibid.*

38   For a biographical sketch of Hallam Tennyson, see Roma D. Hodgkinson, 'Tennyson, Hallam (1852–1928)', *Australian Dictionary of Biography*, National Centre of Biography, Australian National University, http://adb.edu.au/biography/tennyson-hallam-8773/text15379, accessed 11 May 2020.

39   Hasluck (ed.), 1978, pp. 6–7.

40   *ibid.*, pp. 26–27.

41   *ibid.*, pp. 30–31.

42   *ibid.*, p. 34.

43   *ibid.*, pp. 31–32.

44   *ibid.*, p. 35.

45   *ibid.*

46   *ibid.*

47   *ibid.*

48   *ibid.*, p. 106.

49   *ibid.*, p. 38.

50   *ibid.*, p. 53.

51   *ibid.*

52   *ibid.*

53   *ibid.*, p. 50.

54   *ibid.*, p. 44.

55   Howell, 1977, p. 21.

56   Gordon D. Combe, *Responsible Government in South Australia: Volume One – From Foundations to Playford*, 1957, repub. Wakefield Press, Adelaide, 2009, pp. 135–136, 201.

57   Hasluck (ed.), 1978, pp. 37, 40.

58   Gavin Souter, *Lion and Kangaroo: The Initiation of Australia*, Text Publishing, Melbourne, 2000, p. 28.

59   Hasluck (ed.), 1978, p. 110.

60   *ibid.*, pp. 16–17.

61   Souter, 2000, p. 248.

62   Hasluck (ed.), 1978, p. 95.

63   *ibid.*, pp. 66, 70, 89–90, 100, 107,116, 135–137, 160, 165.

64   *ibid.*, pp. 135–137.

65   *ibid.*, p. 323.

66   *ibid.*, p. 14.

67   *ibid.*, p. 61; *Register*, 31 January 1925.

68   Diane Langmore, 'Le Hunte, Sir George Ruthven (1852–1925), *Australian Dictionary of Biography*, National Centre of Biography, Australian National University, http://adb.anu.edu/biography/le-hunte-sir-george-ruthven-7162/text12371, accessed 11 May 2020.

69   *ibid.*

70   Stewart Cockburn assisted by John Playford, *Playford: Benevolent Despot*, Axiom, Adelaide, 1991, p. 1.

71   F.J. West, 'Le Hunte, Sir George Ruthven', *Oxford Dictionary of National Biography*, https://doi.org/10.1093/ref.odnb/5477, accessed 24 August 2020.

72   McCarthy, 2015, pp. 269–287; Philip Payton, *One and All: Labor and the Radical Tradition in South Australia*, Wakefield Press, Adelaide, 2018, pp. 166–167.

73   Brian Dickey, 'South Australia', in D.J. Murphy (ed.), *Labor in Politics: The State Labor Parties in Australia: 1880–1920*, University of Queensland Press, St Lucia, 1975, p. 258.

74   Payton, 2016, pp. 168–169.

75   *ibid.*

76   P.A. Howell, 'Bosanquet, Sir Day Hort (1843–1923)', *Australian Dictionary of Biography*, National Centre of Biography, Australian National University, http://adb.edu.au.autobiography/bosenquet-sir-day-hort-5298/text8941, accessed 11 May 2020.

77   Howell, 1977, p. 24.

78   Payton, 173–174.

79   *ibid.*, p. 22; see also P.A. Howell, *South Australia and Federation*, Wakefield Press, Adelaide, 2002, pp. 301–303.

80   John McConnell Black, *Memoirs*, Hyde Park Press, Adelaide, 1971, p. 66.

81   R.J. Miller, 'The Fall of the Verran Government, 1911–1912: The most determined attempt to abolish the Legislative Council of South Australia, and its failure', unpub. BA Hons thesis, University of Adelaide, 1957.

82   Combe, 2009, p. 145.

83   *ibid.*, p. 146.

84   Keith Bailey, *James Boor's Bonanza: A History of Wallaroo Mines, South Australia*, Bailey, Kadina, 2002, p. 117.

Chapter 5

1   Tom Bridges, *Alarms and Excursions: Reminiscences of a Soldier*, Longmans, London, 1938, p. 62.

2   *ibid.*, p. 64.

3   *ibid.*, p. 330.

4   P.A. Howell, 'Galway, Sir Henry Lionel (1859–1949)', *Australian Dictionary of Biography*, National Centre of Biography, Australian National University, http://adb.anu.edu.au/biography/galway-sir-henry-lionel-6271/text10805, accessed 11 May 2020.

5   P.A. Howell, 'More Varieties of Vice-Regal Life', *Journal of the Historical Society of South Australia*, No. 9, 1981, pp. 4–53.

6   H.L. Galway, 'Pioneering in Nigeria', *Proceedings of the Royal Geographical Society of Australasia, South Australian Branch*, Vol. 16, 1914–1915, p. 78.

7   *ibid.*, pp. 80, 91, 92, 95, 100, 104.

8   Howell, 1981, p. 23.

9   *ibid.*, p. 24.

10   H.L. Gallwey, 'Journeys in the Benin Country, West Africa', *Geographical Journal*, Vol. 1, 1893, pp. 128–130.

11   *ibid.*, p. 96.

12   Howell, 1981, p. 26.

13   *Register*, 4 December 1914.

14   Howell, 1981, p. 29.

15   *ibid.*, p. 4.

16   *ibid.*

17   Marnie Haig-Muir, 'The Economy at War', in Joan Beaumont (ed.), *Australia's War 1914–18*, Allen & Unwin, Sydney, 1995, p. 107.

18   Philip Payton, *Australia in the Great War*, Robert Hale, London, 2015, pp. 25–26.

19   *People's Weekly*, 8 August 1914.

20   Philip Payton, *Regional Australia and the Great War: 'The Boys from Old Kio'*, University of Exeter Press, Exeter, 2012, pp. 27–29.

21   The National Archives (TNA) UK, CO 418/126/114, 19; cited in Howell, 1981, p. 6.

22   TNA, CO 149/138/125, cited in Howell, 1981, p. 6.

23   Philip Payton, *'Repat': A Concise History of Repatriation in Australia*, Australian Government Department of Veterans' Affairs, Canberra, 2018, pp. 5–29.

24   *Register,* 17 May 1916; Howell, 1981, p. 8.

25   *Daily Herald*, 4 December 1915.

26   Howell, 1981, p. 10.

27   *ibid.*, p. 41.

28   P.A. Howell, 'Galway, Marie Carola (1876–1963)', *Australian Dictionary of Biography*, National Centre for Biography, Australian National University, http://adb.edu/biography/galway-marie-carola-10273/text18171, accessed 26 May 2020.

29   Marie Carola Galway, *The Past Revisited: People and Happenings Recalled*, Harvill Press, London, 1953, p. 222.

30   *ibid.*, p. 117.

31   *ibid.*, p. 210. Lady Galway's misgivings about the impact of Imperialism were also transferred to Australia, when at a reception at Government House in Adelaide, she met the remarkable Daisy Bates, who had immersed herself in the study of Aboriginal society. Daisy Bates had written, explained Lady Galway, a book called *The Passing of the Aborigines,* 'a thrilling account of personal courage and devotion'. Bates, like many others, believed that, however regrettably, Indigenous Australians were doomed to extinction, and Lady Galway sadly accepted the conventional wisdom. As she put it, Daisy Bates' book was 'an epitaph on the death of one of the oldest, if not *the* oldest, branch of our human family'; see *ibid.*, p. 230.

32   *ibid.*, p. 211.

33   *ibid.*, p. 52.

34   *ibid.,* p. 221.

35   Adelaide Lubbock, *People in Glass Houses: Growing Up at Government House,* Thomas Nelson, Melbourne, 1977, p. 100.

36   Lady Galway, *Lady Galway Belgium Book*, Hussey & Gillingham, Adelaide, 1916, p. ii.

37   *ibid.*, p. 5.

38   Lady Galway, 'Belgium Unvanquished', *Journal of the Royal African Society*, Vol. 41, No. 165, October 1942, pp. 239–240.

39   Melanie Oppenheimer, *The Power of Humanity: 100 Years of the Australian Red Cross, 1914–2014*, Harper Collins, Sydney, 2014, pp. 15, 17, 23.

40   Galway, 1953, p. 213.

41   *ibid.*, 213–214.

42   *ibid.*, p. 214.

43   *ibid.*, pp. 225–226.

44   Oppenheimer, 2014, p. 64; Payton, 2018, p. 40.

45   *Register*, 15 January 1919.

46   *Advertiser*, 18 December 1918.

47   P.A. Howell, 'Weigall, Sir Ernest George Archibald (1874–1952)', *Australian Dictionary of Biography*, National Centre of Biography, Australian National University, http://adb.anu.edu/biography/weigall-sir-william-ernest-george-archibald-9037/text15917, accessed 11 May 2020.

48   *Evening Standard* (London), 23 January 1920.

49   Howell, 1981, p. 3.

50   *Register News-Pictorial*, 25 September 1929.

51   John Stepak, 'Did One Man Trigger the Great Depression?', *Money Week*, 17 November 2017.

52   J.K. Galbraith, *The Great Crash of 1929*, Marine Books, New York, 2009, p. 91.

53   Howell, *ADB*.

54   Howell, 1981, p. 4.

55   P.A. Howell, 'Pursuing Further Varieties of Vice-Regal Life', *Journal of the Historical Society of South Australia*, No. 17, 1989, p. 87.

56   'Lady Weigall's Report on the Settlements visited by her on the River Murray 1930', Borrow Collection, Special Collections, Flinders University Library.

57   Thomas Pinney (ed.), *The Letters of Rudyard Kipling*, Vol. 6, 1931–1936, University of Iowa Press, Iowa City, 2004, p. 10.

58   *New Zealand Herald*, 6 October 1906.

59   'Grace Emily Blundell Maple (1876–1950), Familypedia, Fandom, https://familypedia.wikia.org/wiki/Grace_Emily_Blundell_Maple_(1876-1950), accessed 6 September 2020.

60   *Lincolnshire Echo*, 23 August 1910.

61   *Daily Mail* (London), 11 January 1932.

62   Carol Henderson and Heather Tovey, *Searching for Grace*, Steele Roberts Publishing, Wellington, 2010.

63   Robert Greenfield, *A Day in the Life: Our family, the Beautiful People, and the End of the Sixties*, Di Capo Press, New York, 2009, p. 12.

64   Winston S. Churchill, 'Foreword', in Bridges, 1938, p. vii.

65   Bridges, 1938, p. 75.

66   *ibid.*, p. 77.

67   Quoted in Richard Holmes, *Tommy: The British Soldier on the Western Front 1914–1918*, Harper Collins, London, 2004, p. 437.

68   Churchill, 1938, pp. v–viii.

69   Bridges, 1938, p. 76–77.

70   *ibid.*, p. 78.

71   *ibid.*, p. 85.

72   *ibid.*, pp. 87–88.

73   Robin Neillands, *The Old Contemptibles: The British Expeditionary Force, 1914*, John Murray, London, 2004, p. 182.

74   Churchill, 1938, p. vii.

75   P.A. Howell, 'Bridges, Sir George Tom Molesworth (1871–1939), *Australian Dictionary of Biography*, National Centre of Biography, Australian National University, http://adb.anu.au/bridges-sir-george-tom-molesworth-5353/text9051, accessed 11 May 2020.

76   Bridges, 1938, p. 7.

77   *ibid.*

78   *ibid.*, p. 8.

79   *ibid.*, p. 13.

80   Churchill, 1938, p. v.

81   Bridges, 1938, p. 37.

82   *ibid.*, p. 50.

83   *ibid.*, p. 55.

84   *ibid.*, p. 56.

85   *ibid.*, p. 84.

86   Michael Bloch, *James Lees-Milne: The Life*, John Murray, London, 2009, p. 195.

87   *ibid.*

88   *ibid.*

89   Bridges, 1938, pp. 195–196.

90   *ibid.*, p. 8.

91   *ibid.*, p. 4.

92   *ibid.*, p. 329.

93   *ibid.*,pp. 329–330.

94   *ibid.*, p. 330.

95   *ibid.*, pp. 332–333.

96   *ibid.*, pp. 333–334.

97   Bloch, 2009, p. 195.

98   Philippa Bridges, *A Walk-About in Australia*, Hodder & Stoughton, London, 1925, p. 148.

99   *ibid.*, pp. 337.

100 P.A. Howell, 'Varieties of Vice-Regal Life with Special Reference to the Constitutional Role of the Governors of South Australia, 1890–1927', *Journal of the Historical Society of South Australia*, No. 3, 1977, p. 43.

101 *ibid.*

102 Bridges, 1938, p. 333.

103 *ibid.*, pp. 339–340.

104 *ibid.*, p. 337.

105 Howell, 1977, p. 39.

106 *ibid.*, p. 45.

107 Bridges, 1925, p. viii.

108 Bridges, 1938, p. 347.

109 *ibid.*, p. 331.

110 *ibid.*, p. 342.

111 *ibid.*, p. 347.

112 *ibid.*, p. 344.

113 *ibid.*

Chapter 6

1   Tom Bridges, *Alarms and Excursions: Reminiscences of a Soldier*, Longmans Green & Co., London, 1938, p. 345.

2   *Advertiser*, 22 November 1926.

3   Jim Moss, *Sound of Trumpets: History of the Labor Movement in South Australia*, Wakefield Press, Adelaide, 1985, pp. 275–276.

4   digital.library.adelaide.edu.au (unidentified South Australian newspaper).

5   *ibid.*

6   Chris Cunneen and Deidre Morris, 'Gowrie, the first Earl of (1872–1955)', *Australian Dictionary of Biography*, National Centre of Biography, Australian National University, http://adb.anu.edu.au/biography/gowrie-first-earl-of-6441/text11023, accessed 11 May 2020; Chris Cunneen, 'Sir Alexander Gore Arkwright Hore-Ruthven', in David Clune and Ken Turner (eds.), *The Governors of New South Wales*, Federation Press, Alexandria (NSW), 2009, pp. 496–505.

7   *London Gazette*, 28 February 1899.

8   *Argus* (Melbourne), 9 July 1909.

9   *Financial Review*, 23 April 2015.

10   *ibid.*

11   *London Gazette* (Supplement), 9 December 1919.

12   digital.library.adelaide.edu.au, accessed 18 September 2020.

13   Anzac Day Memorial Committee, anzacday.org.au/national-war-memorial-adelaide.

14   Cunneen and Morris, accessed 11 May 2020.

15   *Advertiser*, 20 September 1928.

16   Andrew Faulkner, *Albert Blackburn VC: An Australian Hero, His Men, and Their Two World Wars*, Wakefield, Adelaide, 2010, p. 151.

17   *Advertiser*, 21 September 1928.

18   *Advertiser*, 17 April 1959.

19   Cunneenn and Morris, accessed 11 May 2020.

20   *ibid.*

21   Ben MacIntyre, *SAS Rogue Heroes: The Authorized Wartime History*, Viking, London, 2016, p. 334.

22   Patrick Hore-Ruthven, *The Happy Warrior: Poems*, Angus and Robertson, Sydney, 1943, p. 9.

23   Paul Sendziuk and Robert Foster, *A History of South Australia*, Cambridge University Press, Cambridge, 2018, p. 128–129.

24   Dean Jaensch, 'The Playford Era', in Dean Jaensch (ed.), *The Flinders History of South Australia: Political History*, Wakefield Press, Adelaide, 1986, p. 250.

25   *Chronicle* (Adelaide), 2 August 1934.

26   State Library of South Australia (SLSA) D8718/2(L), Letter to Captain R. Wrottesley.

27   *ibid.*

28   *ibid.*

29   *ibid.*

30   P.A. Howell, 'Dugan, Sir Winston Joseph (1876–1951)', *Australian Dictionary of Biography*, National Centre of Biography, Australian National University, http//:adb. anu.edu.au/biography/dugan-sir-winston-joseph-10056/text17737, accessed 11 May 2020.

31   R.G. Harris (rev. H.R.G. Wilson), *The Irish Regiments 1683–1999*, Spellmount, Staplehurst, 1999, p. 119.

32   Gary Sheffield, *The Chief: Douglas Haig and the British Army*, Aurum, London, 2011, pp. 221–222.

33   Howell, accessed 11 May 2020.

34   National Film and Sound Archive of Australia, 404056/Lady Dugan Christens new Miles Hawk plane, 1935.

35   SLSA B7624 The Sir Winston Dugan (Photo).

36   www.monumentsaustralia.org.ay/themes/landscape/settlement/display/50778-pioneer-memorial/photo/5, accessed 26 September 2020.

37   *News* (Adelaide), 28 November 1936.

38   Stuart Sayers, *Ned Herring: A Life of Lieutenant-General the Honourable Sir Edmund Herring*, Hyland House (in association with the Australian War Memorial), Melbourne, 1980, p. 294.

39   *ibid.*, p. 300.

40   *ibid.*, pp. 300–302

41   Howell, accessed 11 May 2020.

42   *Sydney Morning Herald*, 2 January 1947.

43   John Playford, 'Barclay-Harvey, Sir Charles Malcolm (1890–1969)', *Australian Dictionary of Biography*, National Centre of Biography, Australian National University, http://adb.anu.edu.au/biographybarclay-harvey-sir-charles-malcolm-9427/text16573, accessed 11 May 2020.

44   *Mail*, 12 August 1939.

45   *ibid.*

46   *ibid.*

47   Playford, accessed 11 May 2020.

48   *Advertiser* (Adelaide), 22 June 1940.

49   Brenda Hensel, Phyllis McDowall and Judith Mugford (eds.), *Life on the Range: Historical Notes and Reminiscences of the Avenue Range District*, Community of Avenue Range, Narracoorte, 1986, p. 42.

50   *South Eastern Times*, 28 November 1941.

51   *South Eastern Times*, 21 March 1944.

52   *Blyth Agriculturalist*, 9 October 1942.

53   *Northern Argus*, 9 October 1942.

54   *Burra Record*, 7 October 1941.

55   *ibid.*

56   *Quorn Mercury*, 26 September 1941.

57   Nick Anchen, *Outback Railwaymen: Life on the Commonwealth Railways*, Sierra Publishing, Melbourne, 2019, pp. 15–17.

58   Malcolm Barclay-Harvey, *A History of the Great North of Scotland Railway*, Locomotive Publishing Co., London, 1940.

59   Malcolm Barclay-Harvey, *A History of the Great North of Scotland Railway*, Locomotive Publishing Co., London, 2nd edn, 1949.

60   O.S. Nock, *Railways of Australia*, Adam & Charles Black, London, 1971, p. 191.

61   Stewart Cockburn, assisted by John Playford, *Playford: Benevolent Despot*, Axiom, Adelaide, 1991, p. 213. The story was first told by Tom Playford to the well-known Adelaide industrialist Moxon Simpson.

62   Joyce Gibbard, 'O'Brien, Louisa (1880–1957), *Australian Dictionary of Biography*, National Centre of Biography, Australian National University, http://adb.anu.edu/biography/obrien-louisa-11276/text20119, accessed 14 September 2020.

63   Cockburn (and Playford), 1991, p. 213.

64   Harold Guard and John Tring, *The Pacific War Uncensored: A Correspondent's Unvarnished Account of the Fight Against Japan*, Casemate Publishers, Newbury, 2011.

65   *Whyalla News*, 8 October 1943.

66   *News* (Adelaide), 10 August 1944.

67   *Age* (Melbourne), 19 December 1944.

68   *Mount Barker Courier and Onkaparinga and Gumeracha Advertiser*, 14 March 1946.

69   *Advertiser*, 19 November 1945.

70   *Age* (Melbourne), 19 December 1944.

71   https://www.femalefirst.co.uk/books/portals-of-discovery-george-norrie-1036048.html, 17 February 2017, accessed 2 October 2020.

72   *ibid.*

73   P.A. Howell, 'Norrie, Sir Charles Willoughby Moke (1893–1977)', *Australian Dictionary of Biography*, National Centre of Biography, Australian National University, http://adb.anu.edu/biography/norrie-sir-charles-willoughby-moke-11254/text20073, accessed 11 October 2020.

74   General Sir Otway Herbert, interview 8 January 1980, cited in Nigel Hamilton, *Monty: Master of the Battlefield, 1942–1944*, Hamish Hamilton, London, 1983, p. 529.

75   *Evening Advocate* (Innisfail, Queensland), 18 December 1944.

76   Howell, 'Norrie', accessed 11 May 2020.

77   *Advertiser* (Adelaide), quoted in *Daily Telegraph* (Sydney), 20 December 1944.

78 *Evening Advocate* (Innisfail, Queensland), 18 December 1944.

79 *South Eastern Times* (Millicent), 28 June 1949.

80 Howell, 'Norrie', accessed 11 May 2020.

81 *Workers' Weekly Herald*, 5 August 1959.

82 *Workers' Weekly Herald*, 12 October 1945.

83 Jaensch, 1986, p. 252.

84 Walter Crocker, *Sir Thomas Playford: A Portrait*, Melbourne University Press, Melbourne, 1983, p. 51.

85 *ibid.*, p. 52.

86 Cockburn (and Playford), 1991, p. 129.

87 Howell, 'Norrie', accessed 11 May 2020.

88 *ibid.*

89 Report of the Aborigines' Protection Board for the Year Ended 30 June 1945, Adelaide, 1 September 1945.

90 Cited in Rani Kerin, 'Adelaide-based Activism in the Mid-Twentieth Century: Radical Respectability', in Peggy Brock and Tom Gara, *Colonialism and its Aftermath: A History of Aboriginal South Australia*, Wakefield Press, Adelaide, 2017, p. 122.

91 *ibid.*, p. 123.

92 *News* (Adelaide), 26 August 1952.

93 P.A. Howell, 'George, Sir Robert Allingham (1896–1967)', *Australian Dictionary of Biography*, National Centre of Biography, Australian National University, http://adb.anu.edu.au/biography/george-sir-robert-allingham-10292/text18209, accessed 11 May 2020.

94 *West Australian* (Perth), 9 September 1952.

95 Howell, 'George', accessed 11 May 2020.

96 State Records of South Australia (SRSA), GRG 24/140, Records relating to Royal and other Dignitaries visits, 44–73.

97 Peter Spearitt, 'Royal Progress: The Queen and Her Australian Subjects', in John Arnold, Peter Spearitt and David Walker (eds.), *Out of Empire: The British Dominion of Australia*, Mandarin, Melbourne, 1993, p. 211.

98 *ibid.*, pp. 223, 228, 231.

99 Howell, 'George', accessed 11 May 2020.

100 Cockburn (and Playford), 1991, p. 317.

101 *Canberra Times*, 15 September 1967.

Chapter 7

1 Geoffrey Blainey, *A Shorter History of Australia*, Vintage, Sydney, 2000, p. 200.

2 Peter Spearitt, 'Australia and the Monarchy', in Annette Shiell and Peter Spearitt (eds.), *Australia and the Monarchy*, National Centre for Australian Studies, Monash

University, Melbourne, 1993, p. 6.

3   Angela Woollacott, *Don Dunstan: The Visionary Politician who Changed Australia*, Allen & Unwin, Crows Nest (NSW), 2019, p. xi.

4   *Canberra Times*, 7 April 1961.

5   *ibid.*

6   *Australian Women's Weekly*, 19 April 1961.

7   P.A. Howell, 'Bastyan, Sir Edric Montague (1903–1980)', *Australian Dictionary of Biography,* National Centre of Biography, Australian National University, http://adb.anu.edu.au/biography/bastyan-sir-edric-montague-9451/text16619, accessed 11 May 2020.

8   *Derby Evening Standard*, 23 November 1943; see also Grayson Carter (ed.), *Light Amid Darkness: Memoirs of Daphne Randall,* Resource Publications, San Jose, 2015, p. 118.

9   William Slim, *Defeat into Victory*, David McKay, New York, 1961, p. 320.

10   John Grehan and Martin Mace, *The Battle for Burma 1943–45: From Kohima to Imphal through to Victory*, Pen & Sword, Barnsley, 2015, pp. 280–281.

11   Slim, 1961, pp. 320, 437.

12   *Victor Harbour Times*, 21 April 1961.

13   *Victor Harbour Times*, 24 April 1964.

14   Neal Blewett and Dean Jaensch, *Playford to Dunstan: The Politics of Transition*, F.W. Cheshire, Melbourne, 1971, pp. 30–31.

15   *Canberra Times*, 28 March 1962.

16   *ibid.*

17   Howell, 'Bastyan', accessed 11 May 2020.

18   *Canberra Times*, 2 July 1965.

19   *ibid.*

20   *Canberra Times*, 21 March 1968; 22 March 1968.

21   Howell, 'Bastyan', accessed 20 May 2020.

22   Alex G. Castles and Michael C. Harris, *Lawmakers and Wayward Whigs: Government and Law in South Australia 1836–1936*, Wakefield Press, Adelaide, 1987, p. 254.

23   *ibid.*

24   *Canberra Times*, 22 August 1977.

25   Howell, 'Bastyan', accessed 20 May 2020.

26   Don Dunstan, *Felicia: The Political Memoirs of Don Dunstan*, Macmillan, Melbourne, 1981, p. 152.

27   *ibid.*, pp. 152–153.

28   *Good Neighbour* (ACT), 1 June 1968.

29   See obituary, *Canberra Times*, 8 October 1980.

30   Stewart Cockburn and David Ellyard, *Oliphant: The Life and Times of Sir Mark*

Oliphant, Axiom Books, Adelaide, 1981, p. 281.

31   *Canberra Times*, 5 March 1968.

32   Dunstan, 1981, pp. 156–157.

33   *ibid.*, p. 157.

34   Cockburn and Ellyard, 1981, p. 281.

35   *ibid.*, p. 282.

36   *ibid.*

37   P.A. Howell, 'Harrison, Sir James William (1912–1971)', *Australian Dictionary of Biography*, National Centre of Biography, Australian National University, http://adb. anu.edu.au/biography/harrison-sir-james-william-10444/text18521, accessed 11 May 2020.

38   *ibid.*

39   *Canberra Times*, 22 October 1968.

40   Louise Bird and Christine Garnaut, 'From Stock Paddock to Tertiary Education Campus: Fifty Years of Planning and Development at The Levels, 1970–2020', *Journal of the Historical Society of South Australia*, No. 48, 2020, p. 121.

41   Howell, 'Harrison', accessed 20 May 2020.

42   *Canberra Times*, 17 September 1971.

43   Dunstan, 1981, p. 186.

44   *ibid.*, p. 168.

45   Cockburn and Ellyard, 1981, p. 282.

46   *Papua New Guinea Post-Courier*, 10 November 1971.

47   Peter John Boyce, *The Queen's Other Realms: The Crown and its Legacy in Australia, Canada and New Zealand*, Federation Press, Sydney, 2008, p. 157.

48   Dunstan, 1981, p. 186.

49   For biographical details, see Cockburn and Ellyard, 1981, and John Carver, 'Oliphant, Sir Marcus Laurence (Mark) (1901–2000)', *Obituaries Australia*, National Centre of Biography, Australian National University, http://oa.anu.edu.au/obituary/oliphant-sir-marcus-laurence-mark-782/text783, accessed 18 September 2020.

50   Mark Oliphant, *Rutherford – Recollections of the Cambridge Days*, Elsevier Publishing, Amsterdam, 1972, p. 18.

51   *ibid.*

52   *ibid.*, pp. 18–19.

53   *ibid.*, p. 19.

54   *ibid.*, p. vii.

55   *ibid.*, p. 26.

56   *ibid.*

57   *ibid.*, p. 24.

58   *ibid.*, p. 26.

59   *ibid.*, p. 31.

60   *ibid.*, p. 120.

61   *ibid.*, p. 122.

62   *ibid.*, p. 123.

63   *ibid.*, p. 122.

64   Denise Sutherland, 'Just Curiosity . . . Sir Mark Oliphant', University of Melbourne, 1997, http://www.asap.unimelb.edu.au/bsparcs/exhib/journal/as_oliphant.htm, accessed 26 October 2020; see also 'Conversation with Sir Mark Oliphant', 24 July 1967, National Library of Australia, Tape 276, interviewed by Hazel de Berg.

65   Oliphant, 1972, p. 157.

66   *ibid.*, p. 138.

67   Cockburn and Ellyard, 1981, pp. 83–90.

68   *ibid.*, pp. 95–143.

69   *ibid.*, pp. 125–126.

70   Simon Cameron, 'Sir Mark Oliphant, AC KBE (1901–2000) Scientist and Governor of South Australia', in John Healey (ed.), *S.A.'s Greats: The Men and Women of the North Terrace Plaques*, Historical Society of South Australia, Adelaide, 2001, p. 103.

71   Oliphant, 1972, p. 134.

72   Cockburn and Ellyard, 1981, p. 267.

73   Dunstan, 1981, p. 186.

74   *ibid.*

75   Cockburn and Ellyard, 1981, p. 286.

76   *ibid.*, p. 288.

77   Dunstan, 1981, pp. 246–247.

78   Cockburn and Ellyard, 1981, pp. 290–291.

79   Stewart Cockburn, *The Salisbury Affair*, Sun Books, Melbourne, 1979, p. 127.

80   Dunstan, 1981, p. 247.

81   Cockburn and Ellyard, 1981, pp. 304–305.

82   *ibid.*, p. 306.

83   *ibid.*, p. 308.

84   Walter Crocker, *Sir Thomas Playford: A Portrait*, Melbourne University Press, Melbourne, 1983, p. 121.

85   Cockburn and Ellyard, 1981, p. 314.

86   Dunstan, 1981, p. 235.

87   Philip Payton, *One and All: Labor and the Radical Tradition in South Australia*, Wakefield Press, Adelaide, 2016, p. 277.

88   Cockburn and Ellyard, 1981, p. 321.

89   *ibid.*, p. 315.

90   Boyce, 2008, p. 157.

91   According to Cockburn and Ellyard, 1981, p. 319.

92   *ibid.*, p. 317.

93   Letter to the Premier from Sir Mark Oliphant, 22 March 1976, Don Dunstan Collection, DUN/Box 83/341, Special Collections, Flinders University Library; see also Angela Woollacott, *Don Dunstan: The Visionary Politician who changed Australia*, Allen & Unwin, Crows Nest (NSW), 2019, pp. 212–213.

94   Woollacott, 2019, p. 212.

95   Mark Oliphant, 'Foreword', in Charles Duguid, *Doctor and the Aborigines*, Rigby, Adelaide, 1972, p. v.

96   Letter from the Premier to Sir Mark Oliphant, 13 April 1976, DUN/Box 82/341, Dunstan Collection, Special Collections, Flinders University Library; see also Woollacott, 2019, p. 213.

97   *Canberra Times*, 25 May 1976.

98   *Canberra Times*, 26 May 1976.

99   *Canberra Times*, 27 May 1976.

100   *Canberra Times*, 2 December 1976.

101   Speech by the Premier, Don Dunstan, at swearing in of Sir Douglas Nicholls as Governor of South Australia, 1 December 1976, DUN/Speeches/2972, Dunstan Collection, Special Collections, Flinders University Library.

102   *ibid.*

103   Robert Foster and Amanda Nettelbeck, *Out of the Silence: The History and Memory of South Australia's Frontier Wars*, Wakefield Press, Adelaide, 2017, p. 184.

104   Richard Broome, 'Nicholls, Sir Douglas Ralph (Doug) (1906–1988), *Australian Dictionary of Biography*, National Centre of Biography, Australian National University, http://adb.edu.au/biography/nicholls-sir-douglas-ralph-doug-14920/text26109, accessed 11 May 2020; see also Mavis Thorpe Clark, *Pastor Doug: The Story of Sir Douglas Nicholls, Aboriginal Leader*, Lansdowne Press, Melbourne, rev. edn, 1972; Richard Broome, *Aboriginal Victorians: A History Since 1800*, Allen & Unwin, Crows Nest (NSW), 2005; John Ramland and Christopher Mooney, *Remembering Aboriginal Heroes: Struggle, Identity and the Media*, Brolga Publishing, Melbourne, 2006; Richard Broome, *Fighting Hard: The Victorian Aborigines Advancement League*, Aboriginal Studies Press, Canberra, 2015.

105   Broome, 'Nicholls', accessed 11 May 2020.

106   Ramsland and Mooney, 2006, p. 205.

107   Clarke, 1972, pp. 57–67.

108   *ibid.*, p.77.

109   Ramsland and Mooney, 2006, p. 214.

110   Broome, 'Nicholls', accessed 11 May 2020.

111   Clarke, 1972, p. 230.

112   *ibid.*, p. 242.

113 *ibid.*, p. 248.

114 Dunstan, 1981, p. 305.

115 *ibid.*

116 *Victor Harbor Times*, 17 July 2013.

117 Dunstan, 1981, p. 305.

118 *ibid.*

119 Woollacott, 2019, p. 212.

120 *Advertiser* (Adelaide), 24 February 1978.

121 Letter from Robin Millhouse re Keith Seaman, March 1978, Don Dunstan Collection, DUN/B0x 45/022, Special Collections, Flinders University Library.

122 Dunstan, 1981, p. 306.

123 Robert Martin, *Responsible Government in South Australia: Volume Two, Playford to Rann 1957–2007*, Wakefield Press, Adelaide, 2009, p. 90.

124 Arnold D. Hunt, *This Side of Heaven: A History of Methodism in South Australia*, Lutheran Publishing House, Adelaide, 1985, pp. 404–405.

125 For historical background, see Brian Dickey (with contributions from Elaine Martin and Rod Oxenberry), *Rations, Residence, Resources: A History of Social Welfare in South Australia since 1836*, Wakefield Press, Adelaide, 1986, pp. 110–111, 230, 258–259, and Brian Dickey, *No Charity There: A Short History of Social Welfare in Australia*, Routledge, London, 1987, pp. 169–172.

126 *Victor Harbor Times*, 17 July 2013.

127 Keith Seaman, 'The South Australian Constitution Act of 1856', in Dean Jaensch (ed.), *The Flinders History of South Australia – Political History*, Wakefield Press, Adelaide, 1986, pp. 76–94.

128 Keith Seaman, 'The Press and the Aborigines: South Australia's First Thirty Years', *Journal of the Historical Society of South Australia*, No. 18, 1990, p. 28.

129 Crocker, 1983, pp. 136, 126.

Chapter 8

1 Robert Martin, *Responsible Government in South Australia: Volume Two – Playford to Rann 1957–2007*, Wakefield Press, 2009, p. 103.

2 *ibid.*

3 For the origin and distribution of the name Dunstan, see Bernard Deacon, *The Surnames of Cornwall*, CosSERG, Redruth, 2019, p. 57.

4 Philip Payton, *More Than The Last Shilling: Repatriation in Australia 1994–2018*, Australian Government Department of Veterans' Affairs, Canberra, 2019.

5 Clem Lloyd and Jacqui Rees, *The Last Shilling: A History of Repatriation in Australia*, Melbourne University Press, Melbourne, 1994, pp. 355–356.

6 https://anzacportal.dva.gov.au/history/conflicts/australia-and-vietnam-war/australia-and-vietnam-war/vietnam-war, accessed 11 June 2018.

7   Ambrose Crowe, *The Battle after the War: The Story of Australia's Vietnam War Veterans*, Allen & Unwin, St Leonards (NSW), 1999, p. x.

8   Cited in Amanda Laugeson (ed.), *Diggerspeak: The Language of Australians at War*, Oxford University Press, Melbourne, 2005, pp. 158–159.

9   Press Release from Premier Don Dunstan, 30 July 1971, Dunstan Collection, DUN/Speeches/1120, Special Collections, Flinders University Library; see also Angela Woollacott, *Don Dunstan: The Visionary Politician who Changed Australia*, Allen & Unwin, Crows Nest (NSW), 2019, p. 150.

10   Payton, 2019, p. 17.

11   *Advertiser*, 17 October 2011.

12   'In Memoriam: Lieutenant-General Sir Donald Beaumont Dunstan AC KBE CB (1923–2011)', *Australian Army Journal*, Vol. VIII, No. 3, 2011, pp. 187–189; for a short biography of Dunstan's military career see Peter Dennis, Jeffrey Grey, Ewan Morris, Robin Prior, with Jean Bou (eds.), *The Oxford Companion to Australia's Military History*, Oxford University Press, Melbourne, 2nd edn, 2008, p. 190.

13   Paul Ham, *Vietnam: The Australian War*, Harper Collins, Sydney, 2007, p. 165.

14   Mark Dapin, *The Nashos' War: Australia's Servicemen and Vietnam*, Penguin, Melbourne, 2014, p. 349.

15   Ham, 2007, p. 378.

16   *ibid.*

17   Payton, 2019, pp. 15–16.

18   Ham, 2007, p. 551.

19   *ibid.*, p. 552.

20   'In Memoriam', 2011, p. 188.

21   Ham, 2007, p. 565.

22   *Canberra Times*, 1 November 1981.

23   *ibid.*

24   *Advertiser*, 1 December 1990.

25   Diaries of Sir Walter Crocker, 15 April 1990 and 17 April 1985, Special Collections, Barr Smith Library, University of Adelaide; see also Susan Magarey and Kerrie Round, *Roma the First: A Biography of Dame Roma Mitchell*, Wakefield Press, Adelaide, rev. edn 2009, p. 344.

26   Magarey and Round, 2009, p. 344.

27   *ibid.*

28   Magarey and Round, 2009; Susan Magarey (ed.), *Dame Roma: Glimpses of a Glorious Life*, Axiom, Adelaide, 2002; John Healey (ed.), *SA's Greats: The Men and Women of the North Terrace Plaques*, Historical Society of South Australia, Adelaide, 2003, p. 91. Len King, 'The Judicial Career of Dame Roma Mitchell: A Valedictory Tribute', *Adelaide Law Review*, Vol. 22, No. 1, 2000, pp. 1–26.

29   William Deane, 'Memories', in Magarey (ed.), 2002, p. 13.

30   Cited in Deidre Jordan, 'Obituary: The Honourable Dame Roma Mitchell', *Australian Feminist Studies*, Vol. 15, No. 33, 2000, p. 312.

31   Magarey and Round, 2009, p. 339.

32   *ibid.*

33   *ibid.*, p. 169.

34   *ibid.*, pp. 169–170.

35   *ibid.*, p. 172.

36   *National Times*, 20–25 February 1978; cited in Magarey and Round, 2009, p. 173.

37   Healey (ed.), p. 91.

38   Magarey and Round, 2009, p. 202.

39   *ibid.*, p. 203.

40   Healey (ed.), p. 91.

41   Cited in Magarey and Round, 2009, p. 218.

42   *ibid.*, p. 192.

43   *ibid.*, p. 358.

44   *ibid.*, p. 369.

45   *ibid.*, p. 378.

46   Deane, 2002, p. 17.

47   Jordan, 2000, p. 312.

48   *ibid.*, p. 313.

49   https://www.flinders.edu.au/about/investigator-transformed/sir-eric-neal, accessed 27 November 2020.

50   *ibid.*

51   *Canberra Times*, 2 October 1992.

52   https://www.boral.com/history/1980-1989, accessed 27 November 2020.

53   *ibid.*

54   *ibid.*

55   *ibid.*

56   Des Ryan, *The Messenger: Selected Columns from Messenger Newspapers, 1993–2003*, Wakefield Press, Adelaide, 2003.

57   *ibid.*

58   www5.austili.edu.au/au/journals/IndigLawB/2000/3html, accessed 27 November 2020.

59   https://guides.library.unisa.edu.au/specialandarchivalcollections/neal, accessed 27 November 2020.

60   *Advertiser*, 10 October 2017.

61   *Advertiser*, 11 February 2020.

62   https://www.flinders.edu.au/about/investigator-transformed/sir-eric-neal, accessed 27 November 2020.

63   *Veterans' Voice*, Autumn 2012.

64   Flinders University: Citation for the Award of the Degree of Doctor of the University *honoris causa* The Honourable Marjorie Jackson-Nelson AC CVO MBE.

65   Healey (ed.), 2003, p. 98.

66   *ibid.*

67   *ibid.*, p. 99.

68   *ibid.*

69   http://www.womenaustralia.info/leaders/biogs/WLEO397b.htm, *The Encyclopedia of Women and Leadership in Twentieth-century Australia*, accessed 27 November 2020.

70   *Advertiser*, 8 April 2019.

71   Healey (ed.), 2003, p. 98.

72   *Canberra Times*, 16 July 2007.

73   Philip Payton, *More Than The Last Shilling: Repatriation in Australia 1994–2018*, Australian Government Department of Veterans' Affairs, Canberra, 2019, p. 28.

74   https://www.navy.gov.au/biography/rear-admiral-kevin-john-scarce, accessed 11 May 2020.

75   *ibid.*

76   *ibid.*

77   https://en.wikipedia.org/wiki/Kevin_Scarce, accessed 11 May 2020.

78   *Business Defence SA*, 1 September 2010.

79   *Age* (Melbourne), 3 May 2007.

80   Robert Foster and Amanda Nettelbeck, *Out of the Silence: The History and Memory of South Australia's Frontier Wars*, Wakefield Press, Adelaide, 2012, p. 184.

81   *ibid.*, p. 185.

82   https://en.wikipedia.org/wiki/Kevin_Scarce, accessed 11 May 2020.

83   https://scouts.com.au/biog/2019/11/18/president-national-council/, accessed 9 December 2020.

84   ABC News 26 June 2014.

85   *Australian*, 13 December 2014.

86   *Australian*, 25 July 2019.

87   *Defence Connect*, 17 October 2019.

88   ABC News, 10 June 2019.

89   ABC News, 10 June 2019.

90   *Weekend Australian*, 18–19 April 2020.

91   ABC News, 26 June 2014.

92   *SA Weekend*, 27–28 June 2015.

93   Speech by His Excellency the Governor on the Occasion of his Swearing-in Ceremony, 1 September 2014.

94   *Advertiser*, 25 December 2017.
95   *Advertiser*, 25 December 2017.
96   *Weekend Australian*, 18–19 April 2020.
97   ABC News, 26 Jun 2014.
98   Ham, 2007, p. 612.
99   *Advertiser*, 25 December 2017.
100 *Advertiser*, 25 December 2017.
101 *The Signal*, December 2014.
102 *Vietnam Veterans Association of Australia – ACT Branch*, Summer 2014/15.
103 *Advertiser*, 25 December 2017.
104 *Advertiser*, 25 December 2017.
105 ABC News, 26 June 2014.
106 *Advertiser*, 25 December 2017.
107 *Advertiser*, 25 December 2017.
108 *Weekend Australian*, 18–19 April 2020.
109 *Weekend Australian*, 18–19 April 2020.
110 *Weekend Australian*, 18–19 April 2020.
111 *Advertiser*, 7 February 2020.
112 governor.sa.gov.au/vice_regal_news, 14 January 2021.
113 *Advertiser*, 4 December 2020.
114 *Advertiser*, 4 December 2020.

APPENDIX

Governors of South Australia

1 September 2014 – 12 August 2021	The Honourable Hieu Van Le, AC
8 August 2007 – 1 September 2014	Rear Admiral the Honourable Kevin Scarce, AC, CSC, RAN (Rtd)
3 November 2001 – 8 August 2007	The Honourable Marjorie Jackson-Nelson, AC, CVO, MBE
22 July 1996 – 3 November 2001	The Honourable Sir Eric James Neal, AC, CVO
6 February 1991 – 21 July 1996	The Honourable Dame Roma Flinders Mitchell, AC, DBE, CVO
23 April 1982 – 5 February 1991	Lieutenant General Sir Donald Beaumont Dunstan, AC, KBE, CB
1 September 1977 – 28 March 1982	Sir Keith Douglas Seaman, KCVO, OBE
1 December 1976 – 30 April 1977	Sir Douglas Ralph Nicholls, KCVO, OBE
1 December 1971 – 30 November 1976	Sir Marcus 'Mark' Laurence Elwin Oliphant, KBE
4 December 1968 – 16 September 1971	Major General Sir James William Harrison, KCMG, CB, CBE
4 April 1961 – 1 June 1968	Lieutenant General Sir Edric Montague Bastyan, KCMG, KCVO, KBE, CB
23 February 1953 – 7 March 1960	Air Vice Marshal Sir Robert Allingham George, KCMG, KCVO, KBE, CB, MC
19 December 1944 – 19 June 1952	Lieutenant General Sir Charles Willoughby Moke Norrie, KCMG, CB, DSO, MC
12 August 1939 – 26 April 1944	Sir Charles Malcolm Barclay-Harvey, KCMG
28 July 1934 – 23 February 1939	Major General Sir Winston Joseph Dugan, KCMG, CB, DSO

14 May 1928 – 26 April 1934	Brigadier the Honourable Sir Alexander Gore Arkwright Hore-Ruthven, VC, KCMG, CB, DSO
4 December 1922 – 4 December 1927	Lieutenant General Sir George Tom Molesworth Bridges, KCB, KCMG, DSO
9 June 1920 – 30 May 1922	Lieutenant Colonel Sir William Earnest George Archibald Weigall, KCMG
18 April 1914 – 30 April 1920	Lieutenant Colonel Sir Henry Lionel Galway, KCMG, DSO
18 February 1909 – 23 March 1914	Admiral Sir Day Hort Bosanquet, GCVO, KCB
1 July 1903 – 18 February 1909	Sir George Ruthven Le Hunte, KCMG
10 April 1899 – 17 July 1902	The Right Honourable Hallam Lord Tennyson, KCMG
29 October 1895 – 29 March 1899	Sir Thomas Fowell Buxton, Bt, GCMG
11 April 1889 – 10 April 1895	The Right Honourable The Earl of Kintore, GCMG, PC
19 February 1883 – 5 March 1889	Sir William Cleaver Francis Robinson, GCMG
2 October 1877 – 9 January 1883	Lieutenant General Sir William Francis Drummond Jervois, KCMG, CB
9 June 1873 – 29 January 1877	Sir Anthony Musgrave, KCMG
16 February 1869 – 18 April 1873	The Right Honourable Sir James Fergusson, Bt
4 March 1862 – 19 Feb 1868	Sir Dominick Daly, KCB
8 June 1855 – 4 March 1862	Sir Richard Graves MacDonnell, KCMG, CB
2 August 1848 – 20 December 1854	Sir Henry Edward Fox Young, KCMG
25 October 1845 – 2 August 1848	Lieutenant Colonel Frederick Holt Robe, CB
15 May 1841 – 25 October 1845	Captain George Grey
17 October 1838 – 15 May 1841	Lieutenant Colonel George Gawler
18 December 1836 – 16 July 1838	Captain John Hindmarsh, RN

LIST OF ILLUSTRATIONS

Chapter 3

Chapter 4

Chapter 5

Chapter 6

Chapter 7

Chapter 8

75   Major General Donald Beaumont Dunstan inspects a South Vietnamese Guard of Honour at Tan Sun Nhut airport, Saigon (now Ho Chi Minh City) (courtesy Australian War Memorial, 4098124).

76   Governor Dame Roma Flinders Mitchell, 1992 (courtesy *Advertiser*).

77   Dame Roma Flinders Mitchell as Supreme Court Judge, 1965 (courtesy National Archives of Australia).

78   Governor the Honourable Sir Eric Neal, speaking in Adelaide (courtesy Wikipedia).

79   Governor the Honourable Marjorie Jackson-Nelson inspects the Guard at the opening of the State Parliament in 2006 (courtesy SLSA B70703).

80   Governor Marjorie Jackson-Nelson chats with two other women at the International Women's Day lunch at the Adelaide Convention Centre in March 2006 (courtesy SLSA B70666).

81   Governor Rear Admiral the Honourable Kevin Scarce speaking at the Adelaide Convention Centre in 2008 (courtesy SLSA B70753).

82   Mrs Elizabeth Scarce, wife of Governor Kevin Scarce, cutting a cake to celebrate the International Women's Day's 70th birthday on 7 March 2008 (courtesy SLSA B70766).

83   The Honourable Hieu Van Le, Governor of South Australia 1 September 2014 to 31 August 2021, and Mrs Le (courtesy Government House).

84   Governor Hieu Van Le, wearing Companion of Australia decoration (courtesy Government House).

85   East Entrance, Government House, Adelaide

86   Federation Window, Government House

87   The Library, Government House

88   The Small Dining Room, Government House

89   The Small Drawing Room, Government House

90   The State Dining Room, Government House

91   The Adelaide Room, Government House

92   Government House today

93   The State Entrance, Government House

ACKNOWLEDGEMENTS

This book was written at the request of Steven Marshall, Premier of South Australia, and was completed under the aegis of Wakefield Press and the History Trust of SA, where special thanks are due to Wakefield publisher Michael Bollen and Trust CEO Greg Mackie, OAM. Hugh Borrowman, CM, Official Secretary to the Governor at Government House, lent invaluable support and made important suggestions as the project developed.

On 5 August 1977, as a young postgraduate student, I was fortunate enough to attend a lecture entitled 'Varieties of Vice-regal Life', delivered by P.A. (Peter) Howell. To my surprise, I found it a captivating presentation (I had not expected it to be 'my cup of tea'), and awakened an interest in South Australia's vice-regal history to which, at last, I have been able to give full vent. The late Peter Howell, formerly Reader in History at Flinders University, was also the author of several important articles on the same topic, which, together with his various biographical sketches in the *Australian Dictionary of Biography*, were vital in establishing the early groundwork for this project. I remain indebted to Peter for his pioneering work in South Australian vice-regal studies, undertaken so many years ago, and salute his memory.

At Flinders University, I am also indebted to Heidi Ing, who read the text in draft, making numerous suggestions; I am grateful for her constant encouragement and enthusiasm. Likewise, I am grateful to Sandra Kearney for detailed discussion of South Australia during the Great War, including Lady Galway and the Red Cross. Thanks are due too to Pixie Stardust, Special Collections Librarian at Flinders University, who readily made available rare and sometimes obscure items for my perusal. Other colleagues, too numerous to mention individually, have also been extremely helpful, especially those attending my recent Flinders History Seminar Series talk 'Vice-Regal Wives'. Their wry comments and provocative questions gave much food for thought.

At Wakefield Press, I am similarly indebted to my meticulous editor, Julia Beaven, and to Liz Nicholson for her imaginative cover design, Maddy Sexton for assistance with illustration selection, and Jesse Pollard for his expert typesetting.

Above all, I am indebted to my wife Dee, whose love has sustained me in this and so many other projects, and who has worked tirelessly to produce the splendid index which graces this book.

Philip Payton, 2021

INDEX

Wakefield Press is an independent publishing and
distribution company based in Adelaide, South Australia.
We love good stories and publish beautiful books.
To see our full range of books, please visit our website at
www.wakefieldpress.com.au
where all titles are available for purchase.
To keep up with our latest releases, news and events,
subscribe to our monthly newsletter.

Find us!

Facebook: www.facebook.com/wakefield.press
Twitter: www.twitter.com/wakefieldpress
Instagram: www.instagram.com/wakefieldpress